CURRENCY OPTIONS
HEDGING AND TRADING STRATEGIES

CURRENCY OPTIONS

HEDGING AND TRADING STRATEGIES

Henry K. Clasing, Jr., Odile Lombard, Didier Marteau
in collaboration with
Jerome deBontin
and
Ronald Achs

BUSINESS ONE IRWIN
Homewood, Illinois 60430

Project editor: Gladys True
Production manager: Ann Cassady
Designer: Maureen McCutcheon
Art coordinator: Mark Malloy
Compositor: TCSystems, Inc.
Typeface: 11/13 Times Roman
Printer: Book Press, Inc.

Library of Congress Cataloging-in-Publication Data

Clasing, Henry K.
  Currency options : hedging and trading strategies / Henry K.
Clasing, Jr., Odile Lombard, Didier Marteau in collaboration with
Jerome deBontin and Ronald Achs.
     p.   cm.
  Includes bibliographical references and index.
  ISBN 1-55623-170-9
  1. Options (Finance) 2. Hedging (Finance) 3. Foreign exchange
futures. I. Lombard, Odile. II. Marteau, Didier. III. Title.
HG6024.A3C57 1992
332.64'5—dc20   92–3317

Printed in the United States of America
1 2 3 4 5 6 7 8 9 0 BP 9 8 7 6 5 4 3 2

Dedicated to three seeds of the future—Danielle, Jonathan, and Susana

PREFACE

Two developments that characterize doing business in today's more technological world are the greater use of mathematics for investment purposes and the everyday use of computers in measuring facts and making decisions. Currency options are a natural outgrowth of technological progress. Their rapid growth and acceptance prove not only that their time has come but that they are enabling us to cope with an ever-changing world. The most important fact to realize about currency options is they are not a fad or a gimmick but a versatile tool for the management of currency risk. The fact that today's interbank over-the-counter options market quotes options, not in prices, but in terms of volatility is the best possible proof of the acceptance of the mathematical models that are used to characterize options.

Jerome deBontin, Odile Lombard, and Didier Marteau, the three authors who created this book, which was originally written in French, did an excellent job. Making sense out of a complex subject is truly a work of art. As we forge our way into the future, we need better measurements and better tools in order to survive. And that is precisely what this book has given us.

The book begins with basic definitions and descriptions of the varieties of currency options that now exist. Using only words and graphs–without mathematics—it goes on to demonstrate some of the basic strategies.

Chapter 2 introduces and explains the Garman-Kohlhagen model, which is based on the hypothesis of risk-free arbitrage. This model is the most widely accepted means of estimating the "fair value" of currency options. Here and throughout the book, practical examples are given and important concepts are clearly and briefly explained. Such clarity and brevity are welcome when one seeks understanding.

The book then explains the nature of the dominant currency option markets. The largest, the interbank over-the-counter market, owes its size to the easy accessibility to currency markets that it offers option users, to its flexible creation of option strategies tailored to customer needs, and to the technology and communications skills that enable it to perform on an international basis. The largest organized options markets are the Chicago Mercantile Exchange, which trades options that are convertible into currency futures, and the Philadelphia Stock Exchange, which trades options that are directly convertible into currencies. But a trend is afoot to trade options on a worldwide and round-the-clock basis, and London, Tokyo, and Singapore may well develop sizable additions to the existing world of currency options. Globex, a computerized approach to the trading of currency options on a worldwide basis, was formed by the Chicago Mercantile Exchange and Reuters in an attempt to extend the CME's range beyond regular market hours. Rapid technological change is challenging all of the participants in the currency option markets to remain alert.

Next a historical analysis of currency options is provided. This leads into an examination of the areas in which most currency option trading occurs. The first of these areas is arbitrage between the currency and options markets, which is the major source of liquidity in these markets. Then all of the most practical current option strategies are subjected to a thorough treatment buttressed by practical examples for each strategy.

Perhaps the most practical aspect of the book is saved to the end, where everyday importing and exporting problems are considered. As with option strategies, practical examples illustrate each of the problems.

It is rare for a book on an extremely technical subject to provide a thorough overview, but our French authors have done that here. They must be given their justified thanks.

Henry K. Clasing, Jr.

ACKNOWLEDGMENTS

Given the advent of computers and word processing, producing a book has become far simpler. Nonetheless, anything well done in life usually involves a team of capable people. Most thanks must go to Jerome deBontin for his early help in the translation and to Elizabeth Marbach and her staff at Rodman, Renshaw for providing most of the data needed to update the original book. Jerome deBontin was most helpful in giving excellent overviews of the meanings of the paragraphs from the French version. Without these efforts, this new version of *Foreign Currency Options* would not have been possible.

Special thanks need to be extended to Robert Meier, whose support and help made this opportunity possible; to my secretary, Lorene, for many years of unselfish dedication, encouragement, and hard work; to Stan Yabroff, Sid Jones, Oliver Bajor, Van K. Tharp, and Michael Joseph for offering me their insights on option hedging and on the formation of a successful hedge program; to Hiroki Kato and Susan Taylor of the Chicago Mercantile Exchange for helping me with the Glossary; to the good Lord above, for the very blessed life I live; and, finally, to my wife, Amy, whose love and friendship are very much appreciated and worth working for.

Ronald Achs

CONTENTS

CHAPTER 1

BASIC PRINCIPLES FOR THE USE OF CURRENCY OPTIONS

Options on currencies are rights to exchange one currency for another at or prior to an expiration date, termed the *exercise date,* at a predetermined exchange rate, termed the *strike price.* The label *currency option* designates a broad variety of contracts, all of which are based on the principle of the *conditional exercise.* Specific currency options differ from each other with regard to the currencies exchanged, the direction of the conditional exchange (to buy or to sell), and the method of exercise (at the expiration date only or at any time up to the expiration date).

Since familiarity with the terminology of options is the first step toward understanding them, we will begin by defining option terms.

TERMINOLOGY

A *currency option,* unlike a *forward currency contract,* represents a right, not an obligation. An option buyer assumes the right, not the obligation, to exchange currencies at a predetermined price. He will exercise that right only if it is profitable to do so. In contrast, the buyer (or seller) of a forward contract on a currency has a firm obligation to take delivery of (or to deliver) the currency at a specific time in the future.[1]

The right to buy currency A is referred to as a *call option* on A. The right to sell currency A is referred to as a *put option* on A.

---

[1] In practice, the holder of a forward contract often makes a second forward contract for the same date, but for the reverse exchange. This action offsets the initial contract, the result being a profit or a loss, depending on how the exchange rate changed between the two transactions.

1

This terminology originated in options on stocks and other securities. Unfortunately, due to the two-sided nature of currency transactions, it causes certain ambiguities that must be carefully avoided. For example, DM (German mark) calls traded on the Chicago Mercantile Exchange can also be viewed as U.S. dollar puts against the DM.

The currency options traded on the organized stock and commodities exchanges are standardized with respect to the currencies involved, their amounts, and other specific terms. In the principal markets, only options to buy or sell currencies against the U.S. dollar are traded. For example, a German exporter wishing to cover a long dollar position will buy a DM call, the right to buy DM against dollars, which permits him to sell dollars against DM at a predetermined market price. In addition to the markets in standardized currency options operated by stock and commodities exchanges, there is an over-the-counter (OTC) currency options market, operated principally by commercial banks. In this market all forms of customized options can be negotiated, including options on cross exchange rates (i.e., nondollar exchanges). The most commonly traded cross-rate options are the pound sterling–DM and the pound sterling–Swiss franc.

THE UNDERLYING INSTRUMENT

The instrument received if an option is exercised is referred to as the instrument underlying the option. For most currency options, the *underlying instrument* is a cash deposit in a currency. However, it can also be a futures contract or a forward contract.

Options on Cash Currencies

The exercise of options on currencies with cash settlement, commonly called *options on the spot price,* is effected by the exchange of the underlying currency with the counterpart currency. The buyer of call A receives currency A and delivers the counterpart currency. The delivery is executed with cash settlement, which means 48 business hours after the expiration date. The trading price, also known as the *strike price* or the *exercise price,* is, of course, the one established in the contract.

Consider the case of an American exporter who is to receive a payment in DM in three months. He can manage his currency position in three ways:

- Not covering it and therefore being exposed to exchange rate risk.
- Selling his DM three months forward at the prevailing rate, say $1 = 1.80DM.
- Buying DM puts at, say, $1 = 1.80 DM with the settlement date the same as or later than the payment date of the claim.

Suppose that the DM appreciates and that the spot rate is $1 = 1.60 DM on the exercise date. If the exporter covered himself with a forward sale, he has committed himself to sell his DM at the rate of $1 = 1.80 DM and thus cannot benefit from the appreciation of the DM. The forward covering makes him indifferent to the variations of the DM's price in the market. If, instead, he bought puts, he is able to give up his DM in the market at a price of $1 = 1.60 DM and simultaneously to sell back his options (which will have certainly lost some of their value). If the revaluation of the DM is higher than the decrease in the price of the options, he realizes a net profit.

Options on Futures Contracts

A *currency futures contract* is a promise to deliver a currency at a later date and at a price fixed at the origin, the price at which the trade took place. Such contracts, which are traded on organized futures exchanges, are standardized in their amounts and delivery dates. They are the equivalent of interbank forward contracts.

Options on currency futures, traded at the Chicago Mercantile Exchange (CME) and the London International Financial Futures Exchange (LIFFE), are exercised by the delivery of a currency futures contract. Naturally, the exercise date on the options contract must come before the delivery date on the futures contract. Options on currency futures are necessarily traded in markets in which underlying interests are traded.

Options on Forward Contracts

Given the widespread use of currency forward contracts, options on forwards would appear to have considerable potential. Still, options of this kind are relatively uncommon. Options on forwards confer the right to establish a forward position (purchase or sale) in a currency. Such options can vary with respect to amount, date of exercise, and date of forward delivery.

An option on a forward foreign exchange gives its holder both protection from adverse foreign exchange movements and the opportunity to lock in an exchange rate prior to the time when the exchange takes place. This could be useful, for example, to an American exporter who is bidding on a contract that would eventually result in a payment in DM. It will protect the exporter from adverse currency movements between the submission of the bid and the award of the contract. If the bid is successful and the dollar has depreciated against the DM, he can exercise the option, receiving a DM forward sale with the forward exchange rate that was fixed in the option. On the other hand, if the bid is successful and the dollar has strengthened against the DM, the option can be sold at the prevailing price.

In most of what follows, we will concentrate on the general principles that govern spot currency options. The same principles can be applied to options on futures and forwards. We will discuss specific aspects of options on futures and forwards in Chapter 6, which is devoted to hedging foreign exchange exposures.

EXERCISE TERMS AND THE EXPIRATION DATE

An option is said to be "European" if its exercise can take place only at a given date, called the *exercise date,* after which time the option ceases to exist. An option is said to be "American" if it can be exercised at any time until its ending date. An American option is therefore a much more flexible instrument than a European option, and in consequence the price of an American option is higher than that of a European option if the other terms of the options are identical.

THE BUYER AND THE SELLER OF OPTIONS

The buyer of an option controls the exercise of the right of buying (or the right of selling) currencies at the price fixed in the option contract. The seller of an option (also known as the *writer* or *grantor*) is thus dependent on the buyer's decision. The potential losses and profits of the buyer and of the seller are equal and opposite to each other. The buyer has limited risk and the possibility of unlimited gain; the seller has unlimited risk and the possibility of limited gain.

The payment for an option is generally made by the buyer at the time the contract is negotiated; this payment is called the *premium of the option*. For most currency options, the premium is paid in the currency of the counterpart, which is generally dollars.

Buyers and sellers of currency options have three basic motivations: hedging the currency exposure involved in a commercial or financial transaction, investing in the hope of achieving a profit resulting from a favorable change in the exchange rate, and arbitraging between the options market and the spot or forward currency market. In this book we refer to buyers and sellers with the first of these motivations as *hedgers,* to those with the second motivation as *investors* or *speculators,* and to those with the third motivation as *arbitrageurs*. In reality, traders in currency options may have a mixture of motives; however, it is useful for discussion purposes to maintain these distinctions.

THE STRIKE PRICE

The buyer of an option selects a strike price fixed by the exchange at which he will eventually purchase (or sell) a currency. This price is called the *strike price of the option*. It is clear that the value of an option depends on the strike price. On the organized markets, strike prices are spaced from each other by identical amounts. For example, the strike prices in the Chicago Mercantile Exchange DM options are spaced at one-cent intervals per DM. The DM can be bought at . . . 50, 51, 52, 53, 54, . . . cents per DM, which means that the dollar can be sold at . . . 2.00, 1.9608, 1.9231, 1.8868,

1.8518, . . . DM per dollar. Naturally, the choice of the strike price is free on the OTC market.

When the strike price of a call is equal to the spot price of the underlying currency, the option is said to be *at-the-money*. When the strike price of a call is lower than the spot price of the underlying currency, the option is said to be *in-the-money*. An in-the-money call gives the right to buy a currency at a lower price than the spot price, so that exercising the option would yield a profit (ignoring, for the moment, the commissions paid to acquire the option). Conversely, a put is in-the-money when the spot price is below the exercise price.

When the strike price of a call is higher than the spot price of the underlying currency, the option is said to be *out-of-the-money*, which expresses the idea that the option allows the owner to buy a currency at a higher price than its spot price. A put is out-of-the-money when the spot price is greater than the strike price. An out-of-the-money option is purchased in the hope of selling it at a higher price or of guaranteeing its purchaser a fallback price for a transaction.

The choice of the strike price, which is central to the management of an options position, will be discussed at length in this book. At this point we simply note that the further out-of-the-money an option is, the less attractive it is and, consequently, the lower its cost. A German exporter hoping to hedge a dollar receivable with DM calls can buy an in-the-money call and thus assure an exchange rate for the transaction that is more advantageous than the current spot rate; however, the cost of this purchase will be relatively high. On the other hand, he can buy an out-of-the-money call that will assure him of a less attractive rate but will cost less. The advantage of buying the out-of-the-money call is that if the exchange rate does not change or improve, he will have lost very little by buying this form of protection.

The choice of the strike price is equally important for a speculator. If, for example, he expects an increase of the dollar against the DM, he will buy DM puts (the right to sell DM and buy dollars), which he can sell back with a profit if the market has moved to his advantage. If the puts are in-the-money, his initial investment and, therefore, his risk are large. However, he benefits significantly from any decrease in the DM. If he buys an out-of-the-money put, he limits his initial investment but realizes a significant gain only in case of a major fall in the DM. Some traders believe that it is simpler to buy options at-the-money, since the comparison between the cost of the trade and the potential profit is immediate. For example, if the current exchange rate is 55 cents per DM and an at-the-money DM call costs 1 cent, a trader knows that he can profit by the full amount of any rise in the value of the DM greater than one cent. While this is correct, trading only at-the-money options eliminates taking advantage of the profile of risk and reward that is at the heart of options trading.

THE COST OF THE OPTION: THE PREMIUM

The price of an option is commonly called its *premium*. The premium, which is determined in the marketplace, depends, among other things, on the strike price, the spot price, the expiration date, and the volatility of the underlying security. For the reasons discussed above, an in-the-money option on a currency will cost more than an option that is otherwise equivalent but has a strike price that places it out-of-the-money.

The option premium, all other things being equal, increases with the time remaining until maturity. Thus, a long-dated option is more expensive than an otherwise identical option that will expire soon. For an American call option, the reason is obvious. For example, a 55-cent DM call maturing in June 1992 can be exercised at any time prior to June and thus will be at least as valuable as a 55-cent DM call maturing in March 1992. The tendency of premiums to increase with the time to maturity is also typical of the European option. The reason for this is that the probability of profitable exercise is typically greater the more distant the expiration date. This will be discussed at length in Chapter 6.

Intrinsic Value and Time Value

In recognition of the importance of the exercise price and of the time to maturity, it is common to decompose the option premium into the value of the right to exercise at current prices (termed the *intrinsic value*) and the value of the right to benefit from a possibly favorable evolution of prices (termed the *time value*).

For an American call option, the intrinsic value is the amount by which the spot exchange rate exceeds the exercise price of the option. Thus, if the current exchange rate is 55 cents per DM, the intrinsic value of a 50-cent DM American call is 5 cents, while that of a 57-cent call is zero. Conversely, the intrinsic value of an American put option is the amount by which the spot exchange rate for the currency is less than the strike price. Notice that the intrinsic value is positive for in-the-money options and zero for out-of-the-money and at-the-money options. The intrinsic value is simply the degree to which an option is in-the-money.

For a European call option, the forward exchange rate is the rate that can be fixed now for a transaction that is to take place at the time that the option can be exercised. Consequently, we define the intrinsic value of a European call option as the amount by which the forward rate for the same date as the exercise date of the option exceeds the exercise price. Similarly, the intrinsic value of a European put option is the amount by which the exercise price exceeds the forward rate for the corresponding date.

These relationships can be summarized succinctly by using a little notation. We let E denote the strike price of the option, S the spot rate, F the forward rate, and Max(a, b) the limits of a and b. Then the relations of intrinsic value are given in Table 1-1. The symbol "a" represents the out-of-the-money situation, while the symbol "b" represents the degree of in-the-money for the American- or European-style option.

Time value represents the amount paid for the right to exercise an option after realizing a gain. It is measured by the difference between the premium and the intrinsic value. For an American option, the probability of exercise decreases as the exercise date is

TABLE 1-1
Intrinsic Value

	Call	Put
American	Max(0, S−E)	Max(0, E−S)
European	Max(0, F−E)	Max(0, E−F)

approached. In consequence, the time value of the option decreases over time, all else being equal. It is at its maximum when the option is at-the-money. It decreases as the option becomes either more in-the-money or out-of-the-money. However, it can never be negative. The structure of the option premium, expressed as a function of the prevailing exchange rate, is demonstrated in Figure 1–1.

The behavior of the time value as a function of the exchange rate can be understood by considering the behavior of a speculator. When an option is very deeply in-the-money, the probability of exercise is very high and the evolution of exchange rates is not likely to significantly lessen the probability of exercise. The premium will therefore be very close to the intrinsic value, and the time value will be close to zero.

Conversely, if an option is far out-of-the-money, the probability of an evolution of exchange rates that will lead to exercise of the option is very low. Consequently, the premium of the option, and

FIGURE 1–1
The Structure of a Call Premium's Value

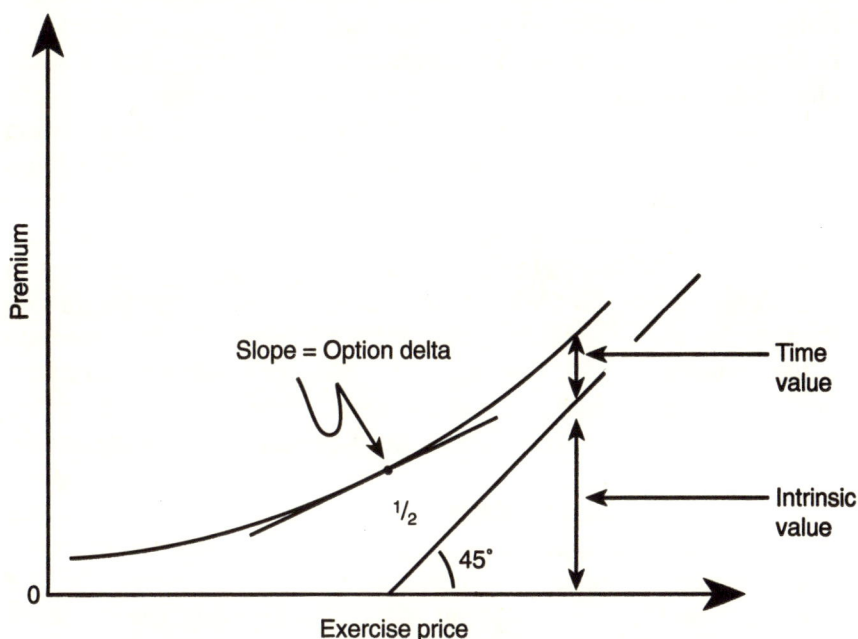

thus the time value, will be close to zero. The time value tends to be at its maximum when an option is just at-the-money because at that point the probability of an ultimate exercise equals the probability of a nonexercise.

Delta

In Figure 1–1 the slope of the curve is the ratio between the variation of the price of the option and the corresponding variation of the price of the currency. Among options traders this slope is called *delta,* that is,

$$\text{Delta} = \frac{\text{Change in option price}}{\text{Change in exchange rate}}$$

Knowledge of an option's delta is extremely useful because it allows traders to precisely hedge an underlying currency position through the sale of options. Furthermore, sellers of options can use delta to hedge their position on the foreign exchange market.

In hedging, a trader has two positions whose fluctuations in value just offset each other. Hedging currency exposure with options is complicated by the fact that option values are related in a nonlinear way to currency exchange rates. This means that in some circumstances, namely when an option is deep in-the-money, every one-cent change in the exchange rate changes the value of the option one cent. This is because the time value is zero and the option premium equals the intrinsic value. In other circumstances, however, namely when an option is far out-of-the-money, the premium is near zero and does not vary significantly with small changes in the exchange rate. In between, the relation between exchange rate fluctuations and changes in option value takes on some intermediate value between 0 and 1. Consequently, the face value amount of the options needed to hedge a given currency exposure will decrease as the option moves from being out-of-the-money to being in-the-money.

Since delta measures the relation between the option price and the exchange rate, it can be used to determine a hedged position. For example, suppose an American importer knows that he will need to pay 10 million DM on March 20 and that the currency quoted forward rate for that date is 55 cents per DM. Now, if he seeks to precisely hedge his exposure with March DM calls, he needs to know the delta of the option. For calls with a strike price of 55 cents, delta = 0.5. Thus, the hedge would be to buy 20 million DM of 55 calls. This may cost $0.02 per DM, or $400,000. Now, if the forward rate rose 1 cent, to 56 cents, the importer's commitment would cost an additional $100,000. However, his options would have risen in price by about 0.5 cents, to $0.025, so that his options position would now be worth $500,000. The result is a combined position that is unchanged.

If, instead, he used 53-cent March calls, their delta would be 0.70, which would require 14.29, say DM 15 million, or somewhat higher (since they are in-the-money) and might equal March DM calls with a strike price of 53 cents. Generally, we can state the hedge relation as follows:

$$\text{Options hedge} = \text{Currency position}/\text{Delta}$$

An important thing to notice is that, as we have already seen, the delta of a given option varies as the exchange rate varies. As a consequence, to maintain a hedge position for a given currency exposure, the options position will have to vary as the exchange rate varies. The full implications of this fact will be explored in Chapter 6.

Delta can also be used to hedge an option position using currency contracts. For example, suppose that a trader has sold call options on 1 million pounds sterling with a strike price of $1.60 and that, at the current exchange rate of $1.64, the delta is 0.35. Then the trader's hedge would be to hold 350,000 pounds sterling. More generally, the relation for hedging an options exposure is

$$\text{Currency hedge} = \text{Options position} \times \text{Delta}$$

Calculation of Option Premiums

Generally, the premium of a currency option is determined through negotiation by buyers and sellers either on an exchange or in the OTC market. But how do these traders determine when a given option is worth buying or selling? Is two cents too much to pay for an at-the-money March DM call? The answer depends on a variety of circumstances. In order to take account of all the relevant factors, traders have increasingly come to rely on mathematical formulas, which, when programmed into computers and fed with data that describe the current market conditions, are able to estimate the "fair value" of a given option. In Chapter 2 we will discuss these options-pricing models in some detail; at this stage, however, it is useful to highlight some of the factors that have been found important in arriving at option premiums.

In the field of international finance, the interest rate parity theory long ago made clear the importance of the interest rates in two countries for determining the long-run rate for forward exchanges of currency between those countries. Thus, if the interest rate is 9 percent in the United States and 4 percent in Germany, a forward DM exchange rate (expressed as cents per DM) will be greater than the spot rate. We say that the DM is at a premium and that the dollar is at a discount. If, as is often assumed, the forward rate is a good predictor of the eventual spot rate, a premium currency can be expected to appreciate relative to a discount currency.

The interest rate differential is also an important determinant of the premium for an option on exchange rates. Since a call on a currency becomes more valuable as the currency becomes more valuable, the premium on a call will increase if, all else being equal, the interest rate on that currency rises relative to that on the counterpart currency. By the same token, the premium of the currency call is a decreasing function of the counterpart interest rate. Thus, we can say that calls on premium currencies tend to be relatively more expensive than calls on discount currencies. Remembering that, for example, a DM call is also a put on the dollar with the DM as its counterpart, it follows that a put on a premium currency will appear cheap relative to a put on a discount currency.

The exercise date of an option is a second important determinant of its premium. The more distant the maturity, the more opportunity there is to exercise the option with a profit. Thus, the more distant the likely option exercise of a given strike price, the greater is the premium. This pattern can be readily observed in tables of premiums for exchange trade operations for both foreign currency options and futures options (see Figure 1–2, shown with currency options quotes below).

Finally, the volatility of the exchange rate is also an important determinant of the premium. If the exchange rate is volatile, the probability that it will change substantially is high and the chances of exercising a given option profitably are correspondingly high. This means that option premiums tend to increase with increases in exchange rate volatility.

VOLATILITY

Volatility is an indication of the amount and frequency of the exchange rate's variation around a mean value over a given period. As we have seen, the greater the anticipated volatility of the underlying currency over the period until the expiration date of an option, the greater is the value of the option. This means, for example, that the premium of an at-the-money pound sterling call against dollars with three months until maturity will be greater than the premium of a three-month at-the-money call of the DM against the Swiss franc. The computation of volatility will be studied in Chapter 2. However, we should note here that two approaches are possible. One approach is to calculate a statistical measure, usually the standard deviation, based on historical observations of the exchange rate. The other more likely approach is to use mathematical models of option premiums. Given an option premium observed in the market in combination with the other parameters of an equation, such as the exchange rate, the strike price, and the interest rates, it is possible to solve the equation for the implied volatility. In this way, the option market can be viewed as a market of volatilities. Option buyers expect relatively high exchange rate volatility; option sellers expect relatively low volatility. The market rate, which just balances supply and demand, is a consensus forecast of future volatilities.

CURRENCY OPTIONS QUOTES

Figure 1–2, taken from *The Wall Street Journal,* gives the quotes of the currency options traded on the principal exchanges active in currency options on June 6, 1990.

Here we will discuss the quotes for options on the Philadelphia Stock Exchange, which are options on spot exchange rates. The

FIGURE 1–2
Foreign Currency Options

CURRENCY TRADING
Wednesday, June 6, 1990

FUTURES OPTIONS

JAPANESE YEN (IMM) 12,500,000 yen; cents per 100 yen

Strike Price	Calls–Settle			Puts–Settle		
	Jun-c	Jly-c	Sep-c	Jun-p	Jly-p	Sep-p
64	1.57	1.87	2.19	0.01	0.14	0.48
65	0.62	1.09	1.54	0.05	0.35	0.81
66	0.06	0.52	1.01	0.49	0.78	1.27
67	0.00	0.22	0.65	1.43	1.48	1.88
68	0.00	0.10	0.40	2.43	2.34	2.61
69	0.00	0.05	0.23	3.43	....	3.44

Est. vol. 3,224, Tues vol. 2,687 calls, 2,491 puts
Open interest Tues; 73,226 calls, 47,938 puts

W. GERMAN MARK (IMM) 125,000 marks; cents per mark

Strike Price	Calls–Settle			Puts–Settle		
	Jun-c	Jly-c	Sep-c	Jun-p	Jly-p	Sep-p
57	2.22	2.30	2.61	0.00	0.09	0.42
58	1.24	1.45	1.90	0.02	0.23	0.70
59	0.35	0.78	1.32	0.13	0.56	1.10
60	0.04	0.36	0.88	0.82	1.13	1.64
61	0.00	0.16	0.57	1.78	1.94	2.31
62	0.00	0.07	0.35	2.78	2.84	3.07

Est. vol. 18,948, Tues vol. 8,738 calls, 10,754 puts
Open interest Tues; 72,224 calls, 69,648 puts

CANADIAN DOLLAR (IMM) 100,000 Can.$, cents per Can.$

Strike Price	Calls–Settle			Puts–Settle		
	Jun-c	Jly-c	Sep-c	Jun-p	Jly-p	Sep-p
845	0.81	0.43	0.79	0.02	0.70	1.07
850	0.36	0.25	0.59	0.10	1.02	1.37
855	0.10	0.14	0.44	0.30	....	1.70
860	0.01	0.10	0.31	0.72	....	2.07
865	0.00	0.04	0.22	1.21	....	2.47
870	0.00	....	....	....	....	....

Est. vol. 509, Tues vol. 207 calls, 1,573 puts
Open interest Tues; 11,603 calls, 15,541 puts

BRITISH POUND (IMM) 62,500 pounds; cents per pound

Strike Price	Calls–Settle			Puts–Settle		
	Jun-c	Jly-c	Sep-c	Jun-p	Jly-p	Sep-p
1625	6.02	3.88	5.16	0.02	0.60	1.92
1650	3.56	2.16	3.70	0.06	1.36	2.92
1675	1.20	1.04	2.58	0.20	2.72	4.26
1700	0.10	0.46	1.68	1.60	4.60	5.84
1725	0.02	0.20	1.10	4.02	....	....
1750	0.004	....	6.52	....	....	....

Est. vol. 1,368, Tues vol. 1,292 calls, 379 puts
Open interest Tues; 13,320 calls, 17,637 puts

SWISS FRANC (IMM) 125,000 francs; cents per franc

Strike Price	Calls–Settle			Puts–Settle		
	Jun-c	Jly-c	Sep-c	Jun-p	Jly-p	Sep-p
68	1.67	1.85	2.35	0.008	0.31	0.82
69	0.75	1.16	1.75	0.08	0.59	1.20
70	0.14	0.65	1.25	0.47	1.07	1.68
71	0.02	0.34	0.88	1.35	1.75	2.29
72	0.01	0.16	0.61	2.34	2.58	2.99
73	0.004	0.08	0.40	3.33	3.49	3.77

Est. vol. 5,224, Tues vol. 1,783 calls, 2,000 puts
Open interest Tues; 19,181 calls, 50,776 puts

OPTIONS

PHILADELPHIA EXCHANGE

Option & Underlying	Strike Price	Calls—Last			Puts—Last		
		Jun	Jul	Sep	Jun	Jul	Sep
50,000 Australian Dollars-cents per unit.							
ADollr	...74	r	r	r	r	0.13	r
77.21	...77	r	r	r	0.42	r	r
77.21	...78	r	0.36	r	r	r	r
31,250 British Pounds-cents per unit.							
BPound	160	r	r	r	r	r	1.30
168.82	162½	6.15	r	r	r	r	r
168.82	.165	3.85	r	4.40	r	1.05	r
168.82	167½	1.60	r	3.02	0.45	r	r
168.82	.170	0.42	r	2.02	1.92	r	r
50,000 Canadian Dollars-cents per unit.							
CDollr	.81½	r	r	r	r	r	0.24
85.41	...83	r	r	r	0.04	0.14	0.55
85.41	.83½	r	r	r	0.04	0.27	0.76
85.41	...84	r	r	r	r	0.35	0.95
85.41	.84½	r	0.94	r	0.12	0.51	r
85.41	...85	0.40	r	r	r	0.83	1.50
85.41	.85½	r	0.41	r	r	r	r
85.41	...86	0.08	0.24	r	r	1.47	2.25
85.41	.86½	r	0.14	0.31	r	r	r
50,000 Canadian Dollars-European Style.							
CDollar	.83	r	r	r	r	0.11	r
85.41	.85½	r	0.38	r	r	r	r
85.41	...86	0.09	r	r	r	r	r
62,500 West German Marks-cents per unit.							
DMark	...56	r	r	r	0.01	r	r
59.15	.57½	r	r	s	r	0.22	s
59.15	...58	r	1.56	r	r	0.30	0.73
59.15	.58½	r	1.18	s	0.14	r	s
59.15	...59	0.53	0.91	r	0.25	0.64	r
59.15	.59½	0.29	r	s	r	r	s
59.15	...60	0.13	r	0.98	r	1.22	r
59.15	...61	0.03	0.22	r	r	1.94	r
59.15	.61½	r	0.15	s	r	r	s
59.15	...62	r	0.10	r	r	r	r
59.15	...63	r	0.05	0.25	r	r	r
59.15	...64	r	0.02	r	r	r	r
62,500 West German Marks-European Style.							
59.15	.60½	r	0.31	s	r	r	s
6,250,000 Japanese Yen-100ths of a cent per unit.							
JYen	...62	r	r	r	r	r	0.16
65.55	...63	r	r	r	0.02	r	r
65.55	.63½	r	r	s	0.02	r	s
65.55	...64	r	r	r	r	r	0.53
65.55	...65	r	r	r	0.16	0.45	r
65.55	.65½	r	0.77	s	r	r	s
65.55	...66	0.20	0.56	1.07	r	r	1.33
65.55	.66½	r	0.39	s	r	r	s
65.55	...67	0.04	0.27	0.65	r	r	r
65.55	...68	0.02	r	0.43	r	r	r
65.55	...69	r	0.06	r	r	r	r
62,500 Swiss Francs-cents per unit.							
SFranc	...64	r	r	r	r	0.01	r
69.71	.65½	4.56	s	s	r	s	r
69.71	...66	4.05	r	r	r	0.06	r
69.71	...67	r	r	r	r	0.15	r
69.71	...68	r	r	r	r	0.26	r
69.71	...69	1.23	r	r	0.24	0.52	r
69.71	...70	0.45	r	r	0.45	0.95	r
69.71	.70½	0.27	0.69	s	r	r	s
69.71	...71	0.16	r	r	r	r	r
69.71	.71½	0.09	r	s	r	r	s
69.71	...72	r	0.28	r	r	r	r

Total call vol. 20,076 Call open int. 378,082
Total put vol. 6,111 Put open int. 378,474
r—Not traded. s—No option offered.
Last is premium (purchase price).

quotes for futures options at the CME and LIFFE follow the same principles.

"Option & Underlying" indicates the different currencies for which options are traded and specifies the spot exchange rate of the underlying currency prevailing at the time options trading was closed. Options on six currencies are reported: the Australian dollar, the British pound sterling, the Canadian dollar, the German mark, the Japanese yen, and the Swiss franc. The exercise of a call option contract on the pound sterling results in 12,500 pounds being deposited in an account in the holder's name.

The counterpart currency for all of these options is the U.S. dollar. Thus, spot exchange rates are expressed in fractions of dollars per unit of currency. More precisely, the yen options are quoted in 100/ths of cents per yen. All of the other options are quoted in cents per unit. For example, the DM spot rate is 59.15 cents per DM, or $1/0.5915 = 1.6906$ DM per dollar.

"Strike Price" lists all the strike prices of the actively traded options. Notice that the regular intervals between strike prices reflect the standardization involved in exchange-traded options. This means that typically no option is precisely at-the-money. The range of available strike prices is much wider for options with a high trading volume (e.g., German marks) than for less popular options (e.g., Australian dollars).

The premiums of call and put options are listed in the right-hand columns of the table, organized with respect to the exercise date and the strike price. Thus, the last DM call for June with a strike price of 57 cents sold for 2.22 cents per mark. This would cost the buyer $62,500 \times \$.0222 = \$1,387.50$.

Reading down vertically, notice that for calls, the higher the strike price, the lower are the option premiums, and that for puts, the higher the strike price, the higher are the premiums. This reflects the point already discussed that the more an option is in-the-money, the more valuable it is. Furthermore, reading horizontally, we see that, for a given strike price and a given type of option (call or put), the more distant the exercise date, the higher the premium is.

The volume (listed as "Total call vol." or "Total put vol.") represents the number of put or call option contracts bought or sold in a day. The open interest ("open int.") specifies the number of outstanding contracts, that is, the number that may still be exercised. As with other exchange-traded term instruments (such as futures), there is no immediate relationship between volume and open interest. If a trader with no position in an option sells the option to a trader who also has no position, this trade adds 1 to the volume and 1 to the open interest. If a trader who has already sold a particular type of option buys the same type of option from a trader with no previous position, the increment to the volume is 1, but there is no change in the open interest (a short position has been transferred from one trader to another). Finally, if a trader who has previously sold a particular type of option buys from a trader who has previously bought the same type of option, the increment to the volume is 1, while the open interest falls by 1.

The ratio between the volume and the open interest gives an indicator of the activity of the options market. For our case, call volume was only 3.4 percent of the call open interest. This means that the average holding period for a call on the Philadelphia Stock Exchange was somewhat more than 29 days. A similar pattern held for puts. In contrast, it is not uncommon in active futures markets for the volume to approach the open interest. Thus, we can see that long-term positions are far more common in the currency options market than in futures markets and that very active intraday trading is the exception rather than the rule.

THE EFFECTIVELY GUARANTEED EXCHANGE RATE

The buyer of an option guarantees himself the right to obtain a specific exchange rate at a given expiration date. This is a "worst case" rate in the sense that he exercises this right only if the eventually prevailing exchange rate would be worse for his purposes. By choosing the strike price, the buyer determines the protected exchange rate; however, the effectively guaranteed rate differs from the strike price.

Let us consider the purchase of a DM option at the prices quoted in Figure 1–2. The buyer of a June call in DM with a strike price of 58 cents must pay 1.24 cents per DM. If he exercises the option, he will have to pay 58 + 1.24 = 59.24 cents per DM. Of course, instead of exercising, he will buy on the spot market if the spot price is less than 58. Thus, in deciding whether to buy the call, he sees that the price ceiling he can effectively guarantee for himself is 59.24.

The premium for a September DM put with a strike price of 60 is 1.64. Thus, the buyer of such a put can be sure that the effective price floor for his eventual sale of DM is 60 − 1.64 = 58.36 cents per DM.

In this discussion we have not taken into account the fact that the premium is paid when the option is purchased. For longer holding periods or high interest rates, it is appropriate to calculate effectively guaranteed exchange rates by multiplying the premium by 1 plus the prevailing rate of interest over the holding period. This makes it possible to calculate the effectively guaranteed exchange rate. Using the Chicago Mercantile DM options from Figure 1–2, we arrive at the data in Table 1–2.

Table 1–2 illustrates an important relationship between the effectively guaranteed prices for calls and puts. Note that the prices effectively guaranteed by July DM calls are greater than the prices effectively guaranteed by July DM puts and that the same relationship holds true for September calls and puts. Otherwise, a risk-free trading profit could be made by buying both calls and puts. The attempts of arbitrageurs to make such a profit would force up option premiums until the profit opportunity was eliminated. This reasoning gives us a more specific relationship:

Guaranteed sell rate < Forward rate < Guaranteed buy rate

The DM spot rate that corresponds to Figure 1–2 was 59.15 cents per DM. At that time, U.S. interest rates were higher than

TABLE 1–2
Effectively Guaranteed Exchange Rates: DM Options

Strike Price	Calls		Puts	
	July	Sept.	July	Sept.
57	59.30	59.61	56.91	56.58
58	59.45	59.90	57.77	57.30
59	59.78	60.32	58.44	57.90
60	60.36	60.88	58.87	58.36
61	61.16	61.57	59.06	58.69
62	62.07	62.35	59.16	58.93

those of Germany, so the DM was the premium currency; the forward rate for late September was 59.31 cents per DM. From Table 1–2 we see that this was above the rate that a trader could guarantee DM sales using September put options. Otherwise, a trader could have a profit no less than the guaranteed sell rate less the forward rate by buying DM forward and September put options. Thus, to prevent risk-free arbitrage between currency puts and the forward market, the guaranteed sell rate is below the forward rate. By analogous reasoning the currency purchase rate guaranteed by long positions in currency calls must be above the forward rate.

The difference between the forward rate and the effectively guaranteed rates reflects the very significant advantage that the currency option holder has compared to the trader who covers himself in the forward market. Like the forward hedger, the currency option holder guarantees an exchange rate for his currency purchase or sale; however, unlike the forward hedger, he can liquidate a position on the spot market if the exchange rate evolves in his favor. In this sense, the option can be understood as a conditional forward cover, and the price of the conditional exercise is the difference between the effectively guaranteed rate and the corresponding forward rate.

The main contribution of currency options is the flexibility they have introduced into international financial management. This flexibility appears at two levels.

1. The risk/reward profile of a position hedged with options is intermediate between that of a forward covered position and that of an uncovered position.[2] An option hedge removes the rigidity of the forward market, making it possible to unwind the hedge if exchange rates favorably evolve. If exchange rates evolve unfavorably, the hedger liquidates his position at a less desirable rate, but the profits he earns by exercising his option reduce his losses.

2. Currency options can be used not only to hedge fixed currency risks but also hedge conditional risks such as bids on foreign contracts or sales based on fixed price lists. In addition, they can be used in more speculative trading strategies that are based on the anticipation of changes in either the direction or the volatility of exchange rates. Since speculative trading strategies do not require

[2] We call the risk/reward profile of an option strategy the potential profits and losses of the trader, depending on the exchange rate at the end of the contract.

a reference to any preexisting currency exposure, they are in a sense more elementary than hedging strategies. The simplest speculative trading strategies are discussed in the remainder of this chapter.

THE BASIC STRATEGIES

There are four basic options positions corresponding to the purchase or sale of calls or puts. The following diagram shows the logic of these positions:

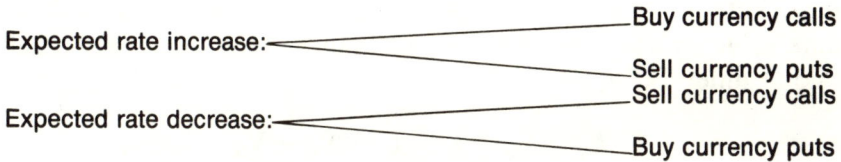

Expected rate increase: — Buy currency calls
— Sell currency puts
Expected rate decrease: — Sell currency calls
— Buy currency puts

A trader who opens one of these positions uncovered is betting on the evolution of the underlying currency exchange rate. If he expects an increase of the exchange rate, he can either buy currency calls or sell currency puts. If he expects a decrease of the exchange rate, he can either buy currency puts or sell currency calls.

If the Exchange Rate Is Expected to Increase

Buy a Call Option on the Currency
A trader who pays a premium C for a call option with a strike price E makes a profit by selling his option at a higher premium than C or by exercising his option and selling the underlying currency at a rate higher than $E + C$.

Purchase and Subsequent Sale of a Call Option
The buyer of a call option sells it with a profit if the increase in its intrinsic value is greater than the decrease in its time value. The result of an option sale at time t before the exercise date can be written as follows:

Premium of the option at t − Premium of the option at the origin = Intrinsic value at t + Time value at t − Intrinsic value at the origin − Time value at the origin

TABLE 1–3
Returns From a Call Purchase and Subsequent Resale

		At Time of Sale	
		In-the-Money	*Out-of-the-Money*
At time of purchase	In-the-money	$S_t - S_0 + V_t - V_0$	$E - S_0 + V_t - V_0$
	Out-of-the-money	$S_t - E + V_t - V_0$	$+ V_t - V_0$

If we note the call premium as C, the intrinsic value as I, and the time value as V, the profit from a call purchase at time 0 and a call sale at time t is

$$C_t - C_0 = I_t - I_0 + V_t - V_0 \tag{1}$$

Of course, the profit will depend on the change of the exchange rate from the time of purchase until the time of sale; however, expressing this in symbols is more complicated than equation (1). Since the intrinsic value of an American call is the minimum of zero and the difference between the exchange rate and the strike price, there are four possibilities. These are given in Table 1–3. At one extreme, a trader buys an in-the-money call and sells it when it is still in-the-money. At the opposite extreme, a trader buys an out-of-the-money call and sells it when it is still out-of-the-money. The result is simply the decrease in time value.

Purchase of a Call Option and Subsequent Exercise
If at some time t the holder of an American option with strike price E finds that the option is in-the-money, he will realize the following return by exercising:

$$S_t - E - C_0 = I_t - I_0 - V_0 \tag{2}$$

If we compare equations (1) and (2), we see that the return for closing out a long American call position through an offsetting sale is greater by the amount V_t than the return from exercising the position. This is intuitively plausible. Through exercise, we lose whatever time value there is in holding the option. In this way, we arrive at a basic rule of thumb when dealing with American options: *An option is more valuable alive than dead.* Consequently, a speculative option position that is terminated before it expires is generally closed out by an offsetting trade.[3]

Risk and Return of Purchase of a Call Option
Using the data from Figure 1–2, the risk/reward profile of the purchase on June 6, 1990, of a September DM call option with a strike price of 59 cents is given in Figure 1–3. If the spot rate is less than 59 cents, the option would not be exercised. Thus, the potential loss is indicated by the horizontal line segment and corresponds to the premium of 1.32 cents. At rates above 61 cents, exercise would result in a gross profit; however, if this gross profit is less than the original premium, the result is a net loss. Thus, the break-even point for this trade is 60.32 cents per DM. At higher rates the net profit potential curve is positive and increases 1 to 1 with the exchange rate. The profit potential of the buyer of a call option is theoretically unlimited. On the other hand, the buyer's risk is limited to the option premium.

Choice of the Exercise Price
The kinked curve in Figure 1–3 describes the basic asymmetry in how call positions make or lose money with exchange rate increases or decreases. The same basic asymmetry applies to call options with different strike prices. However, the balance of risk and reward will depend on which strike price is selected. Generally, for long positions the reward potential is greater the more the option is in-the-money at the time of purchase; however, the risk is also greater the more the option is in-the-money. These basic facts are illustrated in Figure 1–4.

If a trader buys an out-of-the-money call, since the premium is less than that of an at-the-money call, the risk is also less. However, the spot rate would have to be higher before he could realize a gross profit upon exercise; consequently, the profit potential is less.

---

[3] Exceptions to this rule can occur when secondary trading is very illiquid, so that the sale price is so low as to imply negative time value. Other exceptions will be discussed in Chapter 6.

FIGURE 1–3
Risk/Reward Profile of a Call Purchase

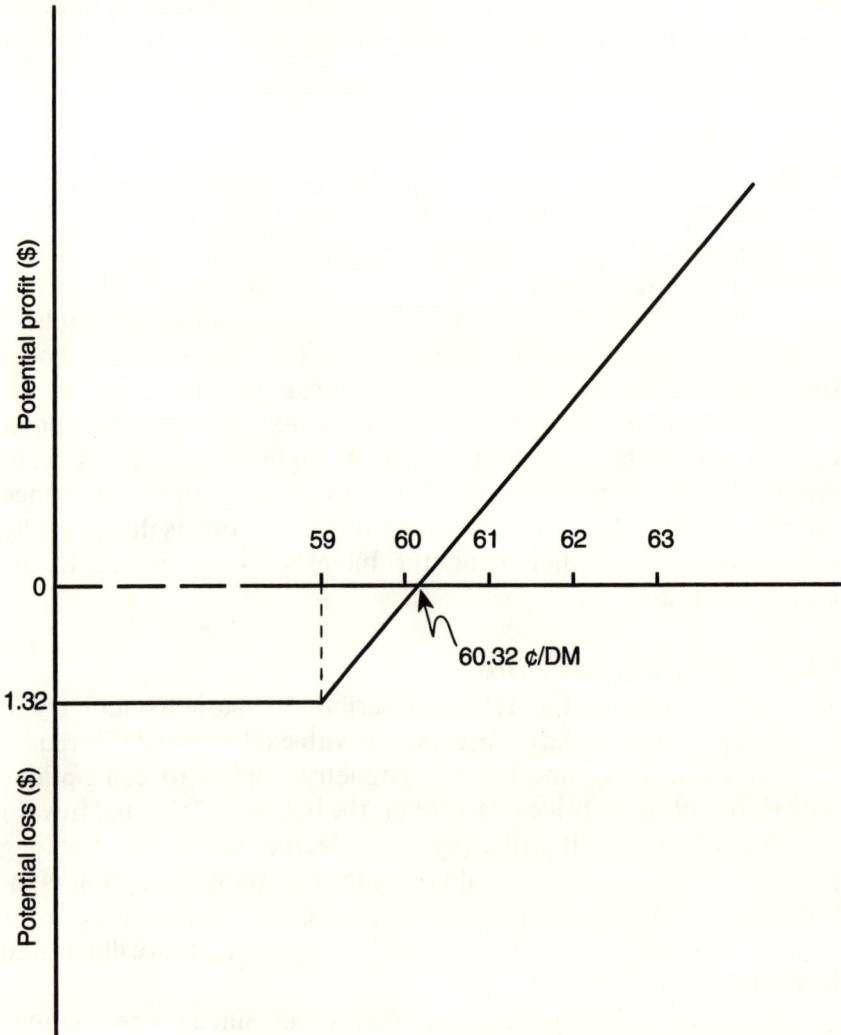

Similarly, we see that an in-the-money call carries more risk and more reward potential than an at-the-money call. In the limit, if the exercise price is zero, we arrive at the simple forward purchase, which has the maximum possible reward potential but carries the maximum risk.

FIGURE 1–4
Buying of Calls with Different Strike Prices

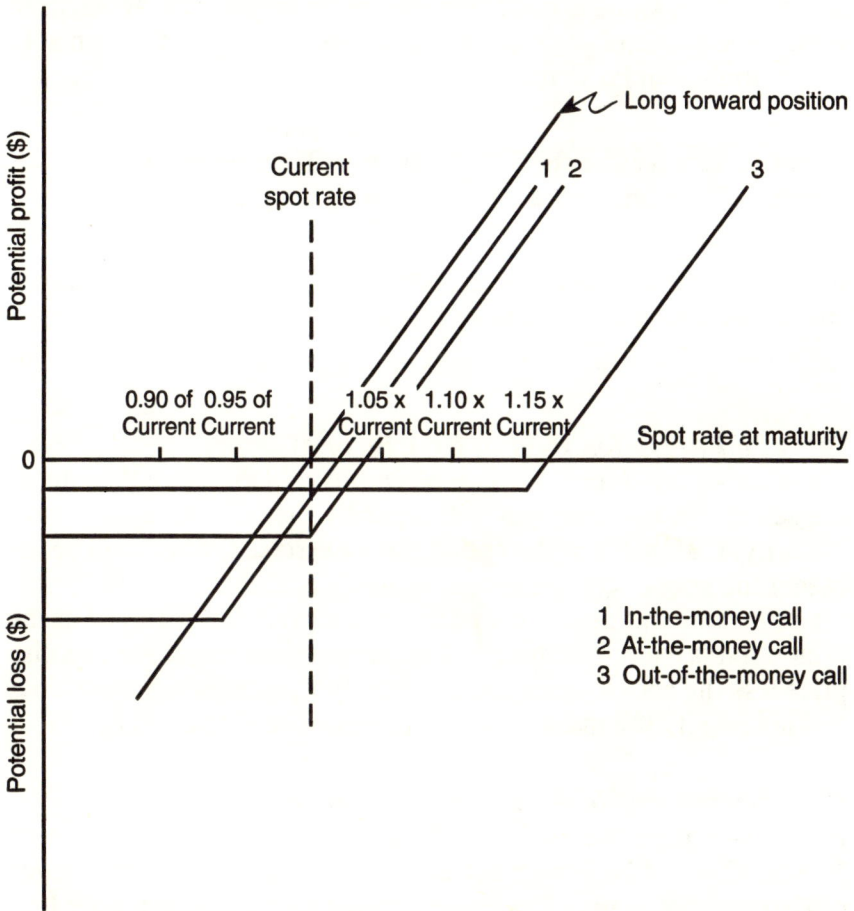

Sell a Put Option on the Currency

For a trader who expects the exchange rate of a currency to increase, an alternative to buying a call is to sell a put option on the currency. The trader who does this hopes to buy back his put right at a lower price, thereby taking advantage of the decrease of the time value as well as a possible decrease in the intrinsic value.

Sale and Subsequent Repurchase of a Put Option

The seller of a put option buys back his right making a profit if the fall in the time value is not overcome by an increase in the intrinsic value. The result of the repurchase at time t of the put option sold at the origin can be written as

Premium received at the origin − Premium paid at t = Intrinsic value at the origin + Time value at the origin − Intrinsic value at t − Time value at t

If we let P be the premium of the put option, then, using the symbols introduced above, the profit of this transaction can be written:

$$P_0 - P_t = I_0 - I_t + V_0 - V_t \qquad (3)$$

Sale of a Put Option Held to Exercise or Maturity

Since, as we have seen, an option is more valuable alive than dead, the seller of a currency put will typically face exercise only upon maturity. If at that time the option is not exercised, which will be the case if the spot exchange rate at maturity is above the strike price, the seller of a put option keeps the entire premium received at the origin. If it is exercised, his profit is the premium minus the exercise price less the spot exchange rate. Thus, his profit from selling a put and holding it until maturity or exercise can be written as $P_0 - I_t$.

Risk/Reward Profile of the Sale of a Put Option

Figure 1–5 gives the profit and loss potential for a trader who on June 6, 1990, sold a September British pound put with a strike price of 170 cents per pound. The figure is based on the data in Figure 1–2. If upon maturity the spot exchange rate was above 1.70, the option would expire unexercised and the trader would make the original premium of 2.02 cents per pound. At lower spot rates the option would be exercised and the profit level of the trader would be reduced by one cent for every cent that the exchange rate was below 1.70. The break-even exchange rate is 167.98 cents per pound.

The profit of the seller of a put option is limited, and the risk is potentially very high. Unlike the buyer of a call option, the seller of a put option does not benefit from a strong appreciation of the exchange rate of the underlying currency. Instead, the seller of a

FIGURE 1–5
Risk/Reward Profile of a Put Sale

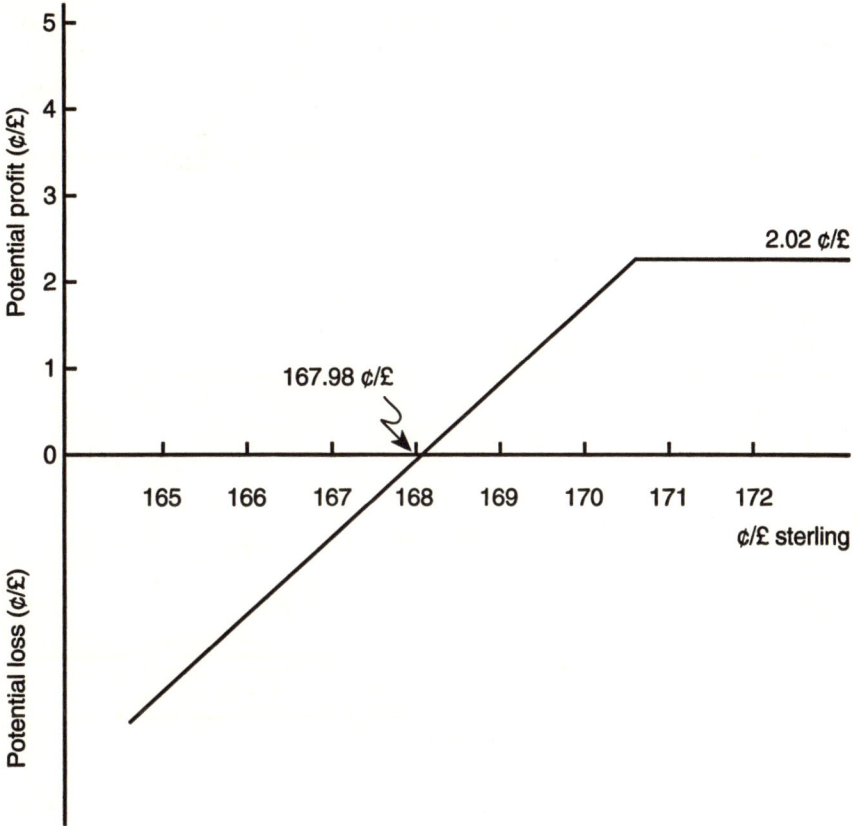

put option profits equally at any exchange rate above the strike price. Selling a put option makes sense when a trader is confident that the exchange rate will not fall sharply but is unsure whether it will be stable or will increase. For if the exchange rate is stable or increases, the put seller will benefit from the steady erosion of time value.

Choice of the Strike Price
The seller of an out-of-the-money put receives a very low premium but is in a position in which the probability of exercise is very

small. Only a major decrease of the exchange rate of the underlying currency leads the buyer to exercise his right. Conversely, the seller of an in-the-money put receives a large premium (reflecting the positive initial intrinsic value) but faces a higher probability of exercise.

Figure 1–6 describes the risk/reward profiles of the sales of put options based on different strike prices. Notice that the higher the exercise price, the greater is the premium but the closer the option approaches the risk associated with a forward purchase.

FIGURE 1–6
Selling Puts with Different Strike Prices

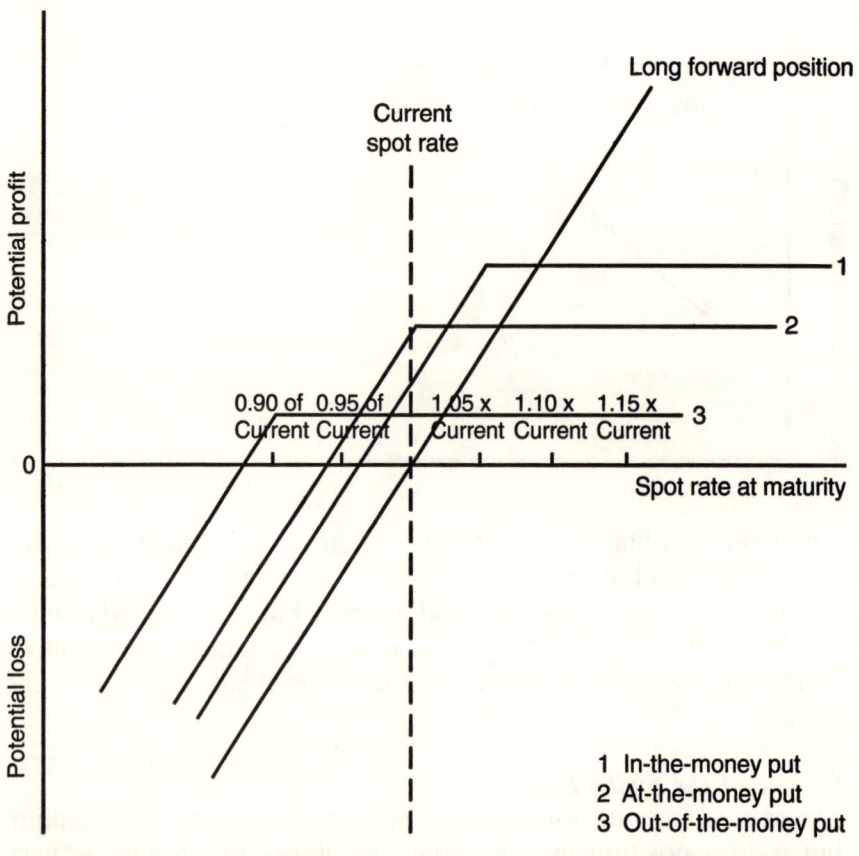

If the Exchange Rate Is Expected to Decrease

Buy a Put Option on the Currency

The buyer of a put option makes a profit if he sells his right at a higher premium than he paid or if upon exercise the spot rate is below the strike price by at least as much as the original premium.

Purchase and Subsequent Resale of a Put Option

By the same type of reasoning that we developed in detail for the purchase of a call, it can be shown that the buyer of a put option makes a profit if the increase of the intrinsic value is at least as great as the decrease of the time value. In symbols, the profit from a put purchase and resale at time t is

$$P_t - P_0 = I_t - I_0 + V_t - V_0 \qquad (4)$$

Purchase of a Put Option and Subsequent Exercise

The buyer of a put option exercises it only if the exchange rate of the underlying currency is lower than the strike price. In this case, he buys the currencies in the market and delivers them at the higher exchange rate. If the difference between the strike price and the spot exchange rate in the market is larger than the premium at the origin, the buyer makes a net profit. In this case, exercising gives the following return:

$$E - S_t - P_0 = I_t - I_0 - V_0 \qquad (5)$$

By comparison with equation (4), we see that exercising a put in advance of maturity involves the loss of time value. For this reason, early exercise of American-style put options on currencies is the exception rather than the rule.

Risk and Return for the Purchase of a Put Option

If at the expiration date the spot exchange rate is higher than the exercise price, the buyer of a put option does not exercise his right and gives up the premium. His loss is therefore limited to P. If, instead, at the expiration date the spot exchange rate is lower than the strike price, the buyer exercises his right and obtains a gross

FIGURE 1–7
Risk/Reward Profile of a Put Purchase

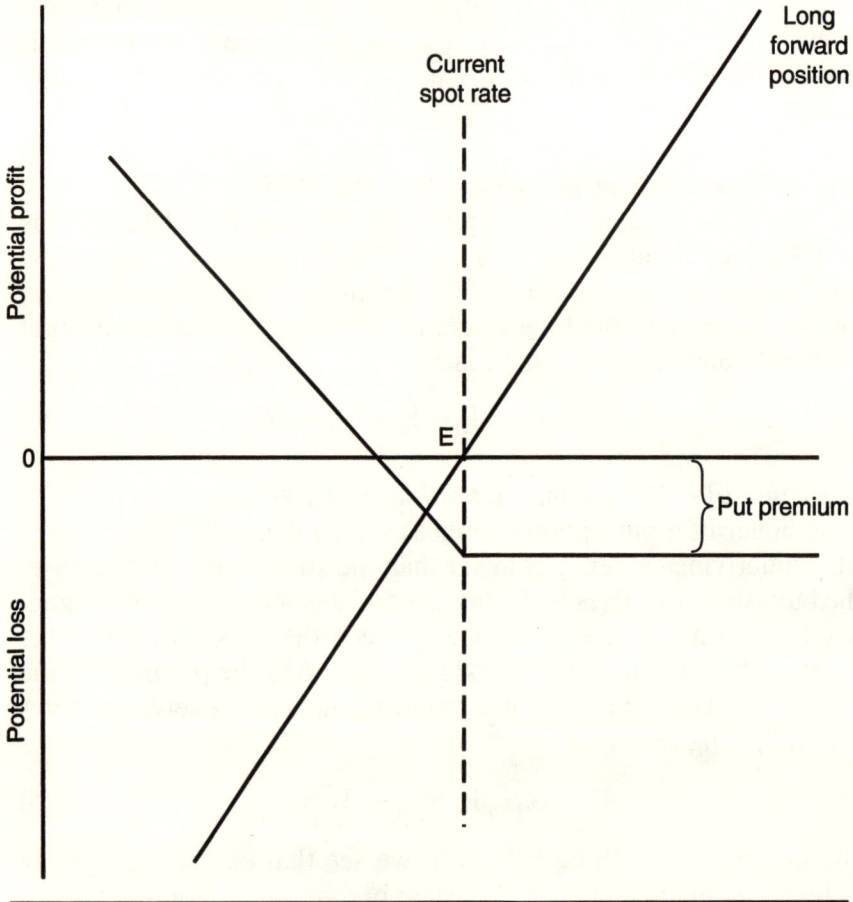

profit. The lower the spot price, the higher is the gross profit. Graphically, this is described in Figure 1–7. Notice that the break-even point occurs where the spot rate is less than the strike price by an amount just equal to the original premium.

Sell a Call Option on the Currency
A trader who sells a call option makes a profit if he later buys back his position at a lower premium than he received earlier. In symbols,

the return from a sale and subsequent repurchase of a currency call is

$$C_0 - C_t = I_0 - I_t + V_0 - V_t \qquad (6)$$

The seller of a call tends to make money from the decline in the time value; however, this decline can be overcome by an increase in the intrinsic value if the exchange rate rises sufficiently. The seller who holds his position until maturity earns a profit if the original premium is greater than the intrinsic value at expiration. If the call expires in-the-money and is exercised, so long as the differ-

FIGURE 1–8
Risk/Reward Profile of a Call Sale

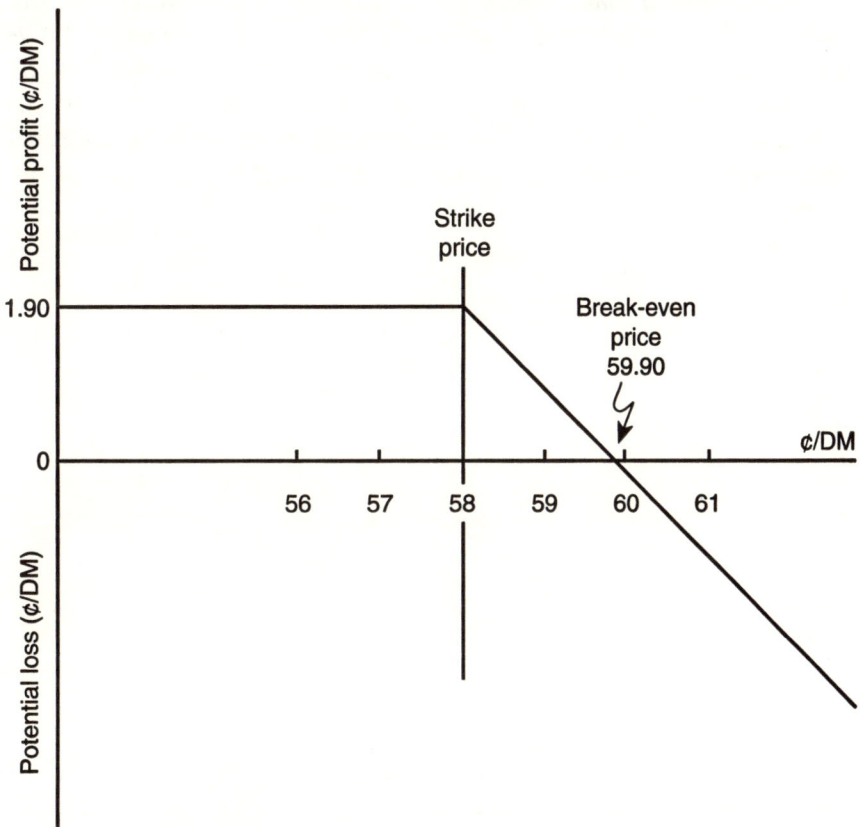

ence between the spot rate and the exercise price is less than the original premium, the seller earns a profit.

If we take the case of a sale on June 6, 1990, of a September DM call with a strike price of 58, we have the potential profits and losses depicted in Figure 1–8. Notice that this graph is perfectly symmetrical to Figure 1–3. This is because, for one transaction, the profits of the seller of an option plus those of the corresponding buyer must sum to zero. Consequently, we see that the profit potential of the call seller is limited to the original premium, while the loss potential of the call seller is theoretically unlimited.

Naturally, in light of our above discussion of the call purchase, the risk/reward profile of the call sale depends on the strike price chosen. If the strike price is high, so that the option is initially far out-of-the-money, the exchange rate must rise considerably before the seller would make a loss through the eventual exercise of the option. The risk associated with such an option will be small; however, the premium earned will be correspondingly small. As the exercise price drops, the premium earned rises, but the loss potential also rises. In the limit, as the exercise price approaches zero, the risk/reward potential approaches that of a forward sale of the currency.

CHAPTER 2

THE DETERMINATION OF THE THEORETICAL OPTION PRICE

The price of an option consists of its intrinsic value and its time value. The intrinsic value is the difference between the option's strike price and the current market price of its underlying security. The time value is the difference between the option price and the intrinsic value. Over time, the marketplace price of an option will fluctuate above and below the theoretical or "fair" value of the option. Rather complex algorithms are required utilizing calculus to compute the theoretical price, and a computer is required to obtain a rapid response to marketplace changes in the conditions measured in the models used. The differences between the models used depend on whether the option is American style, an option whose underlying security is a futures contract, or European style, an option whose underlying security is a forward contract. This chapter explains the two major models used.

THE HYPOTHESIS OF RISK-FREE ARBITRAGE: THE GARMAN-KOHLHAGEN MODEL

In 1982, two American economists, Mark Garman and Steven Kohlhagen, proposed a valuation model for the price of foreign exchange options based on applying the well-known Black-Scholes model, which was designed in 1973 for risk-free arbitrage of common stock options. The key assumption of the Black-Scholes model is that a constant arbitrage occurs in the marketplace between the ownership of an option's underlying security and the sale of just enough call options of a particular maturity to offset any price changes occurring in the underlying security with the price changes occurring in the options. Since this arbitrage is in theory a risk-free operation, its potential reward is the risk-free rate, which is usually assumed to be the 90-day T-bill return. With stock options, a rather busy operation, the returns do in fact approach the T-bill rate less the brokerage commissions involved. Because the rewards are slim, there are always temptations to forecast a bit where the underlying security is heading and therefore not to adjust so much, but that is a subject unto itself.

Professors Garman and Kohlhagen disagreed with the arbitrage assumption because they felt that currency managers tend to specu-late on currency behavior and to involve themselves with options in order to manage risk. Garman and Kohlhagen held that if currency managers desired a hedge against the underlying security, they would simply involve themselves with the forward markets. This approach would force them to account more closely for the behavior of currency fluctuations and interest rates. An important assump-tion of the Garman-Kohlhagen model is that currency fluctuations can best be described by a lognormal probability distribution, which is another way of saying that they are based mainly on percentage changes in price. This assumption is rather sensible, since curren-cies are traded against one another based on the alternative interest returns that they make available. The equations for the lognormal approach are presented in Figure 2–1.

For stochastic processes, Kiyosi Ito has developed a variation regarding "noise"—an uncertain shock that is unanticipated if one expects the mean to follow the normal law. Ito's variation can be described as follows:

$$\text{Log}\frac{(S_{t + \Delta t})}{S_t} = \mu\Delta t + \sigma\text{Agtz}$$

where

z = Variable designed by Wiener with a mean of 0 and σ set equal to 1.

The hypothesis that the lognormal distribution best describes price changes in currency options is currently causing several theo-reticians to reconsider the best way to characterize the price of options. One of the matters being reconsidered is whether plus or minus one standard deviation contains two times the 34 percent of observations that are contained in such an area with the standard normal probability distribution.

FIGURE 2–1

68 Percent of the Variations of the Logs of the Prices Are Contained between μ_1 and μ_2.

The hypothesis for the distribution follows:

$\log S_{t+\Delta t} - \log S_t$ obeys the lognormal form $\aleph\ (\mu, \partial)$

or, $\log \left[\dfrac{S_{t+\Delta t}}{S_t} \right]$ obeys the lognormal form $\aleph\ (\mu, \partial)$

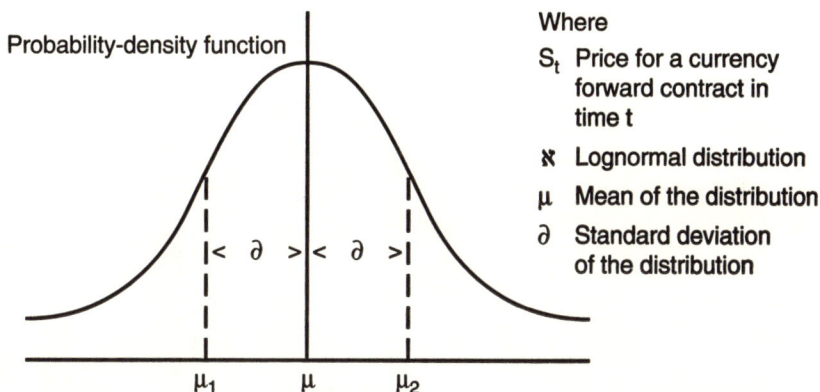

Probability-density function

$|< \partial >|< \partial >|$

$\mu_1 \quad \mu \quad \mu_2$

Where

S_t Price for a currency forward contract in time t

$\aleph$ Lognormal distribution

μ Mean of the distribution

∂ Standard deviation of the distribution

A second important assumption of the Garman-Kohlhagen model is that interest rate levels are constant during the life of an option. Some researchers today introduce a stochastic process to fluctuate interest rates, some dependently, some independently of the fluctuations that actually occur. The increasing volatility of price changes that began in 1970 is a good reason for investigating whether the theories that then existed are still valid. A matter that might be investigated is the behavior of the underlying securities well into the period of greater volatility.

Figures 2–2 and 2–3 show percentage changes on a weekly basis of the U.S. dollar versus the DM and the French franc from January 1983 through November 1984. The graphs in these figures are organized so as to compare the changes that actually took place with a standard normal distribution. As can be readily seen, the empirical data of the percentage changes are skewed to the right and not evenly distributed about the mean, as would be the case if a normal distribution were operating. The differences, which are greatest for the high positive percentage changes, are typical of a

FIGURE 2–2
Comparison of the Frequencies of Percentage Changes versus the
Standard Normal Probability Profile for Dollars/DM

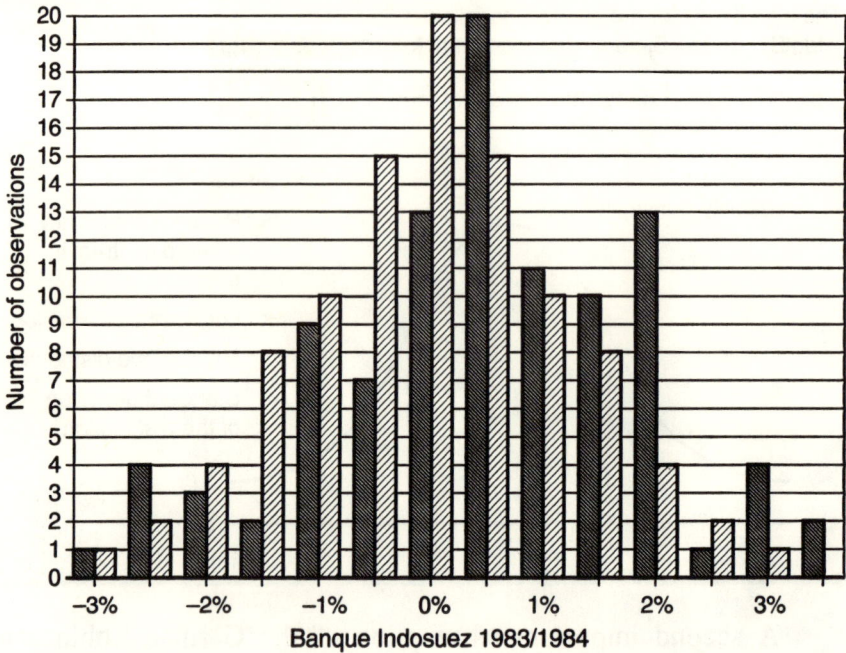

Banque Indosuez 1983/1984

lognormally distributed phenomenon. The sum of the means of the actual percentage changes is a positive number, not zero, as it would be if the percentage changes were normally distributed. The two cases shown confirm the validity of the Garman-Kohlhagen assumption that the logs of the percentage changes for foreign currencies are normally distributed in the readings for +2 percent and +3 percent, the major differences between the actual data and the theoretical ideal for a normal distribution provide all the evidence needed to conclude that the percentage changes in foreign currencies have a lognormal distribution.

An important assumption of the Garman-Kohlhagen model is the constant value of the interest rate return during the life of an option. However, certain researchers have been introducing a stochastic fluctuation in the interest rate as a dependent variable, that is, as a variable independent of the fluctuations in the currency. A question

FIGURE 2–3

Comparison of the Frequencies of Percentage Changes versus the Standard Normal Probability Profile for Dollars/French Francs

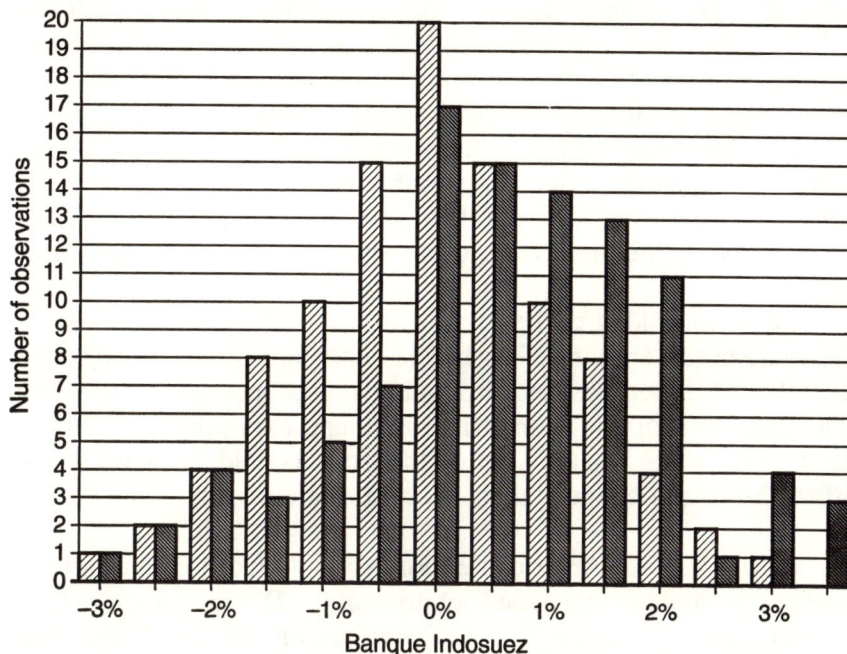

Banque Indosuez

that should be asked is whether the improvements achieved are significant enough to warrant making the model more complex.

The Garman-Kohlhagen model also assumes that no transaction costs are associated with trading options, which is not the case if one has to deal with option brokers and pay them their commissions. With European-style options, which must be held until expiration to be exercised, transaction costs incurred for trading out of an option position are not a consideration. For such options, the assumption of no transaction costs is acceptable. This is not so, however, for American-style options, which are often traded prior to expiration.

An example is perhaps the best way of explaining the use of the Garman-Kohlhagen model.

Suppose that a treasurer wishes to be long a currency. Realizing that there is risk in the price of the currency while the long position is held, to offset that risk he sells call options, which vary in price based on changes in the value of the underlying currency. The revenue received from selling the calls offsets the risk of loss in the currency. The value of the options sold varies inversely with the value of the currency if the currency rises in price. Given too strong a rally in the currency, some of the options may have to be repurchased to offset an imbalanced hedge position.

The movement of the value of a call option as the underlying currency changes in price is a variable that is termed the option's *delta*. Knowledge of how the delta changes in value with changes in the price of the underlying currency is the key to trading with options.

Covering a long currency position by selling call options for the same dollar amount of currencies does not produce the hedge that the treasurer desires. Producing the proper hedge requires selecting the proper option strike price and expiration date, since the inverse price relationship of the options sold must precisely offset the price changes taking place in the currency owned.

Example. An American exporter would like to cover a long position of 1 million DM. The spot price of the DM as of June 6, 1990 (see Figure 1–2), was 0.5915 U.S. dollars or 169 cents/DM. The delta of an American option trading at a strike price of 59 cents is approximately ½. Selling such an option at the Philadelphia Options Exchange (where each call covers 125,000 DM/$) would require

$$\frac{1,000,000 \text{ DM}}{125,000 \text{ DM}/\$} \times \frac{1}{\text{Delta}} = \frac{1,000,000 \text{ DM}}{125,000 \text{ DM}/\$} \times 2$$

$$= 16 \text{ DM July 59 calls at a price of } 0.91 \text{ producing}$$
$$\text{revenues of } 16 \times \$910 = \$14,560$$

If the exporter prefers to sell in-the-money calls, say at a strike price of 58, the delta is 0.59. Repeating the same computations as those used above,

$$\frac{1,000,000 \text{ DM}}{125,000 \text{ DM}/\$} \times \frac{1}{0.59} = 8 \times 1.7$$

$$= 13.6 \approx 14$$

At a premium of 1.56, the revenues produced are $1,560 × 14 = $21,840.

The delta of a call option that is deep in-the-money, roughly 10 percent higher than the strike price, approaches a value of 1, which means that any change in the value of the underlying currency is matched by a change in the intrinsic value of the option. However, there is a very high probability that deep in-the-money calls will be exercised, so that the exporter who sells them loses flexibility in handling his own decision making.

If the exporter decides to go to the opposite extreme and sell severely out-of-the-money calls, a large number of contracts can be involved. For instance, if a July 63 call is sold at the current price of 0.05 ($50), the delta at the futures price/strike price of 59.15/63 = 0.94, which yields a value of 0.15. The standard computation produces the following result:

$$\frac{1,000,000 \text{ DM}}{125,000 \text{ DM/\$}} \times \frac{1}{0.15} = 8 \times 6.7$$
$$= 53.6 \approx 54$$

With a premium of 0.05 the revenues produced are 50 × 54 = $2,700.

Note. An approximate but helpful method for estimating option deltas is shown in Appendix C as a graphic profile of put and call deltas for 0–3 weeks to maturity, 2–3 months to maturity, and 5–6 months to maturity. The graphs are from the article "When to Strike," which appeared in the October 1984 issue of *Intermarket Magazine*.

A position that can be followed by a treasurer who wants to write calls on a neutral basis can be measured in this way:

$$V = S - \frac{C}{C_1}$$

where

V = Value of the position.

S = Value of a long position for the currency in the cash market.

C = Premium of the call.

C_1 = Premium derived from the valuation equation based on the spot price for the currency and the estimated delta.

The variation in the currency position value plus the interest income earned during the life of the option position follows:

$$\Delta V = \Delta S - \frac{\Delta C}{C_1} + r_f S \Delta t \tag{1}$$

where

r_f = Interest rate for the foreign economy.

One consideration regarding the premiums of call options is the change of the spot price over time. A hypothesis proposed by Ito regarding the fluctuations of the currency is shown in the following equation:

$$\Delta C = C_1 \Delta S + C_2 \Delta t + \frac{1}{2} C_{1,1} \sigma^2 S^2 \Delta t \tag{2}$$

where

C_2 = First derivative of the equation for the premium on par with the time remaining.

$C_{1,1}$ = Second derivative of the equation for the premium on par with the value for the spot price.

σ = Standard deviation for the logarithms of the variations in the spot price.

If equations (1) and (2) are combined, one obtains:

$$\Delta V = -(\frac{1}{2} C_{1,1} \sigma^2 S^2 + C_2 - r_f SC_1)\frac{\Delta t}{C_1}$$

This equation is very important because it allows a treasurer to insulate himself globally from any variations in the value of his foreign currency exposures. Carrying the equation to its resolution produces the following result:

$$-(\frac{1}{2} C_{1,1} \sigma^2 S^2 + C_2 - r_f SC_1)\frac{\Delta t}{C_1} = (S - \frac{C}{C_1})r \Delta t$$

$$= rC + (r_f - r)S C_1 - \frac{1}{2} C_{1,1} \sigma^2 S^2 - C_2 = 0$$

The above equation, if differentiated with a constraint of

$C_T - Max[(S_T - S^*),0]$, where S^* is the exercise price at the options expiration, produces the following unique solution:

$$C(S,t) = e^{-r_f(T-t)}SN(d_1) - e^{-r(T-t)}S^*N(d_2)$$

where

$$d_1 = \frac{\log S/S^* + (r - r_f + \tfrac{1}{2}\sigma^2)(T - t)}{\sigma\sqrt{T-t}}$$

$$d_2 = d_1 - \sigma\sqrt{T - t}.$$

N = Cumulative density function for a lognormal distribution.

The price of an option depends on the value of five independent variables regarding the price of the underlying currency during the course of the option's life. The five variables are as follows:

1. The currency spot price.
2. The exercise price.
3. The maturity date.
4. The domestic and foreign interest rate level.
5. The only estimated variable, the volatility of the underlying currency.

As a result, the marketplace behavior of options produces the data necessary to estimate their volatility. The Garman-Kohlhagen model permits one to isolate the time value of options as follows:

$$C(S,t) = Max[(S - S^*),0]$$

For the value of an in-the-money option, the equation is

$$e^{-r_f(T-t)}SN(d_1) - e^{-r(T-t)}S^*N(d_2) = (S - S^*)$$

This equation is too complex to easily offer an idea of what the volatility's value should be. Many traders are able to estimate that value on a more intuitive basis. Constant exposure to the values of the equation with actual marketplace values helps produce that ability.

The Garman-Kohlhagen model is the most popular method for evaluating European options, mainly because it is the preferred approach of the professionals. To become acceptable for common use, the values of a model must be validated in the marketplace. The professionals have instituted the practice of instantly updating the value of the Garman-Kohlhagen model at computer terminals. This has resulted in a new trading custom of simply quoting the value of an option's volatility instead of its price prior to making a trade.

THE SENSITIVITY OF THE FIVE EXPLICATIVE VARIABLES

The results of an option position depend on the interaction of the five variables that determine an option's value. The treasurer must evaluate the various alternatives among the available options in terms of the results he desires. The most important factor that he must consider is the direction in which he thinks the spot price will move during an option's life, because that will determine the option's premiums:

- The call premiums increase if the currency's price increases, decrease if the currency's price decreases. The put premiums do the opposite.
- For both puts and calls, the premium decreases with the passage of time. The seller of the option benefits from the loss in its time value.

The Garman-Kohlhagen model assumes constancy in the first derivative of the available interest rate, which is another way of saying "No change in the value of the available interest rate during the life of the option position." This assumption is in harmony with the model's hypothesis that the volatility of the underlying security is the most important variable that influences the performance of an option position. Despite a drop in the price of the underlying security, which causes a drop in the intrinsic value of a call option, a sharp increase in the underlying security's volatility can increase the time value of the option enough to override the drop in the intrinsic value.

Difficulties for the Garman-Kohlhagen model may be presented by the covariance between measuring variables. The rate of change in the interest rate level is an example of such a difficulty, and one whose effect on option positions is very complex. That is the logic behind the desire to supplement the model with a hypothesis for evaluating the changeability of interest rates during the course of an option position's life. The introduction of such a supplemental hypothesis to the Garman-Kohlhagen model seems a sensible way to improve its effectiveness.

The Sensitivity of the Variation in Premiums versus Changes in the Spot Currency: Management of the Neutral Delta

The sensitivity of the premium to changes in the spot price is measured by the premium's relationship to the spot price as covered by the determination of the option price from the Garman-Kohlhagen model's theoretical price. The equation for changes in the value of a call option versus the spot price is

$$\text{Delta} = \frac{dc}{ds} = e^{-r_f(T-t)}N(d_1)$$

The geometric representation for changes in the value of the premium is contained within a value of 0 to 1 for the delta. As discussed in Chapter 1, the delta is a prime consideration of the seller who wishes to properly open a new option position. Knowledge of the delta is a major concern of the banks and businesses that purchase options.

Assuming stability in the available interest rate return, the delta measurement offers an instant indication of the change that should occur in the value of an option given a specific change in the spot price of the underlying currency. For a pound versus dollar option position with a delta of 0.65, an increase in the spot pound of 5 cents produces an estimated increase of 3.25 cents in the value of the option. A bank that sells pound/dollar calls worth 50,000 pounds per call is selling $0.65 \times 50,000$ pounds/call or 32,500 pounds per each call's worth of currency held. Over a small range of 1–2 percent change in the value of the currency value, the variation in the option position's value compensates closely for the changes taking place in the currency. Over that small range of change, the bank is theoretically operating without risk.

Realistically, the bank cannot perfectly cover its risk because the delta is, by design, the function of four variables—the change in interest rates, the volatility in the spot currency price, the level of the spot price, and the life of the option—all of which must be measured regularly over time. A seller of options who wants to establish a new position must make a calculation with the valuation model in order to determine the number of options needed to produce a perfect hedge. Based on the above example of options hedging a pound/dollar currency position, if at the expiration of the options the calls are trading in-the-money (the spot price is higher than the call strike price), the seller of the calls will receive an exercise notice and is obligated to deliver the pounds covered in the option contracts.

Adjustment of the currency position is a continuous process. Unless one has a systematic approach to this process, the cost of transactions will become prohibitive. In dealing with the currency position, the important fact to realize is that there is no such thing as a permanent perfect hedge position.

The method generally used in adjusting the currency position is to focus on changes in the spot price as the sole determinant of the delta. If the price of the underlying currency is stable, there is no need for any adjustment. However, a growth in the volatility of the underlying currency, without any change in the intrinsic value of the accompanying call, produces a deterioration in the overall position (both the option position and the currency position), forcing the treasurer to adjust his delta-neutral posture. Options become very expensive for a seller, whose desired posture is relative stability in the currency for the remainder of the options' life.

With the passage of time, the probability of exercise—either 0 or 1—is approached. The nature of the delta changes as the time value of the option deteriorates and the value of the call approaches the intrinsic value of the option, as shown in Figure 2–4.

Some option sellers are interested in the *gamma*, a variation of the delta relative to the spot price. The gamma is the second derivative of the premium as it varies with the price of the underlying security according to the option valuation model. The gamma is a measure of the risk of the option seller's position. The approach to zero of a gamma indicates that the margin of error is low and that no adjustment is necessary. Increases in the value of a gamma offer contrary indications. The gamma gives an idea of the concavity of the valuation curve. It tends to approach zero as the option approaches maturity.

FIGURE 2–4
The Relationships between Option Premiums for a Call and Changes due to the Passage of Time

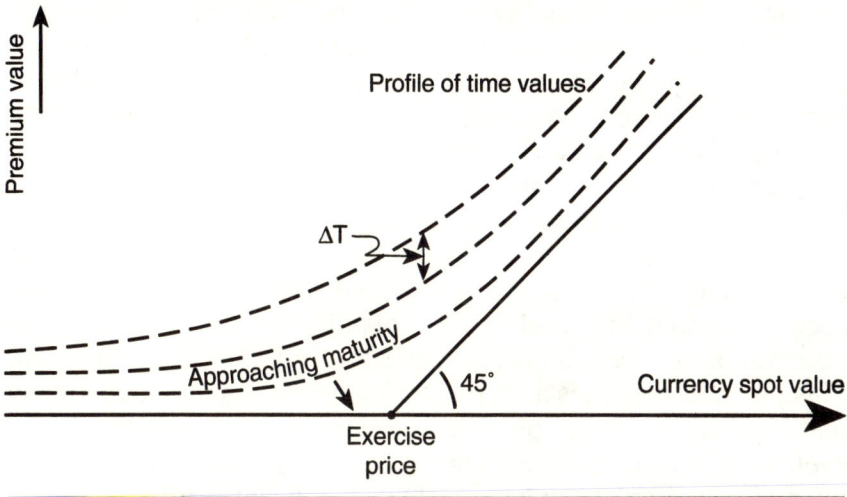

The Sensitivity of Premiums to Volatility

The appeal of *vega* to professionals is that it relates premiums to changes in the volatility of the underlying currency. To measure this relationship, the derivative of call premiums is compared with the derivative of the standard deviation of the probability distribution, which characterizes the price changes of the spot currency. The equation for a call premium's relationship to the volatility of the underlying currency is

$$\text{Vega} = \frac{dC}{d\sigma} = e^{-r(T-t)} S * \sqrt{T - t} \, N(d_2) > 0 \text{ (destination over time)}$$

All growth in the volatility of the underlying currency increases the premiums of options. This explains why buyers of options, whether puts or calls, look for increases in volatility, whereas sellers of options, whether puts or calls, desire stability in the value of the underlying currency.

Such issues emphasize how important it is for options traders to anticipate future volatility.

Estimating Future Volatility Based on the Volatility's History
Some options traders estimate the future volatility of the currency price during the life of an option by computing the past volatility of the currency price. The hypothesis they use is that the underlying security offers indications of the fluctuations in the option price. The methodologies they use, which are questionable, embrace two points of view, the theoretical and the empirical.

The hypothesis used to explain the mode of fluctuation in the price of a currency has not been accepted. One statistical procedure used to explain the level of the volatility for day t is based on observations of the volatility for periods $(t - 1)(t - 2) . . . (t - n)$. This procedure implies a seemingly legitimate assumption, namely that historical volatility provides a certain ability to predict. However, no examples of linear regression analysis based on observations of actual volatility have yielded significant results.

Calculating historical volatility also presents empirical difficulties that engender doubt about the helpfulness of doing so. These difficulties and the ways in which they are resolved are as follows:

- How long a time horizon should be studied? The two most common answers to this question are (1) to choose a time horizon that is equal to the life of the option, usually the three most recent months, and (2) to choose a time horizon of one year.
- What time period should the observation be for—a day, a few days, a week, more than a week? Practical experience indicates that the longer the time period chosen, the greater is the variation in the results.
- How should an annualized statistical measurement be obtained? Since there are usually 260 trading days in a year, most approaches simply take the most recent 260 trading days.

The following equation assumes that the relative variations in the currency price $(S_{t + 1}/S_t)$, are a log/normal phenomenon and therefore uses a standard deviation of the logarithms of the variations in price:

$$\text{Volatility} = \sigma\left[\log(S_{t+1}/S_t)\right] = \sigma\left[\log S_{t+1} - \log S_t\right]$$
$$= \frac{1}{n}\sum_{t=1}^{n}\left[(\log S_{t+1} - \log S_t) - M\right]^2$$

where

n = Sample horizon mean, M, which characterizes the variations in the currency price.

The following steps constitute a methodology for calculating the historical volatility in an orderly manner:

1. Divide the current spot currency price, S, by the past price, and calculate the logarithms of the ratios.
2. Establish a series of variances for every data point between the logarithm and the mean of the logarithms.
3. Put the square of every variance in a series of squares of successive variances.
4. Compute the mean of this series of squares of variances, and compare the values of the most recent prices of the currency with the mean for the entire series.
5. Using the four preceding steps for a total of 260 days, obtain the numbers needed for an entire year's overview of the variation in the price of the currency.
6. Take the square root of the latest figure to obtain the standard deviation of the variation in the currency price.

For an indicative example, the historic volatility of the dollar/ French franc calculated on three months of data at the beginning of 1985 was 16 percent. Based on the New York agreement of the major five industrial nations reached on September 22, 1985, to follow the principle of a "soft landing" in returning to a system of stable parities, one could predict an appreciable drop in the volatility in the month of October. By the end of October, the volatility had dropped below 13 percent.

The Implied Volatility

H. Latane and R. Reudleman[1] proposed a procedure for calculating the volatility that consisted of reversing the utilization of the evaluation model to consider the ideal premiums based on using market prices to compute the theoretical ideal value. Under this procedure, the volatility is the unknown in the valuation of the premiums and is very easily deduced. Such "implication" reflects the anticipation of the marketplace: The *implied volatility* is the volatility that would offer equilibrium in the demand for options and represents the operation of a consensus among the traders. There is no particular reason why anyone can estimate the volatility without also taking into account the level of the exercise price.

The implied volatility is a key variable in the operation of options programs and enjoys the same importance as such factors as the strike price and the expiration date. With options that are deep in-the-money or options that are very out-of-the-money, one can sometimes observe an implied volatility slightly greater than that of options that are at-the-money. The poorer liquidity for such options is mostly explained by the seller's strong demand for options trading at the exercise price, which helps reduce volatility. One can also observe that the implied volatility tends to increase with the lengthening of the time period until exercise. Moreover, the shape of the yield curve influences volatility in the sense that a higher yield should produce greater volatility.

Other influences can also affect volatility. Many buyers of options are treasurers who want to protect the maturity of their companies' long-term assets (six months, nine months, . . .) or speculators who use options to control the risks of their commitments. Such buyers prefer short maturities and provide the liquidity that is especially necessary in the options marketplace prior to the exercise date.

In the final analysis, of all the variables involved in determining the value of options, the volatility is apparently the measure most widely used to anticipate the variability of option prices in the marketplace.

---

[1] H. Latane and R. Reudleman, "Standard Deviations of Stock Price Ratios Implied in Option Prices," *Journal of Finance*, May 1976, pp. 369–81.

The Logic of the Value of Premiums as They Relate to the Length of an Option's Life

With all other things remaining unchanged, an option loses value as its expiration date approaches. This relationship is a basic character-istic of options. The probability of exercise of an out-of-the-money option tends to approach zero as the option's life approaches matu-rity, so the buyer becomes less interested in paying the premium for such an option as the premium becomes lower. Inversely, the proba-bility of exercise of an in-the-money option tends to approach 1 as the exercise date approaches, and the buyer realizes that he will either have to exercise the option or sell his position to avoid going through the exercise process. The buyer also wants to avoid expe-riencing a drop to zero in the time value of the option as maturity approaches.

The seller of an option profits from the drop in the premium with the passage of time, and aspires to unwind his position instead of running the risk that a reversal in the currency price could hurt that position. The seller benefits from the decrease in the option's time value.

Based on the model discussed above, the professionals do not look at the life of an option as the sole determinant of the option's time value, but rather look mainly at the rate of change in the volatility of the underlying currency. The two variables just discussed change independently with the passage of time, but the decrease in time value occurs as shown in Figure 2–4. With regard to Figure 2–4, one must remember that it is unwise to assume that the rate of volatility change is constant, as it is shown to be in that figure.

The Relationship between Premiums and Interest Rates

If one supposes that variations in the interest rate have no effect on the spot price of the currency, the effect of interest rates on premi-ums can be measured from the derivative of the modified Garman-Kohlhagen option model as follows:

- The sensitivity of the domestic interest rate is

$$\frac{dC}{dr} = (T - t)e^{-r(T-t)}SN(d_2) > 0$$

• The sensitivity of the foreign interest rate is

$$\frac{dC}{dr_f} = -(T - t)e^{-r(T-t)}SN(d_1) < 0$$

An increase in the domestic interest rate causes an increase in the value of calls. An increase in the value of the underlying currency causes a corresponding increase in the intrinsic value or the time value of the option.

An increase in the foreign interest rate causes a decrease in the value of calls. A decrease in the foreign interest rate causes a decrease in the value of the underlying currency and reduces the premiums of calls.

The inverse of the above conclusions holds true for the valuation of puts.

THE ELEMENTARY PRINCIPLES OF EVALUATING OPTIONS WITH THE BINOMIAL METHOD

Applying the Garman-Kohlhagen model to European-style options requires the application of differential calculus to a stochastic technique, which necessitates a rather complex statistical analysis. A far simpler alternative model built upon the binomial probability law can be applied to both European- and American-style options.

The alternative model as originally developed by Cox, Ross, and Rubenstein[2] is of definite educational interest, though in their presentation the cumbersome steps required to perform the detailed steps needed to use the model are somewhat hidden. A series of articles on the model have done an excellent job of clarifying its overall methodology.[3]

The model's hypothesis for the margin for an option seller's position in a currency is valid. An option position in foreign funds

---

[2] John C. Cox, Stephen A. Ross, and Mark Rubenstein, "Option Pricing: A Simplified Approach," *Journal of Financial Economics,* September 1979, pp. 229–63.

[3] In particular, see "Binomial Option Pricing," in Robert A. Jarrow and Andrew Rudd, *Option Pricing* (Homewood, Ill.: Dow Jones-Irwin, 1983); R. Geske and K. Shastri, "Valuation by Approximation," working paper 13.82, UCLA; and Robert Merton, "Theory of Rational Option Pricing," *Bill Journal of Economics,* Spring 1973, pp. 141–83.

enables a treasurer who has an option position in domestic funds to use margin to create a position that offers perfect protection by pairing the two positions.

The expectations for a futures position in foreign currencies are no different from the expectations for an option position. Traders are faced with the two possibilities that exist for any position—that is, prices can rise or fall, as shown below:

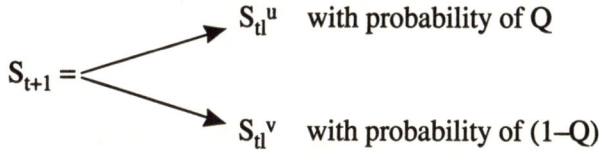

$$S_{t+1} = \begin{cases} S_{tl}^{u} & \text{with probability of } Q \\ S_{tl}^{v} & \text{with probability of } (1-Q) \end{cases}$$

The relative anticipated change in the currency price, S_{t+1}/S_t, is e^u, with a probability of occurrence of q and e^v of $(1 - q)$.

The hoped-for variations in the relative price changes of t versus $(t - 1)$ can be expressed as follows:

$$E[S_{t+1}/S_t] = Q_e^{u} + (1 - Q)_l^{v}$$

The changes in price as one goes forward in time can also be considered. Thus, the next step of S_{t+2} can be described as follows:

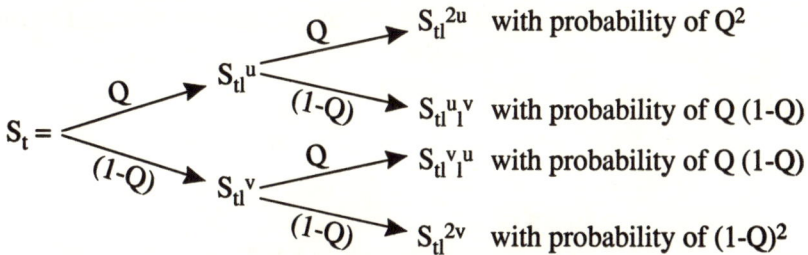

$$S_t = \begin{cases} S_{tl}^{u} \begin{cases} S_{tl}^{2u} & \text{with probability of } Q^2 \\ S_{tl}^{u}{}_{l}^{v} & \text{with probability of } Q(1-Q) \end{cases} \\ S_{tl}^{v} \begin{cases} S_{tl}^{v}{}_{l}^{u} & \text{with probability of } Q(1-Q) \\ S_{tl}^{2v} & \text{with probability of } (1-Q)^2 \end{cases} \end{cases}$$

For a currency position of long French francs, the principle of margin without risk demands an offsetting position in options. The equality in time, T, can be expressed as follows:

$$m_{T-1} S_{T-t} e^{u} + n_{T-1} \times B_T = V_T{}^{u}$$
$$m_{T-1} S_{T-1} e^{v} + n_{T-1} \times B_T = V_T{}^{v}$$

where

m_{T-1} = Number of contracts of the foreign currency at a given interest rate.

n_{T-1} = Number of contracts of the domestic currency at a given interest rate.

B_T = Value of the fixed domestic interest rate.

Acting on a system with two equations with two unknowns causes one to combine optimally for the French franc as [m_{T-1}, n_{T-1}]. One obtains

$$m_{T-1} = (V_{T^u} - V_{T^v})/(e^u - e^v)S_{T-1}$$
$$n_{T-1} = (V_{T^v}e^u - V_{T^u}e^v)/(e^u - e^v)$$

Combining m_{T-1} with n_{T-1} permits one to obtain the value of the option in $T - 1$, V_{T-1}, which is calculated as follows:

$$V_{T-1} = m_{T-1}S_{T-1} + n_{T-1}B_{T-1}$$

These concepts are applied in the same markets in making arbitrage decisions. Here the stepwise iterations are helpful in computing actual premiums for options. Utilization of the logical information is indispensable for the realization of the calculations.

The values of American options give evidence that they are not equal to the values of European options except at the exercise date. The premiums for an American call, for example, are always equal to the maximum premium of a European call and correspond to the intrinsic value, which is truly the option's cash value.

A brief look at the logic follows:

Premium of an American call ≥ Max
[Premium of the corresponding call, $S_t - S*$]
Premium of an American put ≥ Max
[Premium of the corresponding put, $S* - S_t$]

At the opening of the Philadelphia Options Exchange, professionals were not hesitant to quote American options with a European model, often using output from the Garman-Kohlhagen model. However, such an approximation is not acceptable as a quote of a call, a put, or the currency that is the underlying security.

Since the differential in the interest rate is integrated into the premium of the European option, the probability of anticipating the exercise of such an option is poor. Thus, while the utilization of the

European model was very rapid, it took longer for the correct method for estimating American option premiums to be accepted. Corrections therefore needed to be made in the quotes of calls for the yen, Swiss franc, and DM.

Conversely, given the great influence of the interest rate level on whether the underlying currency is rising or falling relative to the domestic currency, the effect of the interest rate level on the statistical analysis of American puts or calls versus European puts or calls is very important.

CHAPTER 3

THE DIFFERENT
OPTIONS MARKETS

Foreign exchange options are negotiable and trade on organized markets (both over-the-counter markets and organized exchanges) that join market traders and the activities of bankers. The following example shows how transactions in foreign exchange options take place between the two types of markets and the role that the participants play.

At the beginning of June 1990, a multinational agriculturally oriented corporation decided to cover its clients in dollars for the next three months by buying options, the credit being $15 million. The treasurer of the corporation requested from its bank a guarantee of call options at a price of 1.65 DM/$ for the three-month period, the spot currency price being 1.69 DM/$ (see Figure 1–2 for the data). The exchange trader at the bank proposed an acceptable quote. The exchange trader immediately communicated the buy order for calls to a floor broker at the Chicago Mercantile Exchange. The floor broker accomplished the order instantly, executing it as part of an overall set of orders transacted in the name of the bank, which had a global network capable of performing such executions.

In this example, a commercial bank and a multinational corporation were able to work with the over-the-counter and exchange markets. The corporation was able to obtain instant execution of an option buying order through the bank. In executing, the bank followed the terms of its contract with the corporation, buying $15 million for the corporation at a price of 1.65 DM/$ for a period of three months.

In the case of a drop in the dollar below the level of 1.65 DM/$, the corporation possessed an option that would permit it to sell the

$15 million at a guaranteed price of 1.65 DM/$ anytime during the next three months.

In a second example, an exchange trader who wanted to execute the sale of an option for a client sought out a market trader at a bank. The client's aim was to combine a purchase in the foreign exchange market with the creation of a delta-neutral hedge in the options exchange market, accomplishing both sides of the trade instantly in the two markets. In effect, he contacted an exchange trader at the Chicago Mercantile Exchange to accomplish both sides of the position simultaneously, so that he was not assuming any risk at any point. The exchange trader negotiated an order for the millions of dollars worth of options necessary according to the standard size of the option contracts ($125,000/call in this case, or eight contracts per million dollars held).

This chapter will consider the options markets available to options portfolio managers and the motivations of options portfolio managers in making use of those markets.

THE ORGANIZED MARKETS

The three major organized currency option markets, begun in the early to mid-80s, are the Philadelphia Stock Exchange Currency Option Market (begun in December 1982), the Chicago Mercantile Exchange's International Monetary Market (begun in January 1984), and the London International Financial Futures Exchange (LIFFE), which introduced pound sterling options in June 1985. While the LIFFE concentrates on the pound sterling, the Philadelphia Stock Exchange trades American-style options for six currencies: Australian dollars, British pounds, Canadian dollars, German marks, Japanese yen, and Swiss francs, all versus the dollar. It recently added trading European-style options for Canadian dollars and German marks. The Chicago Mercantile Exchange trades American-style options for British pounds, Canadian dollars, German marks, Japanese Yen, and Swiss francs.

The general history of the currency option markets will be covered in the order of their birth.

The Currency Option Market of the Philadelphia Stock Exchange

Origin

The Philadelphia Stock Exchange, the oldest stock exchange in the United States (it was established in 1790), authorized the trading of options in 1975. Initially, it traded exclusively in stock options. Its volume for the first year was 137,189 transactions in options for only 14 stocks. From that modest beginning the options operation of the Philadelphia Stock Exchange grew rapidly and the exchange became an important part of overall trading in stock options. By 1984, it traded options of 77 stocks and handled 16,530,206 transactions—8 percent of the transactions for all U.S. options exchange markets.

Encouraged by that success, the managers of the Philadelphia Stock Exchange decided in 1981 to apply options principles to the currency markets. They envisioned the application of options principles to forward currency contracts for the life of the short-term interest rate cycle—90 days. Their initiative made the Philadelphia Stock Exchange the first organized market to offer options for currencies. This initiative was made possible by the flexibility of the regulations of the Securities and Exchange Commission, which supervises the American securities exchanges, and by the reluctance of the Chicago Mercantile Exchange and the Chicago Board of Trade—the two major futures exchanges—to enter the currency markets.

The Philadelphia Stock Exchange began its trading in currency options in December 1982, with the British pound. Later, beginning in January 1983, it successively introduced trading in the German mark, the Swiss franc, the Japanese yen, the Canadian dollar, the French franc, and finally, in 1986, the Australian dollar.

The design of currency options is, in fact, very similar to that of stock options. The standard contracts for these options, all of which are shown in Table 3–1, immediately fell under the jurisdiction of the Securities and Exchange Commission and were made known to the public.

Specifications of the Contracts

The major advantage of the organized options markets is that they offer traders uniform products and identical conditions for each

TABLE 3–1
Specifications for the Philadelphia Options Market's Cash Currency Options

	Australian Dollar	British Pound	Canadian Dollar	German Mark (DM)	European Currency Unit	French Franc	Swiss Franc	Japanese Yen
Unit of transactions	AD 50,000	BP 31,250	CD 50,000	DM 62,500	ECU 62,500 (American style)	FF 250,000	SF 62,500	JY 6,250,000
Strike intervals	U.S. $0.01	U.S. $0.025	U.S. $0.005	U.S. $0.01*	U.S. $0.02	U.S. $0.0025	U.S. $0.01*	U.S. $0.01*
Price quotation	$0.0001 (1 point) or $5	$0.0001 (1 point) or $3.125	$0.0001 (1 point) or $5	$0.0001 (1 point) or $6.25	$0.0001 (1 point) or $6.25	$0.00002 (2 points) or $5	$0.0001 (1 point) or $6.25	$0.000001 (1 point) or $6.25
Minimum authorized fluctuation	U.S. cents per option A quote of 1.20 means $0.0120 per AD or $600 per option	U.S. cents per option A quote of 1.20 means $0.0120 per BP or $375 per option	U.S. cents per option A quote of 1.20 means $0.0120 per CD or $600 per option	U.S. cents per option A quote of 1.20 means $0.0120 per DM or $750 per option	U.S. cents per option A quote of 1.20 means $0.0120 per ECU or $750 per option	Tenths of a U.S. cent per option A quote of 60 means $0.0012 per FF or $300 per option	U.S. cents per option A quote of 1.20 means $0.0120 per SF or $750 per option	Hundredths of a U.S. cent per option A quote of 300 means $0.0003 per JY or $1,875 per option
Delivery months	↓	↓	Quarterly months (March, June, September, December) and the two nearest months that are not quarterly months					↑
Expiration date	↓		Saturday before third Wednesday of the month					↑
Settlement date	↓		Third Wednesday of the month					↑

* Half-point strike price intervals are added in the two nearest term expiration months based on the currency's closing spot value.

Source: Chart courtesy of Rodman and Renshaw, Option Brokers, Chicago, June, 1991.

option. The contracts of the Philadelphia Option Exchange can be described as follows:

- The active underlying currency of all the option contracts is the U.S. dollar.
- The option contracts all have organized expiration dates. They stop trading on the third Wednesday of March, June, September, or December, and they expire on the fourth Saturday of these months.
- All transactions in the option contracts are guaranteed by the Options Clearing Corporation. This nonprofit organization, regulated by the Securities and Exchange Commission, functions mainly to assure that all legitimate options transactions will be honored. It imposes on its members fees proportional to their transaction volume in order to provide the funds necessary to assist members who encounter financial difficulties.

The system has been designed to assure the survival of the exchange. In dealing with the Philadelphia Stock Exchange, one has the assurance that upon the exercise of an option the party that is obligated to deliver the currency covered under the option contract will do so at the exercise price. Moreover, the buyers and sellers of options do not have to deal with each other directly. The Options Clearing Corporation matches the two sides of options transactions and guarantees the proper performance of option contracts.

The Chicago Mercantile Exchange's Currency Option Exchange

Origin

Through the Chicago Board of Trade (CBT) and the Chicago Mercantile Exchange (CME) the city of Chicago is currently the world's most important center for the international trading of financial futures and benefits from the trading of interest rate futures. In 1970, both exchanges transposed their success with merchandise futures into the financial arena.

Chicago, which has long been the prime market for futures options for agricultural products, such as orange juice and pork bellies, has in recent years introduced the adaptation of futures options to the major financial instruments. The Chicago Board of Trade trades mortgage futures and futures for long-term U.S. government bonds. The Chicago Mercantile Exchange and one of its divisions, the International Monetary Market, specialize in active short-term instruments, namely Eurodollars, Treasury bills, and currency futures.

The rapid growth in the use of futures in instruments related to interest rates led the Chicago Mercantile Exchange to originate the development of a market for currency options. The CME's success with its other financially oriented products led it to open its first currency option market, in January 1984. The first contracts it chose were for the DM, and the immediate success of these contracts led it to introduce options for the British pound and the Swiss franc in March 1985. These were followed by options for the Japanese yen and, finally, for the Canadian dollar.

While the currency options designed by the Philadelphia Stock Exchange were appropriate to the activities of that exchange, the currency options developed by the Chicago Mercantile Exchange offered some unique characteristics.

The Contract Specifications
The underlying security for a currency option on the CME is not a foreign currency but a currency future, so that currency options on the CME are deliverable in terms of their currency futures contracts.

The exercise of a currency option on the CME does not transfer a currency between a buyer and a seller. Those who deal in currency options on the CME deal in a currency through a standardized exercise procedure at the time the options expire and take delivery of currency futures following the legal procedures established by the CME.

If a call option is exercised, the call is exchanged for a long future position, which is equivalent to buying the future. On the other hand, if one exercises a put, the put owner becomes short the same contract, which is equivalent to shorting the future. The exercise procedure offers both buyers and sellers an avenue for converting their positions into futures.

After exercise, traders have a choice in handling their position. They can undo their future position in the futures market, or they can transfer their future position through the CME's Office of Compensation and acquire a position in the spot currency.

- The months for the CME's currency option contracts are standardized and have the same expirations as those of the currency futures contracts into which they are convertible (see Table 3–2).
- The quotations are in U.S. cents per dollar equivalent to the currency involved.
- The exercise prices and the expiration dates of the Philadelphia Stock Exchange and the CME are identical.
- Both the Philadelphia Stock Exchange and the CME have the same minimal changes in premiums.
- The exercise dates of the currency options correspond to those of the futures into which they are convertible. The expiration dates of the options naturally precede those of the corresponding futures for the underlying currency to which the options are dedicated. The futures expiration dates are the Saturday following the third Wednesday of March, June, September, and December.
- The currency options of the CME are not guaranteed by the Options Clearing Corporation, which is responsible for all other American option exchanges. The Commodity Futures Trading Commission has established the Chamber of Compensation to meet the exercise needs of CME options.

The owner of a currency option traded on the CME who expects to take delivery of a contract for a particular currency approaches the Chamber of Compensation for the funds corresponding to the value of that contract. On a random basis, the chamber attempts to match up the buyer with an option seller, whose obligation is to forward the appropriate funds according to the specifications of the option. To enter into the transaction, the seller had to establish his credit capabilities. The chamber collects the appropriate funds from the seller and delivers them to the buyer, who possesses the legal claim to those funds upon exercise.

Foreign Currency Options of the London International Financial Futures Exchange (LIFFE)

Origin
The London International Financial Futures Exchange (LIFFE), a futures market for financial instruments that opened in September

1982, decided to enlarge its scope by introducing a market for currency options. The new market, created on June 27, 1985, grew rapidly. Transacting a mere 2,000 options on its first day, after several months it transacted as much business as the CME's options market in the pound sterling. The new mechanism for dealing with currency options offered by the LIFFE, which trades exclusively in the pound sterling, is the main reason for its great success.

The LIFFE option contract for the pound sterling resembles the pound sterling option contract offered on the Philadelphia Stock Exchange. The option contract is deliverable in a standard amount of 25,000 pounds sterling as expressed in dollars, which is the amount received upon exercise of the option. The LIFFE pound sterling option contracts are exercisable quarterly and are quoted in terms of American cents. Table 3–3 indicates the principal char- acteristics of these contracts.

The Contract Specifications
The system of trading currency options embraced by the Philadelphia Stock Exchange and the Chicago Mercantile Exchange placed the responsibility for determining the risk inherent in such options in the hands of both their buyers and their sellers. The LIFFE introduced the option delta as the quotation to be used in trading currency options. This permitted traders to immediately know the risk of the positions they established in these options.

A trader who is given a delta quote for a currency option immediately knows how much the option will fluctuate per 100-point move in the underlying security. An option seller who is given a delta quote of 0.80 knows he faces an option change of 80 if there is a 100-point move in the underlying security.

The LIFFE system not only uses the delta to determine the quote used in selling a currency option, it also uses the delta to determine the deposit required to guarantee the option premium. The payment for an option rising in value is limited to the premium as quoted using the delta, which considerably reduces the cost of the option. The purchase of 200 options with a delta of 0.10 requires the financing of 20 premiums in London, as opposed to the financing of 200 premiums in Chicago or Philadelphia.

The success of the LIFFE currency option since its debut on June 27, 1985, might have been expected to prod other currency

TABLE 3–2
Specifications for the Chicago Mercantile Exchange's Currency Futures Options

	British Pound Future	Canadian Dollar Future	German' Mark Future	Japanese Yen Future	Swiss Franc Future
Underlying asset	One British pound futures contract settling in or after the options month	One Canadian dollar futures contract settling in or after the options month	One German mark futures contract settling in or after the options month	One Japanese yen futures contract settling in or after the options month	One Swiss franc futures contract settling in or after the options month
Quotation and tick size	U.S. cents per British pound. A quote of 106 equals $0.0106 per pound. Each tick is $0.0002 or $12.50 per contract.	U.S. cents per Canadian dollar. A quote of 62 means $0.0062 per Canadian dollar. Each tick is $0.0001 or $10 per contract.	U.S. cents per German mark. A quote of 120 means $0.0120 per German mark. Each tick is $0.0001 or $12.50 per contract.	U.S. cents per 100 Japanese yen. A quote of 150 means $0.0150 per 100 yen. Each tick is $0.000001 or $12.50 per contract.	U.S. cents per Swiss franc. A quote of 115 means $0.0115 per Swiss franc. Each tick is $0.0001 or $12.50 per contract.

Strike intervals	$0.025 or 250 points (i.e., 16,000, 16,250, or 16,500)	$0.005 or 50 points (i.e., 8,400, 8,450, or 8,500)	$0.01 or 100 points (i.e., 50, 51, or 52)	$0.01 or 100 points (i.e., 70, 71, or 72)	$0.01 or 100 points (i.e., 60, 61, or 62)
Expiration months	The next three quarterly months and the next two months that are not quarterly months				
Last trading and exercise day	Two Fridays before the third Wednesday of the contract month. Exercise notices may be delivered up to 7 P.M. of the last trading day.				
Delivery date	The business day following the exercise or assignment notice				

Source: Chart courtesy of Rodman and Renshaw, Option Brokers, Chicago, June, 1991.

TABLE 3–3
Specifications for the LIFFE Contract

	Pound Sterling
Unit of transaction	25,000 GBP
Unit of change for the strike price	5 American cents
Quotations	Expressed in American cents
Minimum fluctuation	1 Centime per cent = 0.01¢
Expiration date	Third Wednesday of March, June, September, and December

option markets into adopting the new LIFFE mechanism. At present, however, the LIFFE is the only organized exchange that uses the delta as a quotation mechanism.

THE OVER-THE-COUNTER MARKET

It is difficult to obtain statistics on the over-the-counter (OTC) currency option market, mainly because such statistics would have to be obtained from the large number of major banks that participate in that market. Another reason for the difficulty in obtaining precise information on that market is that banks have a strong tradition of maintaining secrecy regarding their clients. Moreover, no international interbank trading organization has been created to deal in currency options. No group of traders in the area of foreign exchange is large enough to create such an organization.

Perhaps the best way to organize the available information on the OTC currency option market is to break it down into the four following areas:

1. The traders.
2. The currencies traded.
3. The nature of the options.
4. The size of the operations.

The Traders

Currency option traders in the OTC market can be broken down into three categories: banks, investment management firms, and businesses in general. Most of the trades take place between one bank and another. In many cases, it is advantageous for a bank to have a division that is a member of a currency option exchange.

Banks

Today, each of the top 30 or 40 banks is likely to have a division that guarantees options in the OTC foreign exchange option market. Many of the banks with such a division have offices in New York, but the great majority of them have offices in Europe, mainly in London, Zurich, and Paris, where trading foreign exchange options is an important activity of banks. Moreover, foreign exchange options are the major business of many banks.

Among the top 30 or 40 banks, a dozen are distinguished by their excellent option divisions. Within this group, four or five banks are regarded as the best among the American, British, Swiss, and Parisian banks involved in currency options.

The active involvement of banks in currency options naturally enhances the liquidity of the currency option market.

Investment Management Firms

Many Western investment management firms play a very important role in the OTC currency option market. The technical expertise of these firms imparts a high degree of dynamism and a high degree of professionalism to the options marketplace. Most of the firms operate out of London and New York, mainly because currency risks are a major concern of their large client base in these cities. The major role of the investment management firms is to create hedge contracts that cover the currency risks encountered by their clients.

Businesses in General

The treasurers of many businesses have the same problem that many bank treasurers have, which is how to use currency options as a means of reducing the exposure of their organizations to currency risk. The operations of both banks and investment management firms create a well-regulated environment that makes the OTC market attractive to businesses.

Even if corporate treasurers don't know about currency options, most of them know about the problem they have regarding

currency risk exposure. Nonetheless, there are still major enterprises that have not taken advantage of the OTC currency option
market but could truly benefit from doing so.

Perhaps more than 50 American firms and at least a dozen
French firms have become active in the OTC currency option market. The major participants have been firms that trade agricultural
products and automotive and petroleum firms.

A major activity of firms that trade agricultural products is
taking advantage of the various risk-reducing futures contracts that
apply to such products. Currency options are not a strange concept for these firms, since many of them have participated in risk-
reducing securities for a number of decades.

Automotive and petroleum firms have multinational approaches to their financial activities and were therefore among the
first firms to take advantage of currency options.

The Currencies Traded

The currencies traded on the OTC currency option market obviously include the currencies offered by the currency option exchanges: Australian dollars, British pounds, Canadian dollars, German marks, European Currency Units, French francs, Swiss francs,
and Japanese yen. The Italian lira, the South African rand, and the
Saudi Arabian rial are currencies for which options have been
sought but are not yet available. Stated alphabetically, the principal
currencies traded are the British pound, the German mark, and the
Japanese yen.

The most conservative banks dealing in currency options
are mainly in London. Many petroleum firms use options to protect their pound sterling exposure. Other trade-oriented European
firms use them to protect their DM, yen, and U.S. dollar exposure.

It has been estimated that 75 percent of the OTC currency
option contracts are against the dollar. In these contracts the principal currencies mentioned above are traded against the dollar. In
addition, the British pound is traded against the other major European currencies, while the German mark is traded against the Japanese yen.

The Nature of the Options

The principal reasons for the success of the organized options markets are the standardization of their option contracts and their guarantee that the option writers are sufficiently liquid. But these markets place constraints on conversions to other currencies, such as exercise dates and exercise prices, that limit the choices of treasurers. The lack of such constraints favors the development of the OTC market, especially when special currencies are involved.

- The duration of OTC currency options is not restricted. The traditional exercise periods have been three months and six months, but the exercise period can be as short as a day or a week or longer than a year.

Option sellers prefer short-term contracts, which allow them to manage their affairs better, but important commercial clients may want long-term arrangements (to tie their options into catalog sales or to take advantage of special option offerings), which present special problems in adjustment to the problem of conversion.

The option exchanges do not cover certain months of the year, but some banks offer option contracts that can expire during each of the next 12 months. Most banks now accept option contracts for as long as a year. Moreover, banks may offer warrants, which some clients may prefer over options. For each case, banks focus on the month, which they regard as the key variable of the transaction.

- The exercise prices of OTC currency options are more flexible than the standard exercise prices of the option exchanges. They are usually quoted for the two most popular terms—the three-month term and the six-month term, and not on a quarterly basis, as on the option exchanges.
- An American-style or European-style format may be used.
- The prime focus of the OTC options market is the exercise of options, whereas the prime focus of the option exchanges is to promote the buying of options.

The Size of the Operations

Naturally, the size of the transactions was large enough to launch the OTC currency option market. At first, in the early 80s, the daily transactions of that market were estimated at only $5 million. By 1985, however, about $50 million in contracts were negotiated daily.

By the late eighties, a half-dozen different options were available on the OTC market and as much as $200–300 million were available for each of these options, and the OTC market has been trading at that level or a greater level since then.

OPERATION OF THE ORGANIZED EXCHANGES

The growth in the volatility of foreign currencies that began in 1970 created new operating problems for businesses and banks. New instruments were needed to help business treasurers and bankers to deal with the economic uncertainty and financial risks created by that volatility.

Currency options were rapidly recognized as a possible solution. American banks demonstrated an early interest in this new instrument and supported the initiation of its use by the Philadelphia Stock Exchange.

Within a year, Europeans began to look into currency options. Their curiosity about this instrument was stimulated by its introduction on the Philadelphia Stock Exchange. Efforts to market currency options at many banks and at businesses in general helped to disseminate information about the Philadelphia project throughout Europe.

It is impossible to determine precisely how many traders became involved in the new options market on a monthly basis or to classify these traders by category.

The preceding section discussed the three categories of traders in the OTC currency option market, namely banks, investment management firms, and businesses in general. The structure of an organized exchange introduces these additional categories: "market makers," "locals," and "speculators."

The six categories just mentioned are not mutually exclusive. For example, banks and investment management firms may act as market makers.

The Market Makers

Along with banks and investment management firms, the "market makers" constitute, in effect, a nerve center for the options market. They assure the viability of the option exchange by providing the quotes necessary to arrange trades. To provide the multiple strike prices and expiration dates of option contracts and thus to create viable contracts that possess adequate liquidity, it is essential that quotes be provided instantly. The major benefit of the market makers to the marketplace is the provision of liquidity for both buyers and sellers of options.

For example, a market maker may quote at 36–40 a DM option call that just traded at 37 cents. This quotation signifies that he will pay 36 cents to an option buyer and 40 cents to an option seller. The profit that can be realized by working with the market maker is the difference that he makes available by buying at 36 and selling at 40, or four cents. This offers an option buyer a volatility that is inferior to the mean volatility estimated from the market and offers an option seller a superior implied volatility.

On any given day, at least a dozen market makers are active in the currency option markets of both the Philadelphia Stock Exchange and the Chicago Mercantile Exchange. Banks are the most important participants in these markets. Second in importance are investment management firms, which may have less expertise than the banks in the currency markets but which are very experienced in option dealings. Next in importance are trading companies that are exclusively devoted to the support of market-making operations on the currency option markets. Since their main objective is the immediate profits made by aggressive trading, they generate a major part of the trading volume of these markets. At the Chicago Mercantile Exchange, for example, two or three of the major market makers participate in 75 percent of the transactions. The expertise and capital of such market makers enables a large quantity of options to be traded.

In Chicago, such specialty trading operations make it possible for commercial clients to initiate a major part of the monthly transactions in excess of $50 million. In Philadelphia, banks and investment management firms play a more important role than they play in Chicago.

The function of the market maker is considerably different in Philadelphia than it is in Chicago. In Chicago the traders who act as market makers are special members of the exchange, while in Philadephia the persons who act as market makers are "specialists" whose job is to make quotes in the marketplace and to take the other sides of brokers' trades.

The Locals

The "locals" are members of the exchange who more often than not buy options that they then resell internally to other members. In some cases, they trade between Chicago and Philadelphia.

In the city of Chicago, the locals have a prestige that they lack in other cities. They are an important part of the economics of the Chicago exchanges. Their presence for several generations at the Chicago Board of Trade and the Chicago Mercantile Exchange provided these exchanges with the liquidity they needed to be the successful enterprises that they have been.

The locals stand by their exchanges through both good times and bad, as follows:

1. They always authorize and execute orders according to appropriate rules. Under the open outcry system used in their markets, they respond rapidly and immediately transmit executions to their clients.

2. Following the conditions stipulated by the Chamber of Compensation, they benefit from the effect of considerable leverage. The margin deposits required by the chamber guarantee the ultimate honoring of contracts traded by both the locals and the general public.

3. In executing their orders according to exchange rules, they do so as practically as can be expected. To close out their positions at the best possible prices, they must pay close attention to the actions of the other locals in their respective pits.

The locals do not trouble themselves with the orders or desires of outside clients. They leave that to the "brokers," also known as "paper fillers," who are mainly employees of the major brokerage firms in the futures business. The locals are mainly interested in the consequences of rapid variations in prices. In general, they respond to very minor price changes, and during the course of the day they may trade many times at a given price level. They are very attentive to new highs or lows and to hesitations at those levels, and they may help to ensure that such levels are penetrated. Their style of trading is termed *scalping,* since their main way to profit is to "scalp" the price changes in the marketplace. The locals have a reputation for operating so as to accentuate movements in the value of options, thus causing them to "overshoot" certain price levels as the market reacts to economic announcements.

In general, the locals account for 50–60 percent of the daily trading volume of the Chicago Mercantile Exchange. In the options markets, however, it is very likely that the market makers contribute more than 50 percent of the overall volume.

The positions of the locals vary as a function of their financial capacity. In DM options, for example, their order sizes may vary between 10 and 500 contracts. They tend to adjust their positions to the level of trading activity. They do not want to assume all of the risk inherent in a given movement in the marketplace. They leave the rest to the speculators.

The Speculators

It is important to understand the characteristics of the persons who speculate in currency options. Many visitors to the Chicago or Philadelphia option exchanges think of a speculator as a person who arrives at the exchange in his chauffeur-driven limousine. The following information depicts the speculator more realistically.

A Federal Reserve study[1] on the portfolios of American traders in the futures markets and the options markets contains interesting

---

[1] *A Study of the Effects of the Economy of Trading in Futures and Options,* a book published in 1984 by the Board of Governors of the Federal Reserve System, the Commodity Futures Trading Commission, and the Securities and Exchange Commission.

statistics on the sociocultural characteristics of speculators in currency options:

- Of these speculators, 86 percent claimed that speculating was a minor activity. Most of them had at least one university degree, and 38 percent of them had obtained a master's degree.
- 48 percent of the speculators had an annual income in excess of $50,000 and a stock exchange account worth more than $100,000.
- More than two thirds of the speculators were between 31 and 60 years of age.
- 64 percent of the speculators also invested in other options markets, and 93 percent had a portfolio in common stocks.
- A fourth of the speculators maintained positions in excess of five options, and a majority (59 percent) did not change their positions from one month to as long as three months.
- 68 percent of the speculators stated that they made money from their speculating.

The Federal Reserve study shows that U.S. speculators in currency options do not risk a high portion of their assets on risky trading, that they properly analyze the risks involved in trading, and that they tend to hold their positions for more than a month. It is encouraging to note that the customers of brokerage firms also possess these characteristics.

The Federal Reserve study also observes that the role of U.S. speculators is relatively marginal. The impact of speculators on European and Asian markets may be far more significant. However, the actual impact of speculators' intervention in markets is very difficult to determine.

CHAPTER 4

ARBITRAGE BETWEEN THE CURRENCY AND OPTIONS MARKETS

Given the fact that the profiles of risk of the option exchanges and the interbank currency markets are not identical, it is possible to create certain combinations of option strategies that resemble positions on the currency market itself. Such combinations permit the performance of arbitrage without risk as long as certain fundamental relationships are observed between the spot currency markets and the prices of puts and calls. The arbitrageur who works with options prior to their expiration or exercise takes the position of being either a buyer or a seller of the options.

The arbitrageur takes advantage of the difference between the interbank currency market and the currency option markets, offers the arbitrageur opportunity without risk apart from risks pertaining to the techniques of the arbitrage operation. However, the newness of the options markets limits the possibilities of the arbitrageur to whatever contracts are available to perform arbitrage with.

The arbitrageur must take advantage of the unequal transaction costs of the organized options markets by operating as a member of an option exchange and thereby minimizing these costs. Such costs are an integral part of the computations made to define the results of any arbitrage transaction.

At latest account, the option exchanges are not totally efficient, and this situation offers the arbitrageur opportunities to make a profit.

ARBITRAGE BETWEEN A CALL AND A PUT

The Relationship of Arbitrage between Options and Underlying Currencies

The strategy of buying a currency A that is convertible into currency B is equivalent to selling a currency B that is convertible into currency A. This is based on the reasoning that for money in currency B, buying a call in currency A priced against currency B (term this call A/B) with an exercise price of E is the same as buying a unit of currency A and converting at the exercise price E into currency B. This can be written as

$$1 \cdot A = E \cdot B \text{ or } E\left[\frac{1}{E} \cdot A\right] = E \cdot B$$

If one wants to reason in terms of maintaining currency at locality A and one acquires a Call A/B with an exercise price of E [term this Call A/B (E)], this is equivalent to selling at E a unit of B against 1/E of A, which is equivalent at E to buying Put B/A (1/E), which is logically payable into currency A. Moreover, the premiums for Call A/B and Put B/A should be worth the same amount of money under certain conditions. One can convert in the B currency with Put B/A into the currency rate of A/B done at S, the cash rate for currency B. Expressing this algebraically:

Call A/B (E) = S · [E · Put B/A (1/E)]
(expressed in currency B)   (expressed in currency A)

For an arbitrage, one investigates the quotes on the option exchange versus the quotes in the currency market to seek an equality versus the above relationship. If one exists that is large enough, taking transaction costs into account, a profitable arbitrage is available and is obviously pursued.

Example.   Let us analyze a Call DM/$ for which E = 33 cents; 1/E = 1/33 cents = 3.03 pfennig; Call DM/$ (33) = 0.2 cents; and S = 34 cents. Using the above arbitrage equation, Call DM/$ (33 cents) = 34 cents [33 cents Put $/DM (3.03 pfennig)]. Put DM/$ (33 cents) is quoted as 0.2 cents.
Solving the arbitrage equation:

$$\frac{0.2\text{¢}}{34\text{¢} \cdot 33\text{¢}} = 0.00017825 \text{ pfennig per 100 cents}$$

$$= \text{Put \$/DM (3.03 pfennig)}$$

or

$$\text{Put \$/DM (3.03 pfennig)} = 0.017825 \text{ DM/\$}$$

To seek an arbitrage opportunity, one therefore has to check the OTC market for a quotation on the put that is superior to 0.017825 DM/$ or interest to buy a Call DM/$ at better than 0.2 cents and sell the Put $/DM for at least 0.017825. Inversely, one can seek a cheaper price than 0.017825 to purchase the Put $/DM and sell the Call DM/$ at 0.2 cents, naturally expressing the quote in the DM/$ call in cents and the 33 Puts $/DM in pfennig.

Using symmetrical reasoning, one obtains this relationship:

$$\text{Put A/B (E)} = S[E \cdot \text{Call B/A (1/E)}]$$
(expressed in currency A)   (expressed in currency B)

Profile of the Results

Figures 4–1 through 4–4 represent the four possible profit diagrams that result from buying or selling the puts and calls in the example just given. These figures are purposely paired, the first pair (Figure 4–1 versus Figure 4–2) showing the profit profile of the cost incurred revenues produced in purchasing a call to be offset by selling the matching put, the second pair (Figure 4–3 versus Figure 4–4) showing the inverse relationship, in which revenues are produced by selling a call to be offset by purchasing the matching put. These matched pairs represent the option purchasing that is done in the B/A mode in the call purchase approach and in the A/B mode in the put purchase approach. It must be realized, however, that the currencies dealt with could be reversed as well, with one pair having the call purchase done in the A/B mode and the second, opposite pair having the put purchase done in the B/A mode. Thus, a total of four sets of matched pairs can be investigated for the arbitrage opportunities arising from market inefficiencies. From the foregoing, one can see that the selfish, profit-seeking motive in a freely operating marketplace produces the best-performing markets possible.

The arbitrage cannot be realized only on the OTC market: the organized option exchanges cannot offer the needed prices for the currencies/dollar or the prices for the dollar/currencies as offered by the banks. What is needed are means of communication between the currency markets and the options markets that open the options markets to the European banks.

4–1 Buy a call ^A/B (E)

4–2 Sell E × Put ^B/A (1/E)

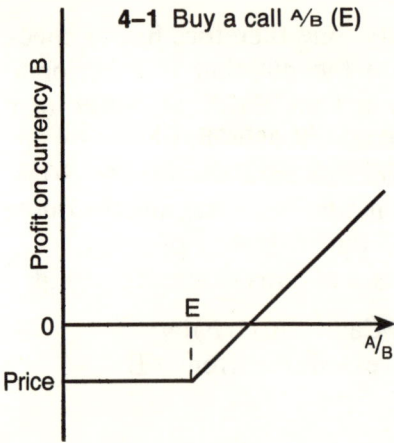

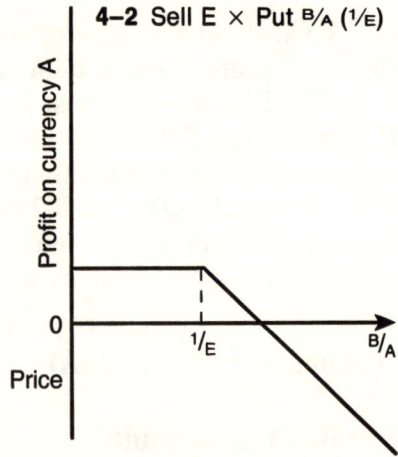

Buy a call ^A/B (E), Sell E x Put ^B/A (1/E)

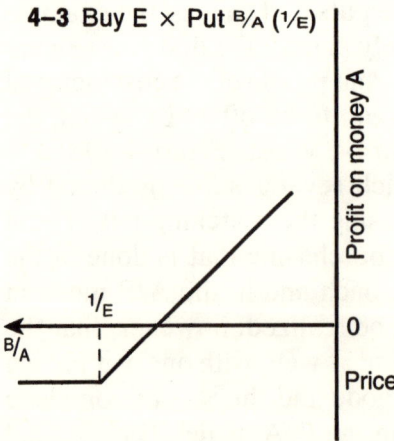

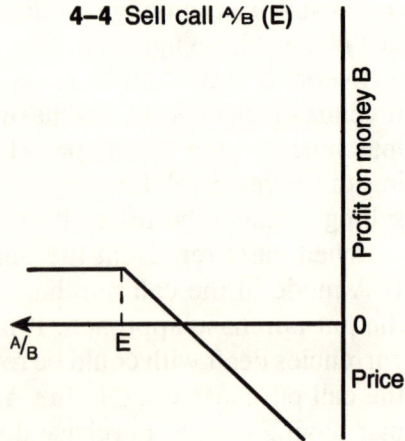

4–3 Buy E × Put ^B/A (1/E)

4–4 Sell call ^A/B (E)

Buy E x Put ^B/A (1/E), Sell call ^A/B (E)

SYNTHETIC FORWARD CONTRACTS AND CONVERSIONS

Buying a Synthetic Forward Contract

Definition
With a little intuitive thought about options, one can conceive an option profit profile that resembles the profit profile obtained from

buying a forward contract: if one can overlook the effect of the maturity of the option contract, the trader has a true long position in currency A that can be converted into currency B.

Buying a Call A/B and simultaneously selling a Put A/B at the same exercise price E and the same expiration constitutes a synthetic forward contract in currency A. In effect, at maturity these operations produce the following alternative results:

- If the price A/B is higher than or equal to E, the buyer of the put does not exercise, while the call owner exercises the Call A/B.
- If the price A/B is lower than or equal to E, the buyer of the put exercises the option.

In both cases, one of the options is exercised and the owner is long an A currency and short a B currency at the exercise price.

The Logic of Working with the Underlying Currency

Buying a synthetic forward contract corresponds to a trader's coverage of a commercial posture as a hedger, in anticipation of an increase in the currency price, especially as it affects the option's exercise price. The hedger seeks to extend his profit by purchasing a synthetic forward, which will permit him to acquire the currency at a higher price. This is similar to the objective of a trader in the currency market who desires a higher price than is available on the option exchange and to that of a speculator in the currency market who seeks to acquire a position at a lower price.

The arbitrageur desires to exploit on an instantaneous basis the difference between the cost of buying a synthetic forward and the price obtained in the interbank currency market.

Examples.   The examples given will illustrate the results that can be obtained with options contracts as compared to the results that are obtained by a hedger who executes his positions in the natural way. The examples will utilize the usual notations:

S = Currency obtained in the currency market.
E = Exercise price.
C = Call premium.
P = Put premium.

These notations will be used to define the logic of buying a synthetic forward:

Initial cash flow = Premium of put sold − Premium of call purchased
= P − C

The price of the purchased synthetic equals the cost of buying currency at the exercise price, plus the premium income of the put sold, minus the premium for the call purchased (while also computing the interest rate return for the cash involved when establishing the position). The value of the arbitrage equation showing the equality between the components (the death point equation) follows:

$$\text{Cost of purchased synthetic} = E - (P - C)(1 + i)^t$$

The resultant equals the price at exercise as expressed by the death point equation, which follows:

$$R = S - E + (P - C)(1 + i)^t$$

The examples will use the June 21 quotations of the PHLEX (Philadelphia Options Exchange), given the price of the currency DM/$, which was s = 32.63 cents (expressed as $/DM = 3.0647).

Example 1. A synthetic forward DM/$ is purchased at an exercise price E = 32 cents (expressed as $/DM = 3.1250) in-the-money, with a life ending September 13 (the expiration of the option).
Executing the operation:

- Buy a DM/$ Sept (32) call: C_1 = 1.43 cents/DM.
- Sell a DM/$ Sept (32) put: P_1 = 0.68 cents/DM.

Buying an in-the-money call while selling an out-of-the-money put shows a negative cash flow:

$$\text{Negative cash flow} = -C_1 + P_1 = -1.43 + 0.68$$
$$= -0.75 \text{ cents/DM}$$

Financing at a flat interest rate, where i = 1.8 percent for the position life, the cost of the position (June 21 through September 13) is

$$-0.75 \times (1.018) = -0.76 \text{ cents/DM}^1$$

The death point exists where the exercise price equals the value of the overall operation, as follows:

$$\text{Death point} = E_1 = (P_1 - C_1)(1 + i)^t$$
$$= 32 - (-0.76) = 32.76$$

The result at expiration is $R_1 = S - 32.76$. Following the equation's logic produces two points about S: S = 32.76, which equates to $R_1 = 0$ (no arbitrage is sensible). (The resulting profit profile is shown in Figure 4–5.)

However, if the call had been exercised at a higher price, such as 33, then

$$R_1 = 33 - 32.76 = 0.24 \text{ cents/DM}$$

If exercise had occurred at a lower price than 32, for example DM/$ = 30 cents, the exercise of the put would have produced

$$R = 30 - 32.76 = -2.76$$

Example 2.   Let's buy a synthetic forward DM/$ at E = 34 cents (which equates to $/DM = 2.9412) out-of-the-money at expiration on September 13.

Executing the operation:

- Buy a DM/$ Sept (34) call C_2 = 0.53 cents/DM.
- Sell a DM/$ Sept (34) put P_2 = 1.76 cents/DM.

Buying an out-of-the-money call while selling an in-the-money put produces an initially profitable position.

$$\text{Initial positive cash flow} = -C_2 + P_2 = -0.53 + 1.76$$
$$= 1.23 \text{ cents/DM}$$

At a flat i = 1.8 percent interest rate during the period from June 21 through September 13, the total gain produced is $1.23\cdot(1.018) = 1.25$ cents per DM.

Death point

$$= E_2 + (C_2 - P_2)(1 + i)^t = 34 - 1.25 = 32.75 \text{ cents/DM}$$

---

[1] For the examples of this chapter, a flat interest rate is used. This avoids the complications that would be introduced if a variable interest rate were assumed.

FIGURE 4–5
Results from Buying a Synthetic Forward

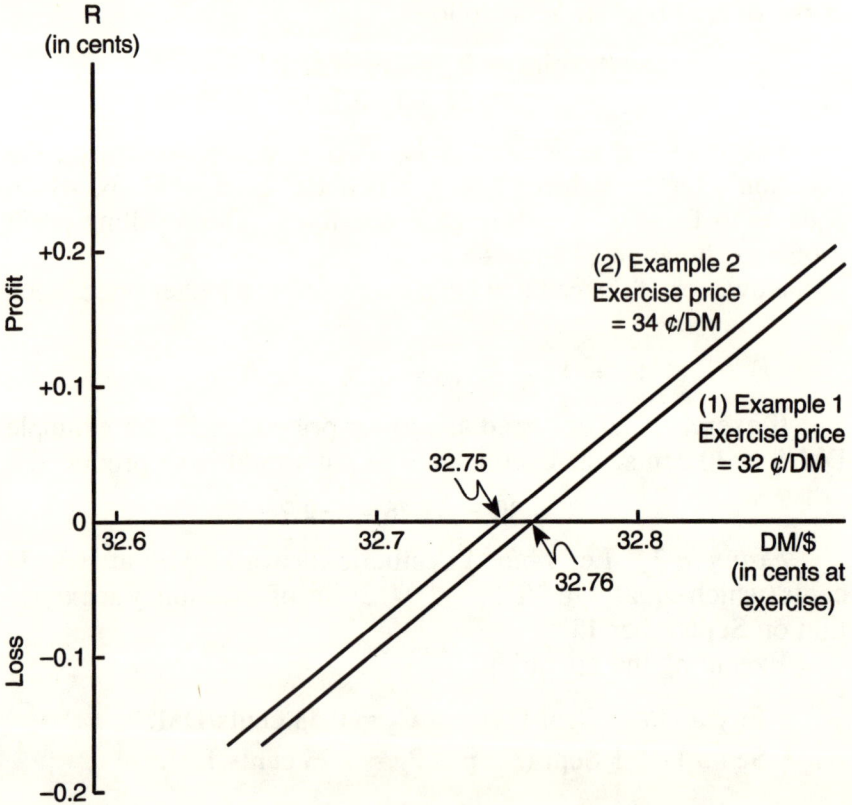

The result at exercise can be written as $R_2 = S - 32.75$. Thus, $S = 32.75$ or $R_2 = 0$ (no arbitrage makes sense).

If exercise had occurred at a different strike price, say 32.5, the result would have been

$$R_2 = 32.5 - 32.75 = -0.2$$

As shown in Figure 4–5, if one draws two parallel lines representing values of R, they pass through the arbitrage death points where $R = 0$ at 32.75 (Example 2) and 32.76 (Example 1). If one formalizes the differences of the resultants, one obtains

$R_2 - R_1 = (S - \text{Death point 2}) - (S - \text{Death point 1})$
$\qquad = \text{Death point 1} - \text{Death point 2} = 32.76 - 32.75 = 0.01$

Also

$$E_1 - (P_1 - C_1)(1 + i) - [E_2 - (P_2 - C_2)(1 + i)] = 0.01 \text{ cent}$$

This leads to

$$[(C_1 - P_1) - (C_2 - P_2)](1 + i) - 0.01 = E_2 - E_1$$

and

$$\frac{E_2 - E_1}{(1 + i)} = (C_1 - P_1) - (C_2 - P_2) - \frac{0.01}{(1 + i)}$$

Since $0.01/(1+i)$ is extremely small, it can be considered negligible. The resulting equation is therefore

$$\frac{E_2 - E_1}{(1 + i)} = (C_1 - P_1) - (C_2 - P_2)$$

This equation will be encountered below in the further discussion of the logical relationship between put and call results as affected by exercise, covered in "The Box Spreads" section.

Based on the exercise price chosen, one can deduce what the profit profile based on actual results will be. The results, which are perfectly normal, show that profitable arbitrages occur only when there are deviations from equilibrium in the marketplace.

Selling a Synthetic Forward Contract

Definition
Selling a Call A/B and simultaneously buying a Put A/B at the same exercise price E and the same expiration constitutes selling a synthetic forward in currency A.

Symmetry occurs in the sense that at expiration the operator of the forward will be either short an A currency or long a B currency at the exercise price.

The Logic of Working with the Underlying Currency
Inversely to the buying of a synthetic forward, the selling of a synthetic forward corresponds to the anticipation of a drop in the currency price below the exercise price. Like the speculator and

the hedger, who want to sell at a price higher than the currency
market price, the operator aims to profit from selling the synthetic
and buying back the currency at a lower price in the market.

Examples.
For this case, we will use the same notations as those used for
buying a synthetic forward.

Initial cash flow = Premium of call sold − Premium of put purchased
= C − P

The price of the sold synthetic equals the price of the currency
that will be sold at the exercise, plus the premium obtained for the
call solid, less the premium paid for the put purchased.

Price of the sold synthetic = $E + (C − P)(1 + i)^t$

That price is also the death point value of an arbitrage in the currency market.

The resultant equals the death point (the price at which the
currency is sold) diminished by the transaction costs (which the
operator incurs when the currency is repurchased).

$$R = E + (C − P)(1 + i)^t − S$$

Example 1. A synthetic forward DM/$ is sold at $E_1 = 32$
cents, out-of-the-money, expiring September 13.
Executing the operation:

- Sell a DM/$ Sept (32) call: $C_1 = 1.43$ cents.
- Buy a DM/$ Sept (32) put: $P_1 = 0.68$ cents.

Based on selling an in-the-money call and buying an out-of-the-
money put, the combination of the two options generates a cash
flow that is initially positive.

Positive cash flow = $C_1 − P_1 = 1.43 − 0.68 = +0.75$ cents

with a total gain potential at expiration of $0.75(1.018) = 76$ cents
per DM.

The death point for an arbitrage equals the price for the currency sale at the exercise price plus the cash gain for the seller of
the synthetic, which is written as follows:

$$E_1 + (C_1 - P_1)(1 + i) = 32 + 0.76 = 32.76$$

The result at expiration can be written as $R = 32.76 - S$. If $S = 32.76$, $R = 0$ (no arbitrage profit). If $S = 33$, exercise of the call costs the difference in the marketplace, as follows:

$$32.76 - S = 32.76 - 33 = -0.24$$

The profit profile is shown in Figure 4–6.

Example 2.   A synthetic forward DM/$ is sold at $E_2 = 34$ cents (in-the-money alternative).

FIGURE 4–6
Results from Selling a Synthetic Forward

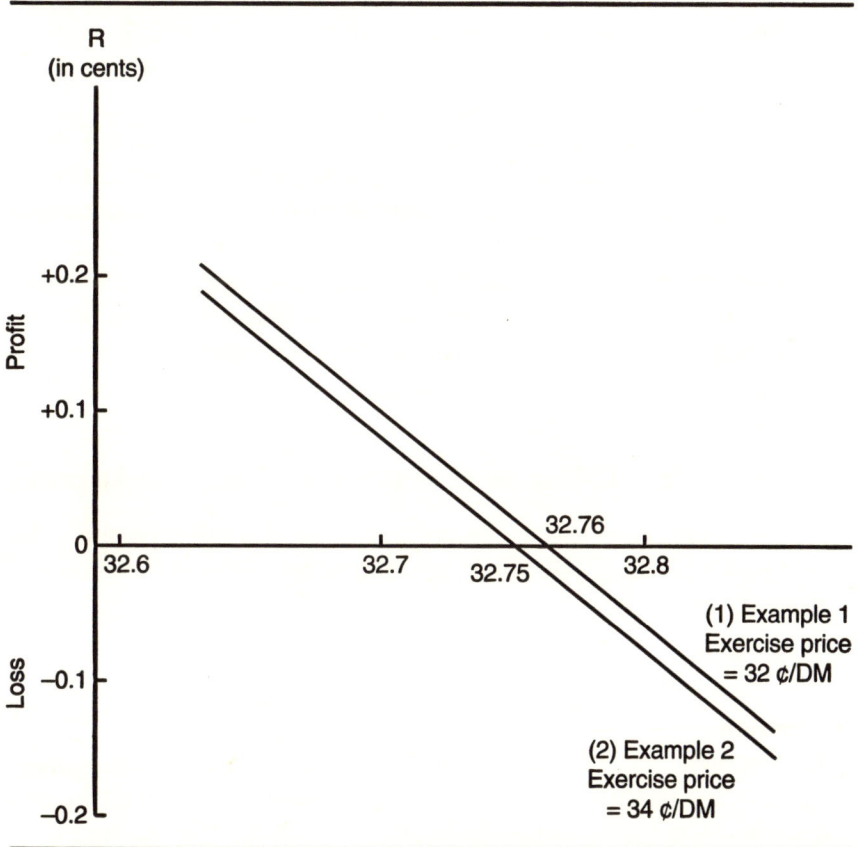

Executing the operation:

- Sell a DM/$ Sept (34) call: C_2 = 0.53 cents per DM.
- Buy a DM/$ Sept (34) put: P_2 = 1.76 cents per DM.

Based on selling an out-of-the-money call and buying an in-the-money put, the combination of the two options produces an initial negative cash flow.

$$\text{Negative initial cash flow} = C_2 - P_2 = 0.53 - 1.76$$
$$= -1.23 \text{ cents per DM}$$

At expiration, the cash flow is $-1.23(1.018) = -1.25$ cents per DM.

Arbitrage death point
$$= E_2 + (C_2 + P_2)(1 + i) = 34 - 1.25 = 32.75$$

The result at expiration can be written as $R_2 = 32.75 - S$. If $S = 32.75$, $R_2 = 0$ (no arbitrage opportunity). If $S = 32.50$, $R_2 = 32.75 - 32.50 = +0.25$ cents.

In both of the cases selected, the same problem exists for the synthetic forward: no matter what exercise price is chosen, it is not possible to produce a profit at expiration no matter what the market price is.

Both the buying and selling of synthetic forwards were shown for a variety of option premium quotations taken from the options marketplace. As the examples show, it is not possible to produce an arbitrage profit without risk because of the parity required for the call and put strike prices, as follows:

Forward price − Call and put premiums at identical strike prices

However, options can be combined in ways that permit arbitrage profit possibilities. Such combinations will now be shown.

Conversions

Definition
The combination of buying a forward in the OTC interbank market and selling a synthetic forward in the options market constitutes a *conversion*. Arbitrage without risk exists between the two markets.

Conditions for Profits

One part of a conversion, buying a forward in A/B in the OTC interbank market at a price F produces at expiration an acquisition of currency A and a selling of currency B at a price at F (noted as −F). The other part, selling a synthetic forward by selling Call A/B (E), which is accomplished on an option exchange, produces a cash flow for the position operator as follows:

$$+ \text{ Call A/B (E)} - \text{Put A/B (E), noted as (C} - \text{P)}$$

At exercise time, one of the two positions will produce a short position in the A currency and a long position at E in the B currency, noted as +E. Based on the conversion, a profit then occurs since at E the difference $(C - P)(1 + i)^t$ is greater than the price of the purchased forward.

The result, R, accounting for the gain produced by the premiums, can be written as

$$R = -F + E + (C - P)(1 + i)^t$$

or

$$R > 0 < = > E + (C - P)(1 + i)^t > F$$

Example.   For June 21, the market price quotes were DM/\$ = 32.63 cents and forward for September 13 = 32.80 cents.

Executing the operation:

- Buy a forward for DM/\$ at 32.80 cents.
- Sell a DM/\$ Sept (32) Call: C = 1.43 cents.
- Buy a DM/\$ Sept (32) Put: P = 0.68 cents.

Interest for the period from June 21 through September 13 equals 1.8 percent flat.

The conversion produces a positive cash flow equal to C − P or 1.43 − 0.68 = +0.75 cents/DM.

Cash flow at expiration = 0.75 (1.018) = 0.76 cents/DM

Results of arbitrage:

$$R = -32.80 + 32 + 0.76 = -0.04 \text{ cents}$$

At these quotes, conversion is not profitable. However, the alternative strategy, the inverse conversion, can produce a gain.

FIGURE 4–7
Arbitrage Results via Conversion

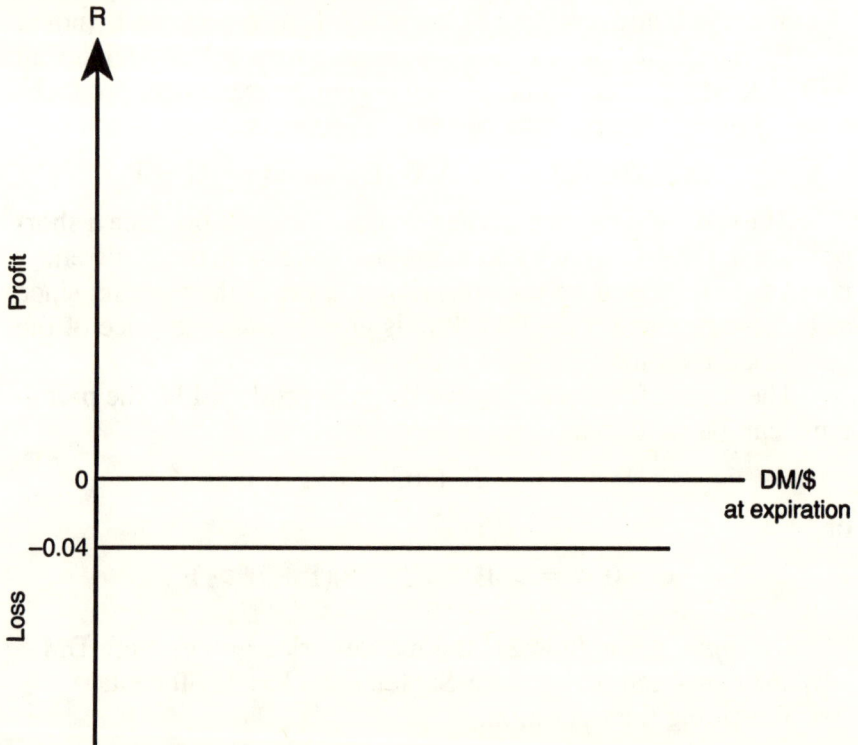

The results at exercise, which are linear and negative (as shown in Figure 4–7) do not produce the profit necessary to make a risk-free arbitrage possible. The converter ends up short DM and long dollars, which demands that he sell dollars and buy DM in the marketplace in an attempt to obtain the neutral result of zero.

The Inverse Conversion

Definition
Combining the selling of a forward in the interbank market and the buying of a synthetic forward in the options market constitutes an inverse conversion.

Conditions for Profits

Given the symmetrical nature of a conversion, the results of an inverse conversion are to attempt a higher price for the forward sold at F, which is diminished by the cost of the synthetic forward purchase, shown as $-E - (C - P)(1 + i)^t$.

$$R = F - E - (C - P)(1 + i)^t$$

where

$$R > 0 <=> E + (C - P) < F.$$

Arbitrage profits at the exercise price are increased by the difference $(C - P)(1 + i)^t$ and reduced by the cost of the forward at F.

Example.   On June 21, the spot price DM/\$ was 32.63 cents and the forward for September 13 was 32.80 cents.
Executing the operation:

- Sell a forward DM/\$ at 32.80 cents.
- Buy a DM/\$ Sept (34) call: C = 0.53 cents.
- Sell a DM/\$ Sept (34) put: P = 1.76 cents.

Positive cash flow $= -(C - P) = -0.53 + 1.76$
$$= +1.23 \text{ cents}$$

Cash flow at expiration $= 1.23(1.018) = 1.25$ cents

The results of the arbitrage can be written as:

$$R = 32.80 - 34 + 1.25 = +0.05 \text{ cents/DM}$$

The inverse conversion is profitable. (Moreover, it is possible to close out an American put prior to expiration and to maintain a long DM position and a short dollars position, thus avoiding an exercise and protecting the gain made.)

Parity: Forward Price—Call and Put at the Same Exercise Price

Relationship to the Base Currency

The notation F is the price for a forward contract in A/B, and what one wants to investigate is the possibility of an arbitrage for different values of F prior to exercise of an option position executed at the exercise price E, in which the maximum cash flow is established by the initial premiums and exists until expiration as a source of funds earning an interest rate return. The arbitrageur operates between the option and currency markets, attempting to produce a profit by following the logic rules as shown below.

$$F = [\text{Call A/B (E)} - \text{Put A/B (E)}] (1 + i)^t + E$$

for the particular case in which E = S.

Given a situation in which the option exercise price equals the market price at the moment an arbitrage is contemplated, the difference between the premiums, enhanced by the interest rate earned in currency B, is equal to the cash produced less the cash spent.

In effect,

$$F = S + \text{Cash inflow} - \text{Cash outflow}$$

and

$$F = [\text{Call A/B (E)} - \text{Put A/B (E)}] (1 + i)^t + S$$

or

$$[\text{Call A/B (E)} - \text{Put A/B (E)}] (1 + i)^t = \text{Cash inflow} - \text{Cash outflow}$$

This interesting fundamental relationship between the two equalities is expanded in the following section.

Relationship between the Premiums of the Call and the Put at the Same Exercise Price

$$[\text{Call A/B (E)} - \text{Put A/B (E)}] = \frac{F - E}{(1 + i)^t}$$

The difference between the call and the put at the same exercise price is equal to the difference between the price of the forward and the exercise price, relative to the interest rate return earned on currency B held during the life of the option position.

The case for the equality between the call premium and the put premium at the same strike price is as follows:

$$\text{Call A/B (E)} = \text{Put A/B (E)} \langle = \rangle \frac{F - E}{(1 + i)^t} = 0$$

$\frac{F - E}{(1 + i)^t} = 0$, as verified in the two cases just shown; F = E, that is, the exercise price equals the forward price, and $(1 + i)^t$ tends to infinity.

The two cases would occur only if a position were held until expiration and the time for the interest rate return was not infinity. In truth, the interest rate return would rarely exceed 20 percent, or the expiration time for the options would rarely be any longer than a year. The two cases would most likely be expressed in reality as

$$\text{Call A/B (E)} = \text{Put A/B (E)} \langle = \rangle \text{ E} = \text{F}$$

The premiums for the put would not be equal to those for the call at the same exercise price, and at the expiration date the exercise price would rarely be equal to the forward price.

As was discussed in Chapter 1, for an at-the-money option whose intrinsic value is zero and whose maximum time value occurs at that price, the probability is equal (i.e. 50/50) that either the put or the call will end up above or below the at-the-money value. When evaluating the case in which the strike prices for both the call and the put equalize the value of the forward price, the probability that the call will be profitable at expiration equals the probability that it will not be profitable and that the put will be profitable instead.

The Basis for Evaluating a Spread

When one investigates the parity relationship (Forward price = Put = Call), one must compute the spread between the price of the forward when selling (the bid) and its price when buying (the ask), which will be noted as F_B and F_A, with $F_B < F_A$, as well as the placement of the order for whatever financial instrument is used to obtain an interest return, using notations of i_B and i_A, with $i_B < i_A$.

The arbitrage of a forward—the synthetic approach without interest—has two cases, which are evaluated as follows.

1. The Conversion That Is Not Profitable. When the price for buying a forward is greater than the price for selling a synthetic, this can be written

$$F_A \geq [\text{Call (E)} - \text{Put (E)}] (1 + i_l)^t + E \qquad (1)$$

or $i_1 = i_A$ if the interest cost is negative (the premium of the call sold is less than the premium of the put purchased) and $i_1 = i_B$ if the interest return is positive (the premium of the call sold is greater than the premium of the put purchased).

2. The Inverse Conversion That Is Not Profitable.   When the price of the forward sold is less than the price of the synthetic purchased, this can be written

$$F_B < [\text{Call (E)} - \text{Put (E)}] (1 + i_2)^t + E \qquad (2)$$

or $i_2 = i_B$ is the interest cost since the premium cash flow is negative (the premium of the call purchased is greater than the premium of the put sold) and $i_2 = i_A$ is the interest return since the premium cash flow is positive (the premium of the call purchased is less than the premium of the put sold).

If one isolates the exercise price, E, in the inequalities between equation (1) and equation (2) one obtains an interval for E in which a profit is not possible.

$$F_B - [\text{Call (E)} - \text{Put (E)}] (1 + i_2)^t \le E \le F_A$$
$$- [\text{Call (E)} - \text{Put (E)}] (1 + i_1)^t$$

One also compares F_A from the inequality in equation (1) and with F_B from the inequality in equation (2) (the cases in which the arbitrage is not interesting).

The equation (1) deviation is

$$F_A - F_B \ge \underbrace{[\text{Call (E)} - \text{Put (E)}] (1 + i_1)^t}_{\substack{\text{product of selling a} \\ \text{synthetic forward}}} + \underbrace{E - FB}_{\substack{\text{product of selling} \\ \text{a forward}}}$$

And, contrarily, arbitrage is profitable if

$$F_A - F_B < [\text{Call (E)} - \text{Put (E)}] (1 + i_1)^t + E - FB,$$

the case in which the spread is less than the difference between selling a synthetic and selling a forward.

The equation (2) deviation is

$$-F_A + F_B \le - F_A + [\text{CALL (E)} - \text{Put (E)}] (1 + i_2)^t + E$$

or

$$F_A - F_B \geq \underbrace{F_A}_{} - \underbrace{[Call\,(E) - Put\,(E)]\,(1 + i_2)^t + E}_{}$$

cost of buying
a forward

cost of buying
a synthetic forward

And, contrarily, arbitrage is profitable if

$$F_A - F_B < F_A - [Call\,(E) - Put\,(E)]\,(1 + i_2)^t + E,$$

the case in which the spread between the forwards is less than the difference between buying a forward and buying a synthetic.

The final decision for the arbitrage is to decide which case is better, the exception to case 1 or the exception to case 2. Or, stated more completely, the final decision for the arbitrage is to choose the case in which the spread is less than the difference between selling a synthetic and selling a forward or the case in which the spread is less than the difference between buying a forward and buying a synthetic.

With the first case, selling a synthetic forward is superior to selling a forward plus a spread, with the arbitrage of buying the forward against selling the synthetic (a conversion).

With the second case, buying a forward is superior to buying a synthetic plus a spread, with the arbitrage of selling the forward against buying the synthetic (inverse conversion).

If one bears in mind the relationship between the premiums for a call and a put at the same strike price, the possibilities for an arbitrage are

1. $$[Call\,(E) - Put\,(E)] > \frac{F_B + spread - E}{(1 + i)^t},$$

which is equivalent to

$$[Call\,(E) - Put\,(E)] > \frac{F_A - E}{(1 + i)^t},$$

and

2. $$[Call\,(E) - Put\,(E)] < \frac{F_A - Spread - E}{(1 + i)^t},$$

which is equivalent to

$$[Call\,(E) - Put\,(E)] < \frac{F_B - E}{(1 + i)^t}$$

The equilibrium in the market (offering arbitrage possibilities) is as follows:

$$\frac{F_B - E}{(1 + i)^t} < [\text{Call (E)} - \text{Put (E)}] < \frac{F_A - E}{(1 + i)^t}$$

THE BOX SPREAD

The Box Spread Arbitrage

Definition

The "box spread" is a combination vertical spread (discussed in Chapter 5) that is best analyzed by viewing it as buying and selling synthetic forwards having the same expiration dates but two different strike prices, E_1 and E_2. The box spread can also be viewed as simultaneously doing a conversion with exercise price E_2 (also written as buying a forward and selling a synthetic at E_2) and an inverse conversion with exercise price E_1 (also written as selling a forward and buying a synthetic at E_1). If it is not possible to obtain a forward in the currency market, one can simultaneously buy a conversion and sell an inverse conversion in the options market.

This approach achieves independence of the currency market and provides the following arbitrage opportunity in the options market:

R = − Price of buying a synthetic forward + Price of selling a
 synthetic forward

Conditions for Profits

Given that the price of the currency at expiration of the contract is greater than both exercise prices, at exercise the resultant of the two call options can be written as

R = − Exercise of purchased call E_1 − $(C_1 - P_1)(1 + i)^t$
 + Exercise price of call sold E_2 + $(C_2 - P_2)(1 + i)^t$

This results in the gain from the call purchased minus the loss from the call sold, shown as

R = − E_1 − $(C_1 - P_1)(1 + i)^t$ + E_2 + $(C_2 - P_2)(1 + i)^t$
 = $E_2 - E_1 + [(C_2 - P_2) - (C_1 - P_1)](1 + i)^t$

If the price of the currency is lower than both exercise prices, the two put options are exercised, which can be written as

R = Gain from the put purchased − Loss from the put sold
$= E_2 + (C_2 - P_2)(1 + i)^t - E_1 - (C_1 - P_1)(1 + i)^t$
$= E_2 - E_1 + [(C_2 - P_2) - (C_1 - P_1)](1 + i)^t$

Finally, if the currency price is between E_1 and E_2, the operator exercises his options (if $E_1 < E_2$) or faces an exercise (if $E_1 > E_2$). The resultant for the two cases can be written as

$R = E_2 + (C_2 - P_2)(1 + i)^t - E_1 - (C_1 - P_1)(1 + i)^t$
$= E_2 - E_1 + [(C_2 - P_2) - (C_1 - P_1)](1 + i)^t$

Given the two cases, the resultant is equal to the difference between the two exercise prices $(E_2 - E_1)$ helped by the difference between the premiums of the sold synthetic $(C_2 - P_2)$ and the premiums of the purchased synthetic $(C_1 - P_1)$. If the difference between the two exercise prices is greater than the final cash flow of the premiums,

$$[(C_2 - P_2) - (C_1 - P_1)](1 + i)^t,$$

there lies the profit of the arbitrage.

Example. On June 21, an arbitrage was realized on a box spread with the prices E_1 of DM/$ = 34 and E_2 of DM/$ = 32.
Executing the operation:

- Sell a synthetic at E_2 = 32 cents.
- Sell a DM/$ Sept 32 call at 1.43 cents.
- Buy a DM/$ Sept 32 put at 0.68 cents.

- Buy a synthetic at E_1 = 34 cents.
- Buy a DM/$ Sept 34 call at 0.53 cents.
- Sell a DM/$ Sept 34 put at 1.76 cents.

The fixed interest rate for the period is 1.8 percent. The cash flow from the premiums at expiration is

$$(C_2 - P_2)(1 + i) - (C_1 - P_1)(1 + i)$$
$$= (1.43 - 0.68)(1.018) - (0.53 - 1.76)(1.018)$$
$$= 0.76 - (-1.25) = 2.01$$

FIGURE 4–8
Result of an Arbitrage for a Box Spread.

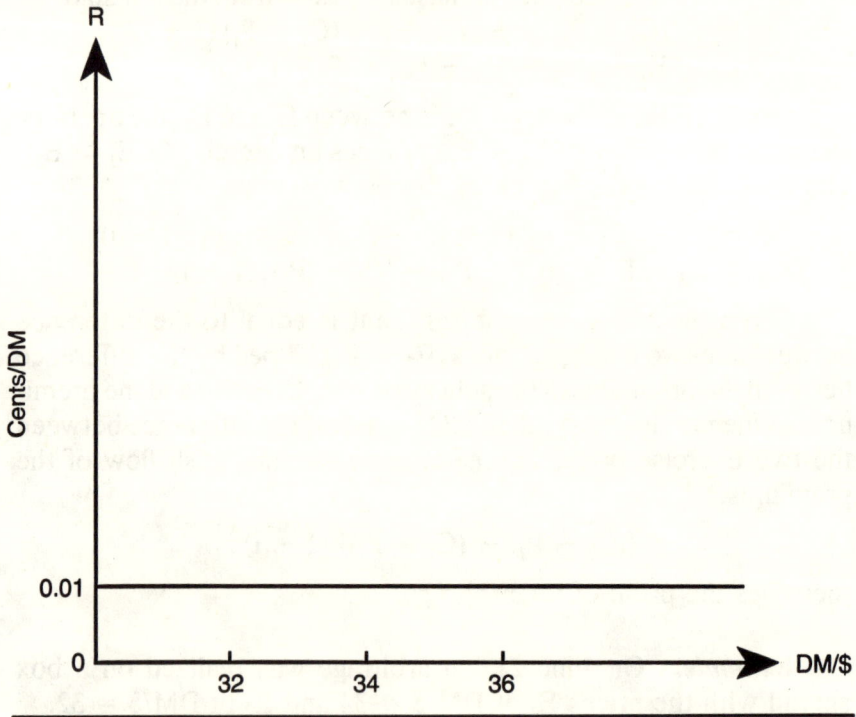

The resultant at expiration is as follows:

$$R = 32 - 34 + 2.01 = 0.01 \text{ cents per DM}$$

Therefore, the arbitrage is profitable (assuming that the transaction costs are negligible). The profits are diagramed in Figure 4–8.

Relationship between Puts and Calls with Different Strike Prices

Within the logic of the arbitrage for the box spread, the relationship of parity between the forward and the put versus the call presents a predicament.

In effect,

$$\text{Call } (E_1) - \text{Put } (E_1) = \frac{F - E_1}{(1 + i)^t}$$

and

$$\text{Call } (E_2) - \text{Put } (E_2) = \frac{F - E_2}{(1 + i)^t},$$

which can be combined as

$$\underbrace{[\text{Call } (E_1) - \text{Put } (E_1)]}_{} - \underbrace{[\text{Call } (E_2) - \text{Put } (E_2)]}_{} = \underbrace{\frac{E_2 - E_1}{(1 + i)^t}}_{}$$

| cash flow for buying synthetic forward at E_1 | cash flow from selling synthetic forward at E_2 | resultant realized at exercise |

The logic of the relationship is that given the act of buying a synthetic forward at E_1 and selling a synthetic forward at E_2, the cost of the difference between the two strike prices equals the cost of the operation. Also, the difference between the two pairs of synthetic premiums approaches the difference between the two strike prices, the difference being the interest rate cost on the net cash flow paid for the option premiums.

The resultant, R, for the arbitrage on the box spread tends to zero.

For the particular case, E_1 and E_2 are equidistant from the cost of the forward:

$$E_1 = F - X$$

Thus, buying a synthetic forward at E_1 and selling a synthetic forward at E_2 generally produces an opposing cash flow, as follows:

$$\text{Call } (E_1) - \text{Put } (E_1) = \frac{F - F + X}{(1 + i)^t} = \frac{X}{(1 + i)^t}$$

$$\text{Call } (E_2) - \text{Put } (E_2) = \frac{F - F - X}{(1 + i)^t} = \frac{-X}{(1 + i)^t}$$

Example. On June 21, the spot price of DM/$ was 32.63 and the forward was 32.80. Premiums from the OTC market were

E_1 = Forward − 0.5 = 32.3; Call (E_1) = 1.30; Put (E_1) = 0.83
E_2 = Forward + 0.5 = 33.3; Call (E_2) = 0.85; Put (E_2) = 1.35

The interest rate, i = 1.8 percent, was fixed for the period.

$$\text{Call}\,(E_1) - \text{Put}\,(E_1) = 0.47$$
$$\text{Call}\,(E_2) - \text{Put}\,(E_2) = -0.5$$

Following the above logic,

$$\frac{X}{(1+i)^t} = \frac{0.5}{1.018} = 0.4912$$

The market did not offer an arbitrage possibility.

Initially, the cash flow to the treasurer did not show the exact opposing values, producing a box spread profit, with the following result:

$$(C_2 - P_2) - (C_1 - P_1) + \frac{E_2 - E_1}{(1+i)^t},$$

which gives

$$-0.5 - 0.47 + \frac{1}{1.018} = -0.97 + 0.982 = 0.012 \text{ cents}$$

Note. In the OTC market, the costs are generally near zero. The calculations for the arbitrage for the entire analysis performed after looking only at the premium quotations need to be corrected, since they show only a marginal profit.

RELATIONSHIP BETWEEN THE SPOT PRICE AND THE OPTION PREMIUMS

A well-known relationship between the currency spot price and two equations for the option premiums will now be examined.

In effect, as can be shown,

$$\text{Call A/B (E)} - \text{Put A/B (E)} = \frac{F - E}{(1 + i)^t} \quad \text{(parity between the} \quad (3)$$
forward and the puts
and calls)

$$F/S = \frac{(1 + i)^t}{(1 + i^*)^t}, \text{ where } F = \frac{S(1 + i)^t}{(1 + i^*)^t} \quad \text{(definition of the} \quad (4)$$
forward contract in
the interbank market)

where

i^* = Interest rate in the country of currency A.

i = Interest rate in the country of currency B.

$$\text{Put A/B (E)} = S \times E \times \text{Call B/A} \left(\frac{1}{E}\right) \quad (5)$$

Combining equations (3) and (4) produces

$$\text{Call A/B (E)} - \text{Put A/B (E)} = \frac{S(1 + i)^t/(1 + i^*)^t - E}{(1 + i)^t},$$

which reduces to

$$\text{Call A/B (E)} - \text{Put A/B (E)} = \frac{S}{(1 + i^*)^t} - \frac{E}{(1 + i)^t} \quad (6)$$

Expressing equation (6) solely in terms of the put and comparing it to the put equation shown in equation (5) produces the following:

$$\text{Call A/B (E)} - S \times E \times \text{Call B/A} \left(\frac{1}{E}\right) = \frac{S}{(1 + i^*)^t} - \frac{E}{(1 + i)^t},$$

giving

$$S[\frac{1}{(1 + i^*)^t} + E \times \text{Call B/A} \left(\frac{1}{E}\right)] + \text{Call A/B (E)} + \frac{E}{(1 + i)^t}$$

Solving in terms of S gives

$$S = \frac{\text{Call A/B (E)} + \dfrac{E}{(1 + i)^t}}{\dfrac{1}{(1 + i^*)^t} + E \cdot \text{Call B/A}\left(\dfrac{1}{E}\right)}$$

Replacing the Call A/B (E) expression in equation (6) with the
S × E × Put B/A (1/E) value in equation (5) produces the following
value for S expressed solely in terms of puts:

$$S = \frac{\text{Put A/B (E)} - \dfrac{E}{(1 + i)^t}}{E \times \text{Put B/A}\left(\dfrac{1}{E}\right) - \dfrac{1}{(1 + i)^t}}$$

CONCLUSION: THE LIMITS OF ARBITRAGE BETWEEN THE CURRENCY AND OPTIONS MARKETS

Limits due to the Differences between Forwards and Options

An operation in forwards involves a buyer and a seller in the delivery
process of the currency exchanges, whereas an operation in options
does not involve the sellers.

A synthetic forward involves the buying and selling of an option. The counterparties to these transactions can complicate the
process by delivering exercises. Exercises can be anticipated by
the treasurer who has handled his financing of the transactions
based on the expectation of either an increase or a decrease in the
currency price.

An American option can be exercised at any time during the
course of its life. Nevertheless, exercise of such options is neglected
for the most part, mainly because their buyers prefer to take a profit
prior to exercise. The time value of an American option deteriorates
markedly in its final weeks of life, and a buyer should avoid such
a loss. Nonetheless, the seller should anticipate the risk of exercise
and be prepared to accept exercise at the expiration of an option.

Example. In the case of selling a put A/B, to be exercised in
time t', the seller should contemplate the final gain attainable by the
delivery of currency A and the financing of currency B for the period
(t − t').

Given all of the simulation programs available for estimating
results, we can appreciate how many hypotheses can be contem-

plated during the course of an option's life. However, no matter how many hypotheses we evaluate, it is not possible to produce all of the possible profit profiles that will allow us to predict precisely the results at expiration of our options.

The Limits of the Options Markets

During the early stages of the options markets, in the early to mid-80s, an arbitrageur was not able to obtain decent quotes on both the call side and the put side of a hoped-for trade. In the early 90s, however, with the option exchanges open on both sides of the Atlantic and round-the-clock trading beginning to become a reality, the arbitrage possibilities have become far greater. The option exchanges and the far larger interbank markets have expanded tremendously, and the techniques for estimating and communicating option values are far superior to the rather crude techniques of the early stages. The quotation of options in strictly volatility terms in today's interbank market is one example of how far the currency option game has come.

CHAPTER 5

THE STRATEGIES FOR SELECTING A POSITION

ANTICIPATING THE TENDENCY OF PRICE

Description of the Basic Strategies

Applying the strategies for selecting a position is simply a matter of work, since there is no one best position. The principal objective here is to foster a facility for properly anticipating profits in the face of the risks involved.

An important purpose of all the detailed studies that will now be shown is to create an awareness of the proper choice of the strike price that is best for a particular strategy.

Buying or Selling a Forward Contract

Whether a tendency for an increase or a decrease in price is anticipated, a look at a simple forward contract offers an overview of the available opportunities.

Example. On October 2, a quotation of the DM/$ from the currency market offers the following information: Price quote for the cash DM/$ = 64.47 cents per DM; 90-day forward quote for December 31 = 64.39 cents per DM.

A speculator who anticipates an increase in the DM above the 64.65 level by mid-November would buy the DM/$ forward (i.e., sell a dollar forward). A speculator who anticipates the opposite would sell the DM/$ forward (i.e., buy a dollar forward). The profit/loss profiles of such transactions are shown in Figures 5–1 and 5–2.

These strategies simply demonstrate the risk inherent in the forward contract: the obligation to deliver the currency based on its price at the contract's expiration. The outcomes of the option

FIGURE 5–1
Anticipating a Rise in the DM

Purchasing a DM/$ forward

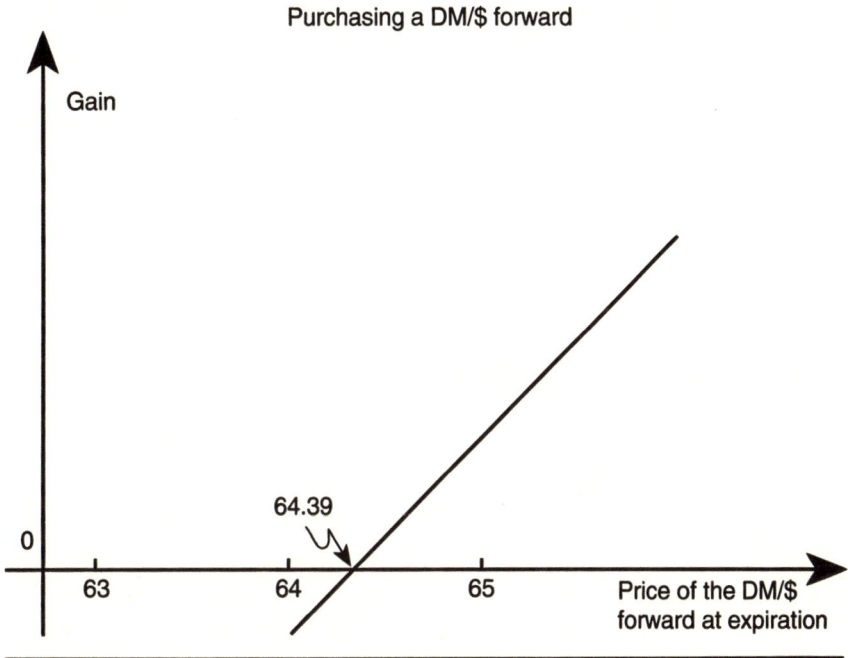

strategies that will be covered here will be compared with the possibilities offered by the forward contract.

We now present the change in premiums over time for the basic option strategies, the proper selection of the exercise prices, and profiles of the risk inherent in each of the option strategies.

Buying a Call: Anticipation of a Rise in the Currency Price
Purchasing a currency option focuses one's attention on obtaining a profit. One monitors the price of the currency from the moment the option has been purchased, the key variable being the intrinsic value of the option. Moreover, one realizes that the increase in the intrinsic value must overcome the decrease in the time value. In the case of stability or increase in the currency price, the maximum risk one is exposed to is the cost of the option premium.

The choice of the exercise price determines the attractiveness of the gains curve and the price potentials. The three exercise price

FIGURE 5–2
Anticipating a Drop in the DM

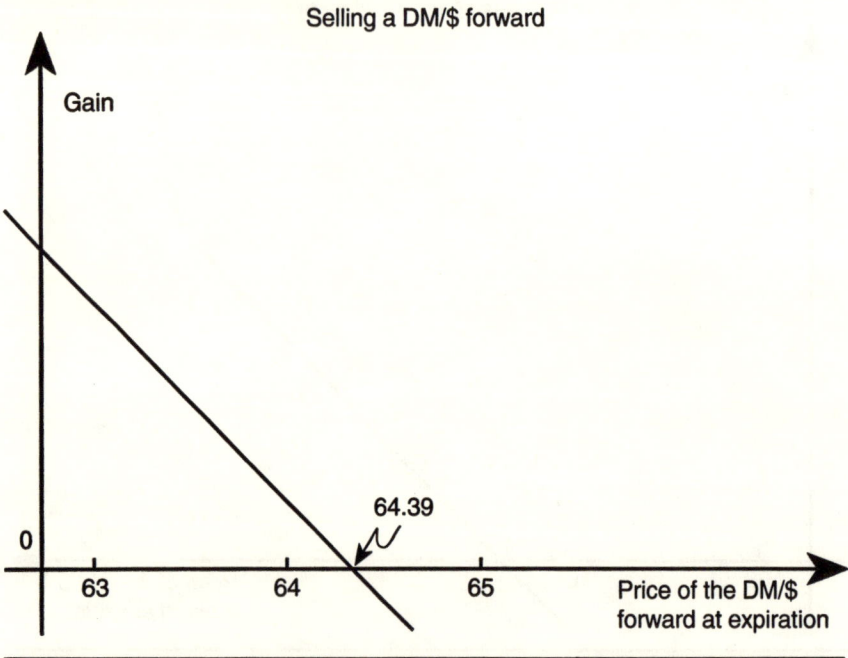

Selling a DM/$ forward

possibilities—at-the-money (parity), in-the-money (within), and out-of-the-money (outside)—will now be examined. The examples presented will be done in comparison with our introductory DM/$ forward example for October 2, for which the currency price was DM/$ = 64.47 cents, with a price of 64.39 for the forward expiring on December 31.

Buying a Call At-the-Money

Example.   A December 64.50 DM call costs 1.23 cents per DM, as compared to a currency spot price of 64.47 cents and a 90-day forward price of 64.39 cents. The initial cost, 1.23 cents, corresponds to a maximum time value and an intrinsic value of zero.

Risk versus Reward Profile.   The at-the-money option changes in value for each one-cent change in the spot DM/$ price at a rate of 0.50 in the option premium (Delta $= \frac{1}{2}$, as discussed in Chapter 1).

The risk variation of the premiums is equivalent to the option delta times the variation of a long position in the underlying cash currency values. The gain for the option buyer can be determined from the value of a long position in the cash value of a spot DM/$ rate. The increase in this value must overcome the deterioration in the option time value and therefore there must be hope that the deterioration in the time value is not rapid. The deterioration is slow over a two- to three-week period three months from expiration but accelerates during the final two–three weeks of the option's life.

The risk for the option position is the risk of loss due to the value of the underlying currency plus the interest rate paid on the cash used to purchase the option. The maximum loss is incurred if the price of the currency remains stable until expiration, thus producing a total loss of the time value and no increase in the intrinsic value. The interest rate cost is the prime rate over the 90-day holding period. We will estimate this to be a flat rate of 1.8 percent, producing a total option cost of $1.23 * (1.018) = 1.25$ cents per option.

Death point at exercise
$$= E + C * (1 + i) = 64.50 + 1.23 * (1 + 0.018) = 65.75$$
where

$S < 64.50$, $R = -1.25$ cents.

$64.50 < S < 65.75$, $R = S - 65.75$ or $-1.25 < R < 0$.

$S > 65.75$, $R > 0$.

Evolution of Results with Passage of Time.   In Figure 5–3, one can see the profit curve as expiration is approached. One can also see the evolution over time of the option time value. The curve of the option time value changes with changes in the volatility of the underlying currency.

For the sake of simplicity, all of the figures presented in this chapter assume that volatility is a constant.

Buying a Call Out-of-the-Money

Example.   A DM/$ December 65.60 call is bought at 0.82 cents/DM.

FIGURE 5–3
Buying a Call At-the-Money (Volatility Assumed to Be Constant)

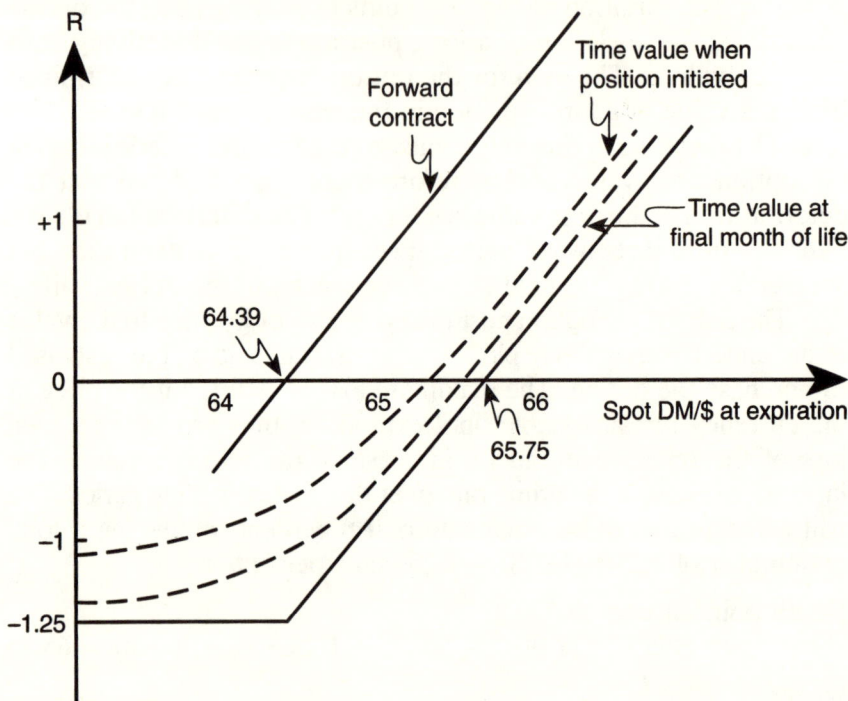

The initial debit of this strategy includes not only the time value but also the distance from the spot currency price to the strike price of the option. The risk of the option position is dependent solely on the value of the underlying currency. The risk of an out-of-the-money purchase is less than that of an at-the-money purchase, since a far lower gain results from an equal gain in the spot currency.

Risk versus Reward Profile.   The delta ratio is very small, to the point that the premium hardly responds to variations in the currency price. The risk of the option is far less than the risk of an outright position in the currency. The value of the option is almost beyond measure, since the time value hardly reflects movements in the spot, thus not giving any regularity to the option value. The option value becomes sensitive to the spot price only as it approaches the strike price. The owner of a call has an attachment to the option only as long as a rise above the strike price, and thus a profit, can be anticipated.

A profit can be realized from the call even if the spot price does not rise above the strike price. If the variations in the spot price are large enough to overcome the gradual loss in the time value during the option's life, a profit can be realized from the increase in the time value alone.

The purchase of an out-of-the-money call may be triggered by two different sets of circumstances:

1. Anticipation of an important rise in the currency price prior to the option's expiration.
2. Anticipation of a major increase in the volatility of the currency, which leads to an increase of the out-of-the-money delta, so that the option becomes more sensitive to changes in the spot currency price.

FIGURE 5–4
Buying a Call Out-of-the-Money (Volatility Assumed to Be Constant)

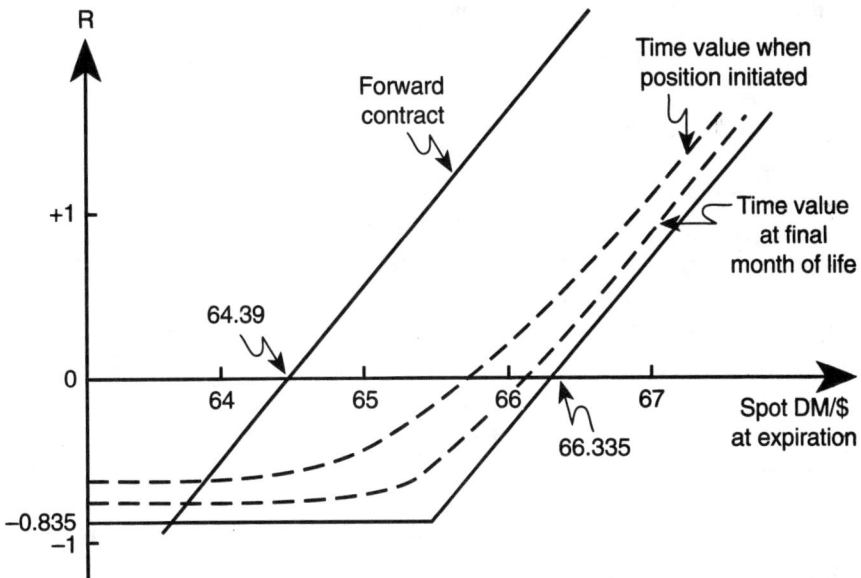

The maximal risk is limited to the prime rate interest cost plus the initial option premium, as follows:

$$(-0.82 \text{ cents/DM})(1 + 0.018) = -83.5 \text{ cents/DM}$$

Death point at exercise

$$= E + C * (1 + i) = 65.50 + 83.5 \text{ cents} = 66.335 \text{ cents/DM}$$

where

$S < 65.50, R = -0.835.$

$65.60 < S < 66.335, R = S -$ Death point or
$\quad -0.835 < R < 0.$

$S > 66.335, R > 0.$

This is shown in Figure 5–4.

Buying a Call In-the-Money

Example.   A DM/\$ December 63.50 call is bought at 1.79 cents/DM. The initial debit is equal to the amount that the spot price is above the option strike price or the intrinsic value of $64.47 - 63.50 = 0.97$ plus the time value, which is equal to the option premium less the intrinsic value, or

$$1.79 \text{ cents/DM} - 0.97 = 0.82 \text{ cents/DM}$$

Risk versus Reward Profile.   The option delta is elevated and approaches the value of 1, which means that the value of the option reflects very closely the value of the underlying currency. This means that the profit or loss of the option position depends almost exclusively on the value of the underlying currency. The buyer of the option should realize that the currency price change is a very strong factor in this strategy, that variations in volatility are not an important consideration. The in-the-money call purchaser is mainly a speculator in the value of the currency spot price.

At expiration the increase in the value of the currency has to be greater than the increase in the value of the option, the difference being the time value of the option.

The important difference between the cash strategy and the option strategy is that in the cash strategy the risk of the forward contract is unlimited, while in the option strategy the risk is limited to the premium paid at purchase of the option. The holder of a long currency position has to protect himself with a stop-loss order, while the holder of an in-the-money call has the choice of simply not exercising his option. Moreover, the holder of a currency has to get his stop-loss order executed properly in the marketplace, which could be a problem in a runaway currency market, while the holder of a call is protected by legal contract, with the option strike price determining precisely where the value of his position will be calculated. Yet another advantage of an in-the-money option over a long currency position is that the option is independent of the market's volatility, while the currency position can be taken out inadvertently in a "whipsaw" market.

Maximum risk at exercise

$$= (-1.79 \text{ cents/DM}) * (1 + 0.018) = 1.82 \text{ cents/DM}$$

Death point at exercise

$$= E + C * (1 + i) = 63.50 + 1.82 = 65.32 \text{ cents/DM}$$

where

$S < 63.50, R = -1.82.$

$63.50 < S < 65.32, R = S - \text{Death point}, -1.82 < R < 0.$

$S > 65.32, R > 0.$

The figure for buying an in-the-money call is shown in Figure 5–5.

Figure 5–6 demonstrates the following truths regarding the three strategies for buying a call:

- The purchase of an in-the-money call approaches most closely the purchase of a forward contract. This is evidenced by the option's delta, which approaches the value of 1. The major handicap that has to be overcome is the high premium paid for the option. The option owner prefers owning an in-the-money call to owning a forward contract mainly because since the call premium, however high it may be, is the only loss that he will incur if there is a meaningful change in the direction of the currency price.

- The out-of-the-money call permits the enjoyment of profits from a meaningful rise in the underlying currency at a minimum cost. In terms of its profit potential, however, its case is weaker than that of an in-the-money call or an at-the-money call.

FIGURE 5–5
Buying an In-the-Money Call (Volatility Assumed to Be Constant)

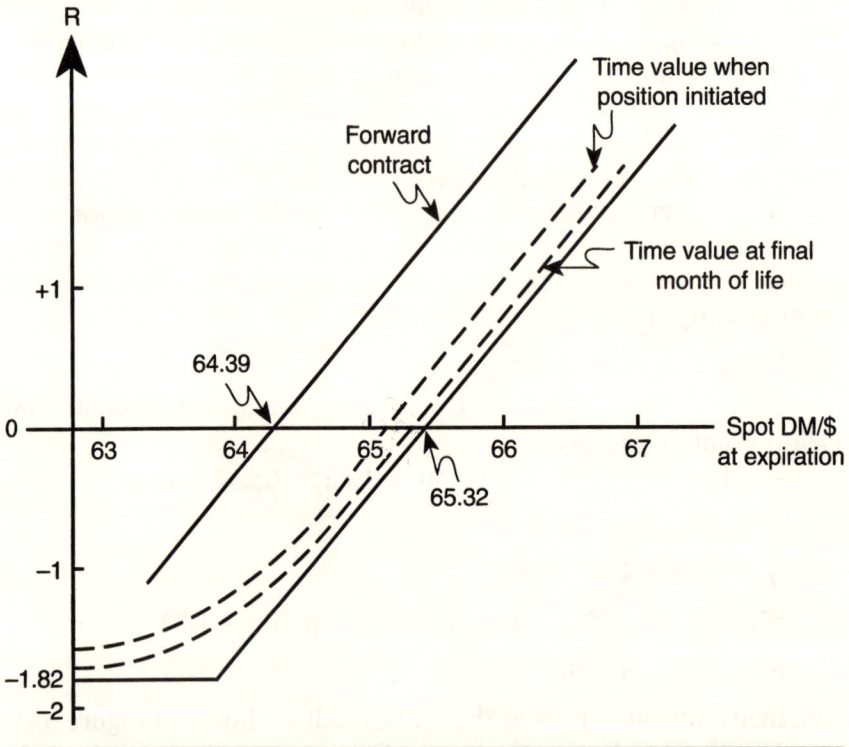

- The at-the-money call offers performance intermediate to the performance of the two more extreme cases. It possesses a higher probability of success than the out-of-the-money case, while, having a far lower premium than the in-the-money case, it incurs far lower costs if a major change occurs in the direction of the currency price. The at-the-money alternative is the most popular of the three strategies and forms the main basis for the options markets. A figure comparing the three strategies is shown in Figure 5–6.

Selling a Call: Anticipation of a Drop in the Currency Price
The position acquired by selling a call is the inverse of the position acquired by buying a call. Selling a call implies that an attempt

FIGURE 5–6
Buying a Forward Contract versus Buying Calls At-, In-, and Out-of-the-Money

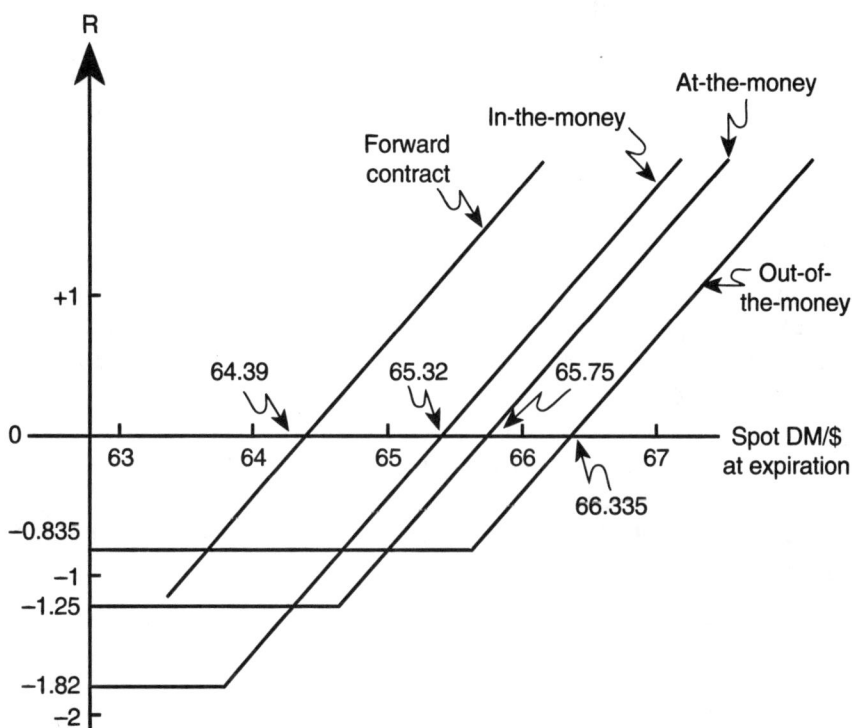

is being made to achieve a profit that has a high likelihood of occurring.

The seller of a call thinks that the high likelihood of a drop in the currency price makes it very unlikely that the option he sells will be exercised, which means that he is very likely to hold onto the profit he obtains from the premium. He also thinks that if he should have to repurchase the option, the likelihood is high that he will be able to repurchase it at a price lower than the price at which he sold it. In addition, he believes that the position of the option buyer will be maintained for a certain period of time, so that the decrease in the option's time value, a loss to the buyer, will naturally accrue to him.

Selling a Call At-the-Money

Example.   A December 64.50 DM call is sold for a premium of
1.23 cents/DM, compared with a currency spot price of 64.47 cents
and a 90-day forward price of 64.39 cents. The initial credit is 1.23
cents, while at exercise, taking into account the 1.8 percent interest
earned until expiration, the total amount earned is 1.25 cents.

Risk and Profit Expectations.   The risk profile of an option
seller is more attractive than the risk profile of an option buyer.
When the trade is executed, the seller receives the credit of the
premiums immediately. As long as the option price remains below
the exercise price, the seller possesses the maximum profit. The
main variables that the option seller has to estimate are the likelihood of an increase in the currency price and the volatility. Once
the call has been sold, the sensitivity of the option to an increase in
the underlying currency is only one half of the value of an increase
in the currency price.

The resultant, R, is exactly the inverse of the resultant obtained
when a call is purchased.

$$\text{Maximum gain} = 1.23 * (1.018) = 1.25 \text{ cents}$$
$$\text{Death point} = 65.75$$

where

$S > 65.75, R < 0.$

$64.50 < S < 65.75, 0 < R < 1.25.$

$S < 64.50, R = 1.25.$

Evolution of Results of Time Value.   The curves for the seller
of options are convex, and their convexity increases with the passage of time. Note that Figure 5–7 shows this strategy.

Selling a Call Out-of-the-Money

Example.   A December DM 65.50 call is sold at 82 cents. The
initial credit is the premium of 82 cents, which becomes 83.5 cents
at expiration due to the 1.8 percent interest return.

FIGURE 5–7
Selling an At-the-Money Call (Volatility Assumed to Be Constant)

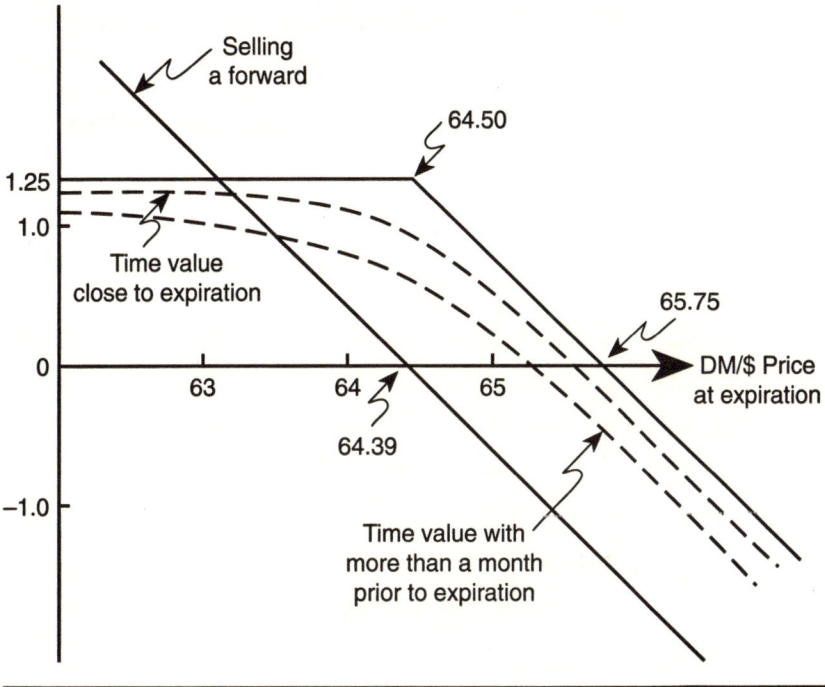

Risk and Profit Expectations.   The delta in this case is between slightly more than 0.3 and slightly more than 0.4, depending on the level of volatility. The seller in this case is willing to accept a somewhat lower profit in order to decrease the likelihood of exercise.

An option seller selects two strategies relative to the possibilities of gain in the underlying currency:

1. Anticipation that either a drop in the currency prior to exercise is likely or that if a rise does occur, it has a very low probability of exceeding the premium prior to exercise and that he will therefore retain most of the premium he receives.

Since the seller's profits are based on the diminution of the option's time value, even if a rally approaching the strike price occurs at some point prior to expiration, time will have passed and the delta will have decreased, so that the seller of the out-of-the-money call will still have a fair probability of obtaining a net profit.

2. Anticipation that the volatility of the currency will decrease.

A seller is likely to profit from a drop in the currency price even if the currency's volatility increases, because it is still probable that the seller will buy back the option at a lower premium than the premium at which it was sold.

The seller's greatest risk is that a strong rally will increase the intrinsic value of the option. It is therefore prudent for the seller to have a stop order in place to repurchase the option if such a rally occurs.

The seller's resultant, R, is exactly the inverse of the resultant experienced by the buyer.

Maximum gain at expiration = (0.82 cents) * (1.018) = 0.835 cents

Death point at exercise = 66.335 cents

where

S > 66.335, R < 0.

65.50 < S < 66.335, 0 < R < 0.835.

S < 65.50, R = 0.835.

Figure 5–8 portrays this strategy.

Selling a Call In-the-Money

Example.   A DM/$ December 63.50 call is sold at 1.79 cents. The initial cash flow is 1.79 cents, which grows to 1.82 cents at expiration.

Risk and Profit Expectations.   Due to a higher delta (usually greater than 0.7), the movement of the option relative to that of the underlying currency approaches 1.

At expiration the currency price is superior to the exercise price, which assures the occurrence of an exercise if the position has been maintained. In addition, the time value at the establishment of the position has a high probability of being the maximum obtain-

FIGURE 5–8
Selling an Out-of-the-Money Call (Volatility Assumed to Be Constant)

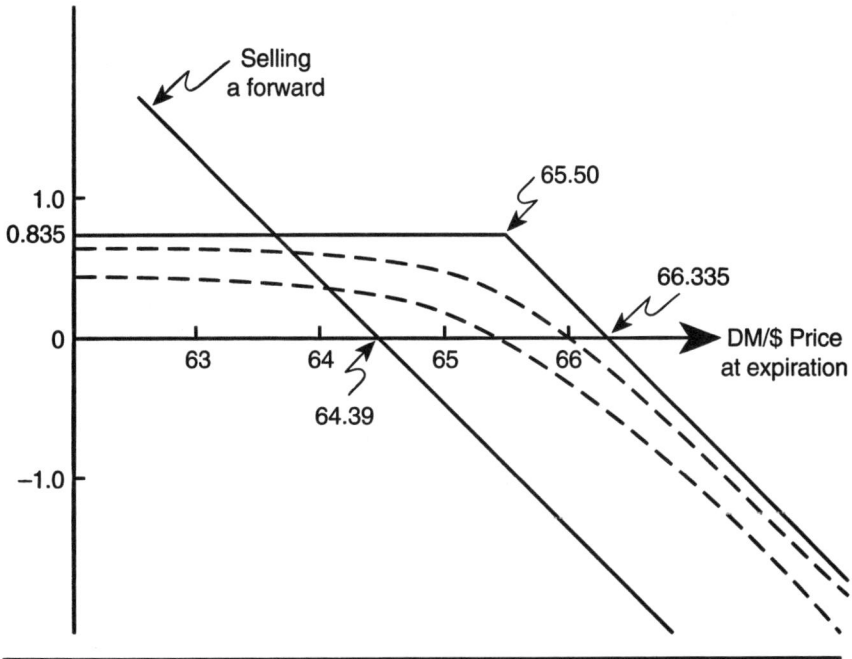

able, since the time value of an in-the-money option is very insensitive to change in the underlying currency.

If a severe drop does occur in the underlying currency, the maximum gain possible is the premium obtained when the position was established.

The seller of an in-the-money call anticipates an immediate drop in the currency. For protection against loss if a rally occurs instead, the seller should have a tighter stop order than is desirable with the two other selling strategies. Since the likelihood of exercise is highest for an in-the-money call, the seller must be prepared to face that outcome.

The maximum gain is 1.79 cents initially and grows through interest to 1.82 cents at expiration.

Death point at exercise = 65.32

where

$S < 63.50$, $R = 1.82$.

$63.50 < S < 65.32$, $1.82 > R > 0$.

$S > 65.32$, $R < 0$.

The profile for selling an in-the-money call is shown in Figure 5–9.
There is a great deal of symmetry between the buying and selling of calls:

- Selling an in-the-money call most closely follows the profit profile of selling a forward contract.
- Selling an out-of-the-money call offers the smallest profit potential but is also the option-selling strategy that is most

FIGURE 5–9
Selling an In-the-Money Call (Volatility Assumed to Be Constant)

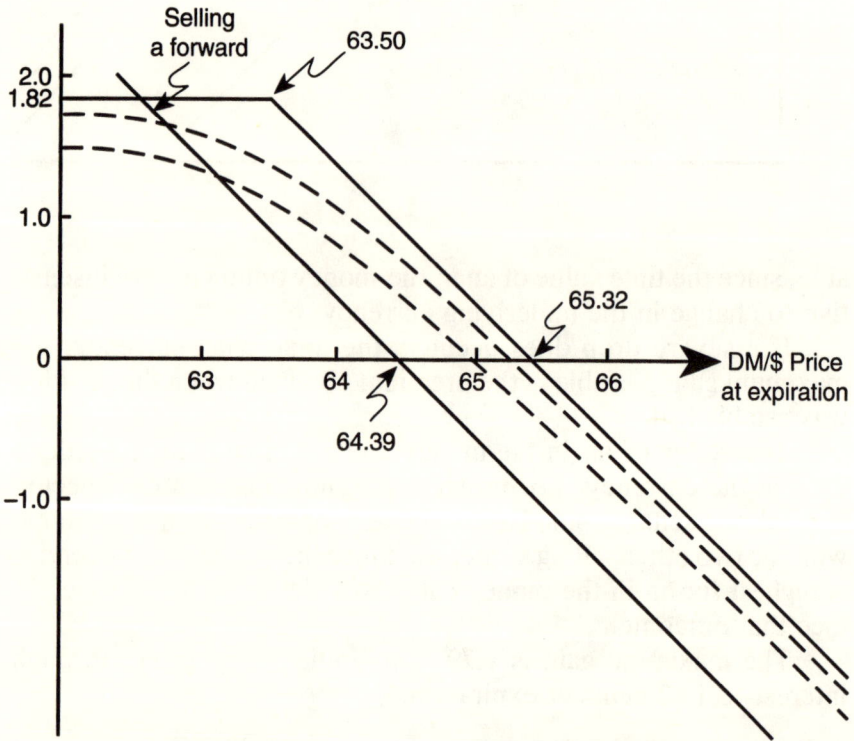

likely to succeed relative to the alternative of simply dealing in the currency market.

• Selling an at-the-money call offers results intermediate to those of the two extremes if the currency markets are unstable and a large rally or decline occurs. Given stability in the currency market, the results of selling an at-the-money call are superior to those of the two extremes.

To review the most important aspects of selling call options:

1. The most important fact a call writer must be alert to is a major market movement that is contrary to his original expectations, since his objective in selling call options is the profit he obtains from the deterioration in their time value as they age.

For this reason, it makes more sense to sell short-term options than to enter into long-term contracts and thus become more vulnerable to unpleasant accidents.

2. The seller of in-the-money options faces the highest risk of receiving an exercise notice.

3. As protection against contrary price movements in the currency marketplace, the seller should always consider the placement of stop-loss orders to buy back the options and close the positions.

Buying a Put: Anticipation of a Drop in the Currency Price
A put buyer has two objectives: either to buy back the option at a profit or to exercise the option at a favorable price. Once a put position has been established, the ideal outcome is for an immediate drop to occur in the currency market. The risk to the put buyer is at a maximum if either stability or a rally occurs, due to the resulting drop in the put's premiums. In order to cover all of the put outcomes properly, the at-the-money, in-the-money and out-of-the-money cases will be investigated.

Buying a Put At-the-Money

Example.   In October, the spot DM/$ was 64.47 cents and the December 64.50 put, very close to parity, was trading at 1.30 cents. The initial debit was 1.30 cents.

Risk and Profit Expectations.   Like the position of an at-the-money call, the at-the-money put position varies with the price of the underlying currency at one half of the change in the currency price. The risk for the option position equals one half of the risk for a short currency position.

The maximal risk occurs at expiration if the currency price remains unchanged or rises above the exercise price. That risk is equal to the premium charged for the option plus the prime rate, assumed to be flat at 1.8 percent until expiration: $(-1.30) * (1.018) = -1.32$ cents.

Death point at expiration
$$= E - P(1 + i) = 64.50 - 1.32 = 63.18 \text{ cents}$$

where

64.50 < S, R = -1.32.

63.18 < S < 64.50, R = 63.18 - S, producing -1.31 < R < 0.

S < 63.18, R > 0.

Buying an at-the-money put is shown in Figure 5–10.

Buying a Put Out-of-the-Money

Example. A DM/$ December 63.50 put is bought at 0.86 cents. The initial debit is the maximum risk and is close to the minimum risk available since the option is well out-of-the-money. For that reason, the probability of gain is small.

Risk and Profit Expectations. Due to the low delta incurred in such a situation, somewhere between 0.3 and 0.4, depending on the volatility at the time, the variation relative to that of the underlying currency is rather small. If the change in the currency price is small, it will not offset the loss in the time value of the put. If the currency merely drops to the exercise price, the entire time value will be lost. With an out-of-the-money option, a large price change is necessary to create a profit.

FIGURE 5–10
Buying a Put At-the-Money (Volatility Assumed to Be Constant)

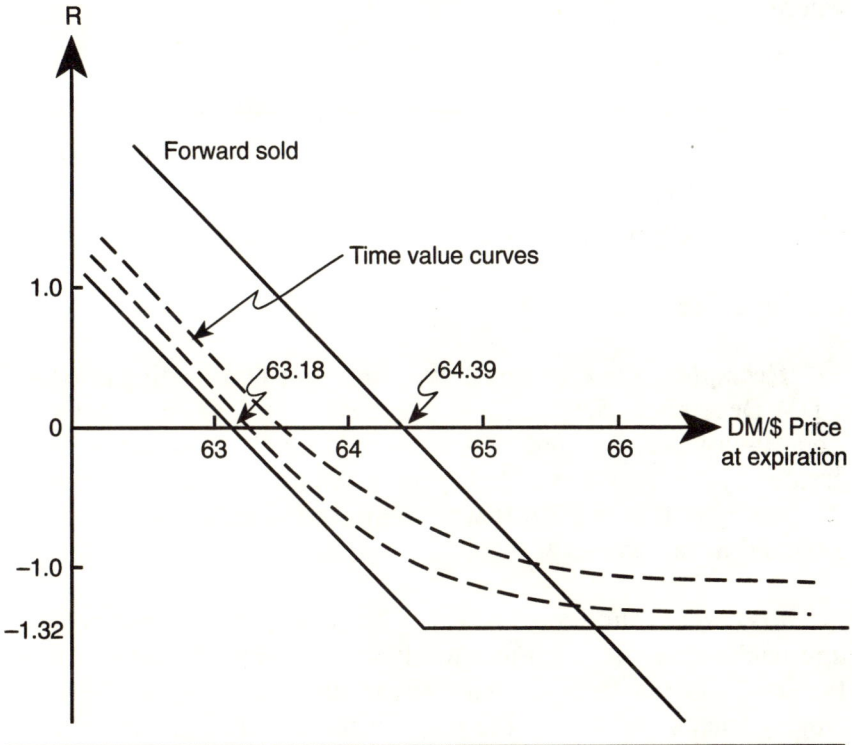

Two situations are anticipated when an out-of-the-money put is bought:

1. Anticipation of a major drop in the underlying currency.
2. Anticipation of a major increase in the volatility of the option corresponding to a major drop in the underlying currency.

The maximum risk is limited to the initial premium paid times the interest rate on the cash used, which equals $(-0.86) * (1.018) = -0.875$ cents.

Death point at expiration
$$= E - P(1 + i) = 63.50 - 0.875 = 62.62 \text{ cents}$$

where

63.50 < S, R = −0.875.

62.62 < S < 63.50, R = 62.62 − S, equating to
−0.875 < R < 0.

S < 62.62, R > 0.

The profile of buying an at-the-money put is shown in Figure 5–11.

Buying a Put In-the-Money

Example. On October 2, with the spot DM trading at 64.47, a DM December 65.50 put was purchased for 1.89 cents per DM. The 90-day DM forward was trading at 64.39. The initial debit, greater by far than that of either an at-the-money put or an out-of-the-money put, was 1.89. It was composed of an intrinsic value of 1.03 and a time value of 0.86.

Risk and Profit Expectations. The risk for this option position approaches the risk for the underlying currency. The delta is between 0.7 and 0.8, depending on the existing volatility, and therefore closely tracks changes in the price of the underlying currency.

Changes in the option closely follow changes in the values of the forward contract. A small change in the currency makes for a large change in the option's premiums, which is why stop-loss levels are an important consideration for this strategy. The put buyer's attitude has to be that the risk of a rally is very small.

An advantage of buying the option over buying the forward is that the total risk of the option is defined, while the risk for being short the forward is virtually unlimited. On the profit side, buying the option is inferior to being long the forward, since the option buyer must always suffer the loss of the time value paid when the position was established.

For both the forward and the option, a stop-loss order is an essential means of providing automatic protection against a rally. A stop order protects the risk side of the position but still allows the speculator to benefit from a new drop in the currency.

FIGURE 5–11
Buying an Out-of-the-Money put (Volatility Assumed to Be Constant)

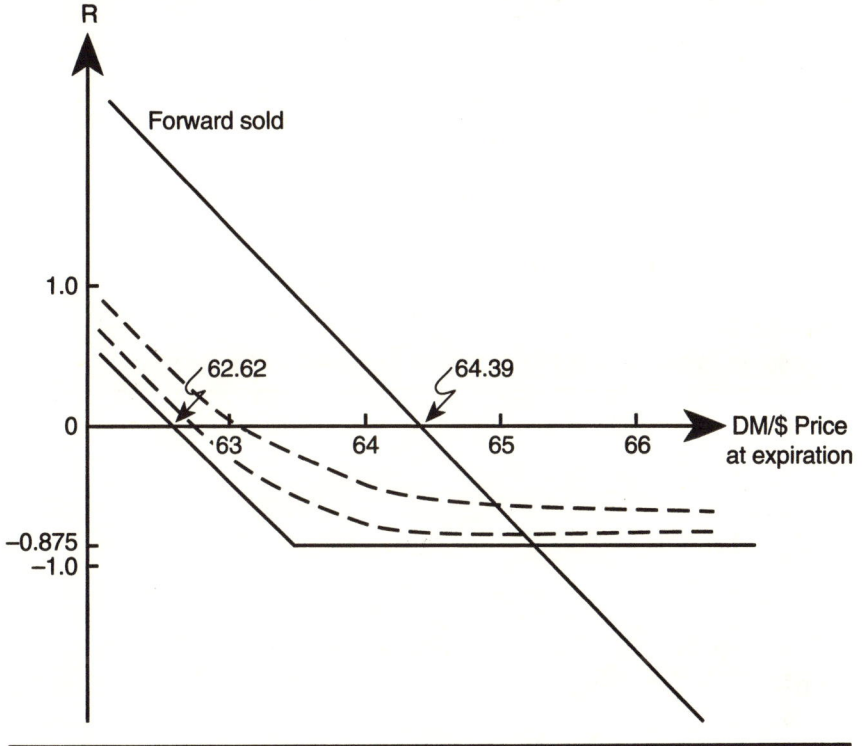

The maximum risk for the in-the-money put is incurred when the position is established. It equals the premium paid for the option plus the interest lost on the capital tied up in the option, shown as follows:

$$(1.89) * (1.018) = 1.92 \text{ cents per DM}$$

Death of position point
$$= E - P * (1 + i) = 65.50 - (1.89) * (1.018) = 63.58$$

where

$65.50 < S, R = -1.92.$

$63.58 < S < 65.50, R = 63.58 - S$, producing $-1.92 < R < 0.$

$S < 63.58, R > 0.$

Figure 5–12 shows buying an in-the-money put.

In summary, the three strategies for buying a put can be compared as follows:

- The most important fact about the in-the-money strategy is that it closely approximates the selling of a forward. The profile of the resultant varies very much like a short position in the underlying currency.
- The out-of-the-money strategy limits the risk of an unexpected rally, but it also limits the available profit.

FIGURE 5–12
Buying an In-the-Money Put (Volatility Assumed to Be Constant)

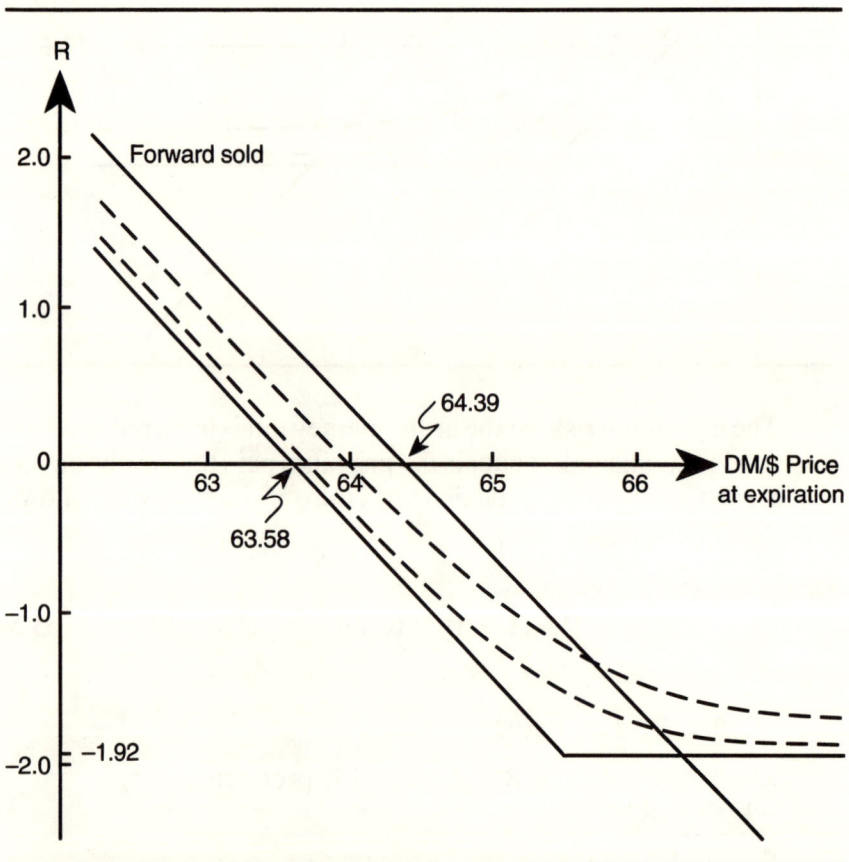

- The at-the-money strategy offers an intermediate performance, but it is the least interesting if the market becomes stable and the currency price does not change.

Selling a Put: Anticipation of a Rise in the Currency Price
The put seller benefits from a search at the treasurer's level for the ability to obtain a well-defined profit. The put seller anticipates an increase in the currency price and desires the avoidance of an exercise of the option sold. If necessary, he will repurchase the option prior to exercise in order to secure a profit.

In the ideal case, with the passage of time the put seller benefits from the decrease in the time value of the option and in the likelihood of its exercise.

Like the call seller, the put seller faces unlimited risk.

Selling a Put At-the-Money

Example.   A DM/$ December 64.50 put was sold on October 2, for 1.30 cents, with a spot DM price of 64.47 cents and a 90-day forward of 64.39 cents. The initial credit of 1.30 increased through interest at a 1.8 percent rate until exercise to reach a value of 1.32 cents.

Risk and Profit Expectations.   The probability of gain of a put seller is identical with that of a call seller in the sense that both receive the profits to be made immediately. Their risk is also identical in the sense that the risk of both is unlimited.

If the currency price does not drop below the average price or at least does not drop more than the value of the premiums received, the put seller is able to earn a profit prior to expiration.

While the put seller faces the adverse possibilities of a drop in the price of the currency and an increase in its volatility, these possibilities must overwhelm the benefit of the drop in time value, which accrues to the put seller with the passage of time. The put seller estimates that such possibilities are slim.

The profile of the put seller's profit expectations at expiration, R, is the inverse of the put buyer's profile.

$$\text{Maximum gain} = 1.30 * (1.018) = 1.32 \text{ cents}$$
$$\text{Death point at expiration} = E - P * (1 + i) = 63.18$$

where

$$64.50 < S, R = +1.32.$$

$$63.18 < S < 64.50, R = -63.18 + S, \text{producing}$$
$$0 < R < 1.32.$$

$$S < 63.18, R < 0.$$

The profit profile for selling an at-the-money put is shown in Figure 5–13.

FIGURE 5–13
Selling an At-the-Money Put (Volatility Assumed to Be Constant)

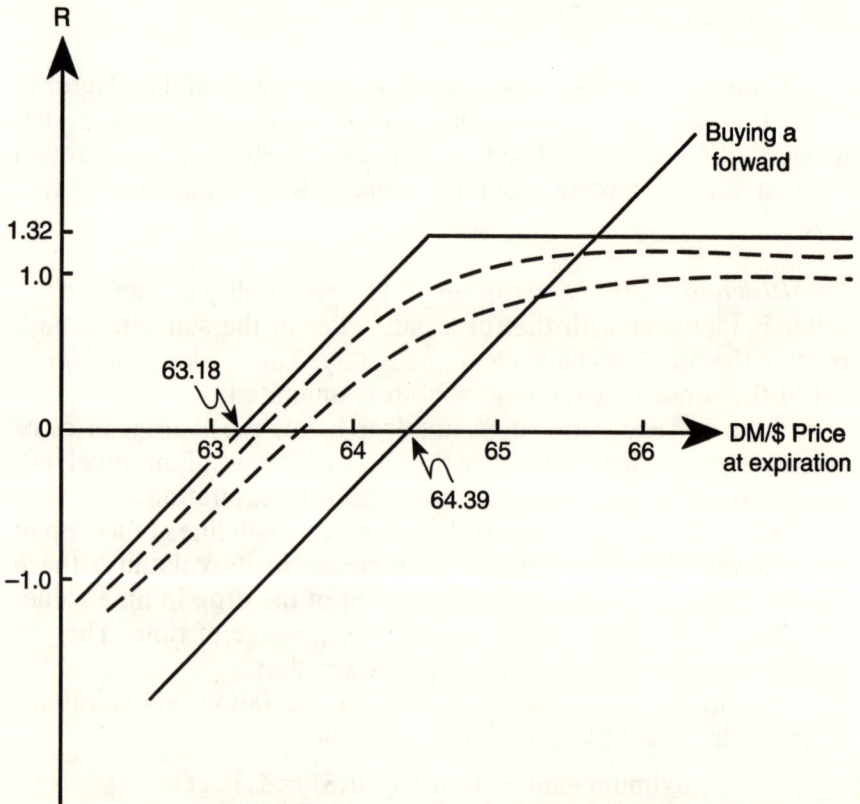

Selling a Put Out-of-the-Money

Example.   A DM/$ December 63.50 was sold at 0.86 cents. The initial credit, 0.86 cents, grew through interest until expiration to 0.875 cents, which was the lowest total among the three alternatives.

Risk and Profit Expectations.   The assumption of an out-of-the-money posture is based on the following anticipations regarding the behavior of the currency price:

1. Anticipation of either a rally in the currency price or a drop prior to expiration that is limited to the amount of the option premium.

The put seller's point of view is that the erosion of the option's time value will accrue to him with the passage of time. He expects the delta to approach zero as time passes, but he must always be ready to repurchase the option if there is a sharp drop in the currency price.

2. Anticipation of weak volatility as the most likely tendency for the currency, with the idea of repurchasing the option in case the exact opposite occurs. Diminution in volatility promotes a drop in the option's time value.

The profit resultant, R, of a put seller is the inverse of a put buyer's profit resultant.

The maximum gain, which occurs at expiration, equals

$$0.86 * (1.018) = 0.875 \text{ cents}$$
$$\text{Death point at expiration} = E - P * (1 + i) = 62.62$$

where

$S < 62.62, R < 0.$

$62.62 < S < 63.50, R = S - 62.62, \text{producing } 0 < R < 0.875.$

$63.50 > S, R = 0.875 \text{ cents}.$

The profile of selling an out-of-the-money put is shown in Figure 5–14.

Selling a Put In-the-Money

Example.   A DM/$ December 65.50 put was sold for 1.89 cents, with the spot currency at 64.47 and the forward at 64.39. The

FIGURE 5–14
Selling an Out-of-the-Money Put (Volatility Assumed to Be Constant)

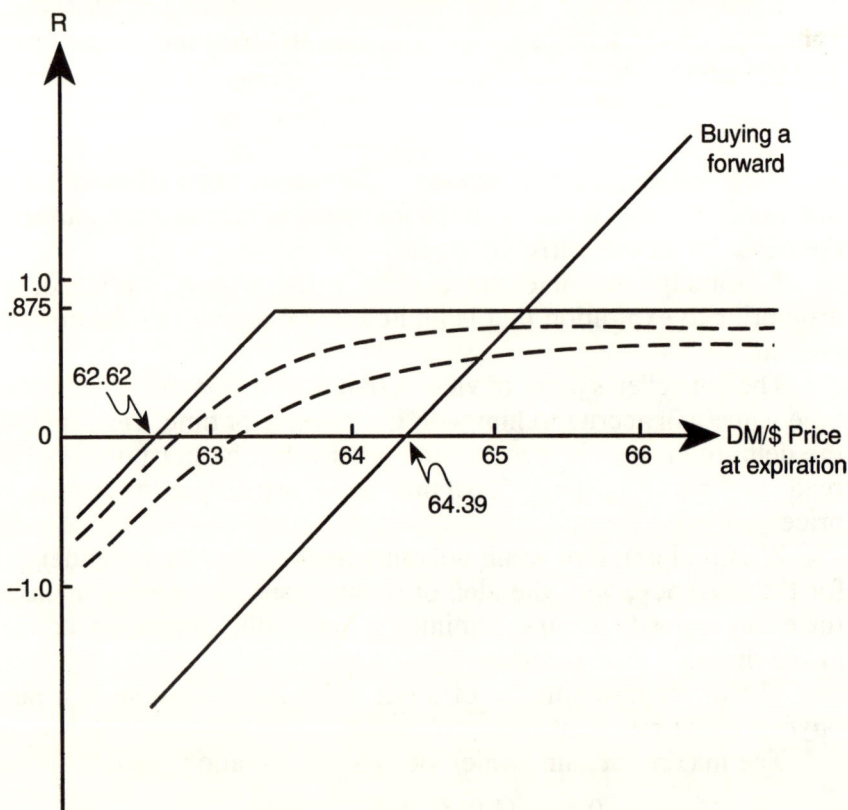

initial credit consisted of an intrinsic value of 1.03 cents and a time value of 0.86 cents, totaling 1.89 cents. This initial credit was higher than that of the other two alternatives.

Risk and Profit Expectations. The delta of the position is greater than 0.7 and can approach 1 if the currency rallies, which means that the position's risk approaches that of a short position in the underlying currency.

If the currency price is that of the exercise price at expiration, the resultant for the option is superior to that of owning the currency at the strike price. The difference between the two alternatives is the time value of the option when the position was established. If the currency price rises above the strike price of the option, the profit obtainable from the option is limited to the option premium, while the profit obtainable from the currency is unlimited.

The option seller prefers the immediate benefit of the option premium received to speculation on a rally in the currency. However, the option seller must always be prepared to protect himself from an unwanted exercise, which is more likely to occur with the sale of an in-the-money put than with the sale of an at-the-money put or an out-of-the-money put.

$$\text{Maximum gain} = 1.89 * (1.018) = 1.92 \text{ cents}$$

Death point at exercise

$$= E - P * (1 + i) = 65.50 - 1.92 = 63.58 \text{ cents}$$

where

$65.50 < S, R = 1.92.$

$63.58 < S < 65.50, R = S - 63.58, \text{ producing } 0 < R < 1.92.$

$S < 63.58, R < 0.$

The profile of an in-the-money put is shown in Figure 5–15.

In evaluating the three strategies of selling puts, one arrives at these conclusions:

- The profile of the risk resulting from the selling of an in-the-money put very closely approaches the profile of the risk resulting from the buying of a forward.
- The selling of an out-of-the-money put is the least risky of the three alternatives, but it also gives the put seller the lowest profit.
- The selling of an at-the-money put offers a profit and risk profile that is intermediate to the profit and risk profiles of the other two alternatives.

Synthetic Calls and Puts

The combination of two positions, a currency forward contract and either a put or a call option, produces the equivalent of the option

FIGURE 5–15
Selling an In-the-Money Put (Volatility Assumed to be Constant)

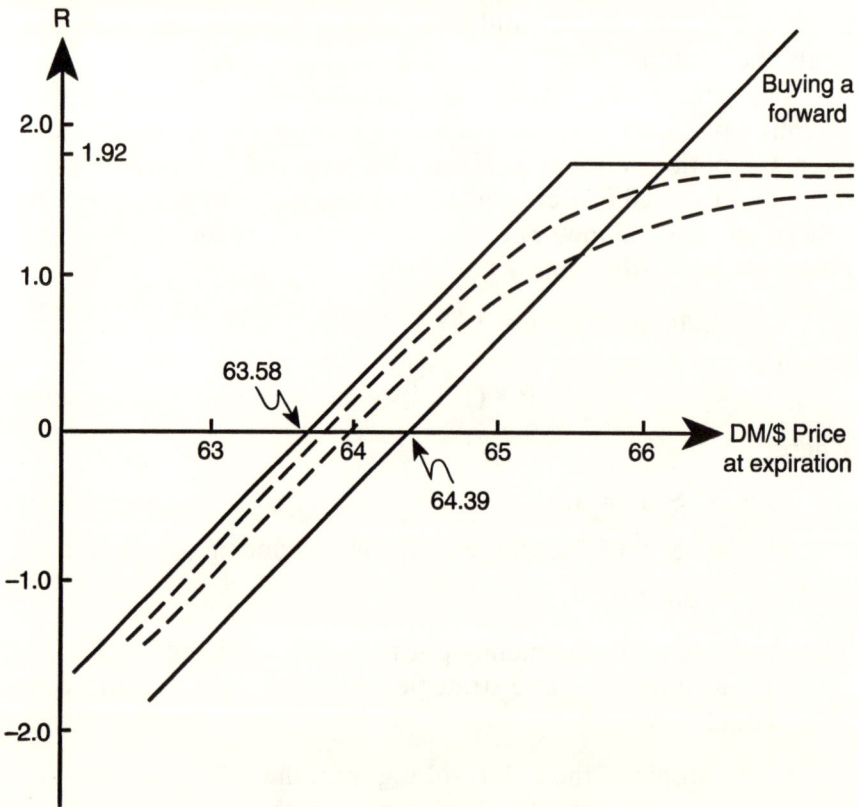

that is the inverse of the option used in the combination. Based on the logic involved, four strategies can be created on this "synthetic" basis.

Also, the treasurer who takes advantage of both the currency and option markets can produce a strategy that has the logic of an option strategy while avoiding complicating margin problems caused by an adverse price movement.

Buying a Synthetic Call: Buying a Forward Contract and Buying a Put
The profile that creates a synthetic call is shown in Figure 5–16. The configuration presented is the equivalent of owning an invisible

put. For our example, we are choosing an at-the-money option (Exercise price = Forward price).

The profile shown assumes that the forward is purchased at the same price as the spot currency and that the option strike price equals the spot price of the currency. (Such strategies can be most easily executed in the interbank market.)

The profile of the resultant for buying a put runs into all of the predicaments involved in owning a put, while the overall result of combining the two strategies is the equivalent of buying a call at-the-money (see Figure 5–16).

Selling a Synthetic Call: Selling a Currency Forward and Selling a Put
The combination of selling a forward and selling a put is shown in Figure 5–17. The configuration for this strategy is equivalent to selling a hidden put.

- The profile of the resultant shown is produced by selling a forward that is the equivalent of the currency with a spot price that equals the strike price of the put sold.
- The profile of the resultant shown may be the profile for selling a call at-the-money, but it incurs all of the predicaments involved in selling a put.

Buying a Synthetic Put: Selling a Currency Forward and Buying a Call
The configuration shown in Figure 5–18 is the equivalent of buying a hidden call, but it still involves the trader in all of the predicaments involved in owning a call.

Selling a Synthetic Put: Buying a Currency Forward and Selling a Call
The configuration shown in Figure 5–19 is the equivalent of selling a hidden call, but it involves the trader in all of the predicaments involved in selling a call.

Vertical Spreads for Rallies or Declines

In general, the spreads for these positions offer limited gains. If the anticipated gain does not occur, because the price change is contrary to what was hoped for, they result in a limited loss.

FIGURE 5–16
Buying a Synthetic Call At-the-Money

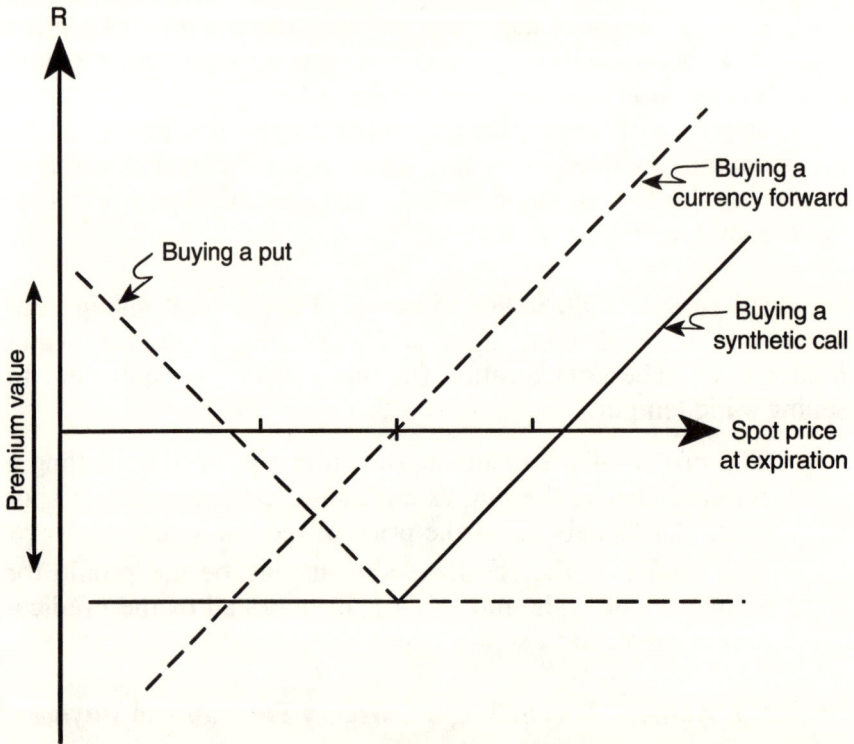

Vertical spreads are positions in which an option is purchased while another option of the same kind (a put or a call) and with the same expiration date is sold. Only the strike prices of the two options are different.

The exact gains and losses of such a spread are dependent on the quotations available in the marketplace.

A Vertical Spread for a Rally
A vertical spread for a rally is established by purchasing an option with a lower strike price, usually a price below the current market price, and selling an option of the same kind with a strike price above the current market price. As the name indicates, the expected

FIGURE 5–17
Selling a Synthetic Call At-the-Money

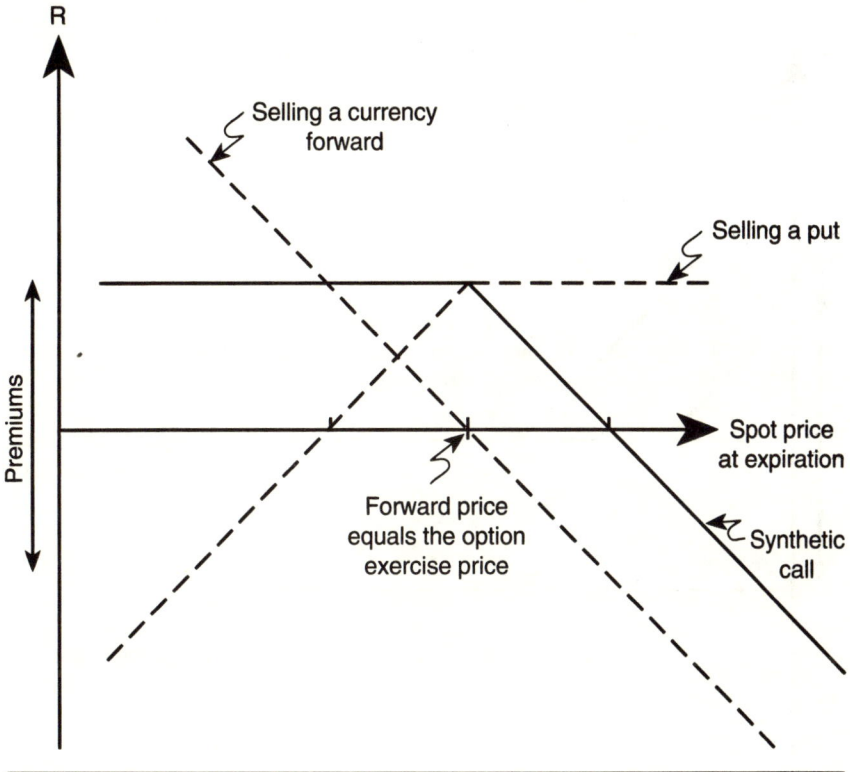

gain depends on the occurrence of a price change in the underlying currency.

The initial cash flow experienced by the treasury office that uses call options for the spread is a debit, shown as follows:

$$|\text{Call } (E_2)| < |\text{Call } (E_1)| \text{ or Call } (E_2) + \text{Call } (E_1) < 0$$

In this case, one sells a call (E_2) whose strike price is higher than the spot. The initial cash flow is the maximal loss obtained during the life of the option.

The initial cash flow experienced by the treasury office that uses put options for a rally in the market is shown as follows:

$$|\text{Put } (E_2)| > |\text{Put } (E_1)| \text{ or Put } (E_2) + \text{Put } (E_1) > 0$$

FIGURE 5–18
Buying a Synthetic Put At-the-Money

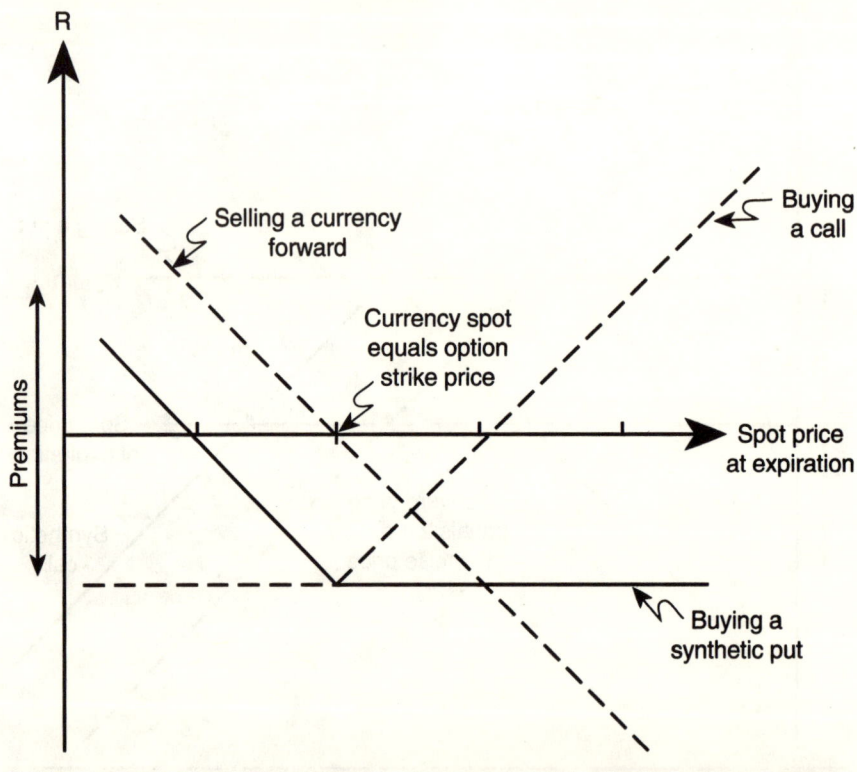

In this case, one sells a put (E_2) whose strike price is higher than the spot, but in this alternative the cash flow is the maximal gain obtained during the life of the option.

Risk and Profit Expectations. The risk of the spread has two aspects:

- If the price behavior of the currency is contrary to expectations, the extent of the loss is limited.
- If the spread operator allows the sold option to be exercised, the spread becomes a more complex affair.

The spread operator can also choose between using puts to initiate an initial positive cash flow, which he can then attempt to

FIGURE 5–19
Selling a Synthetic Put At-the-Money

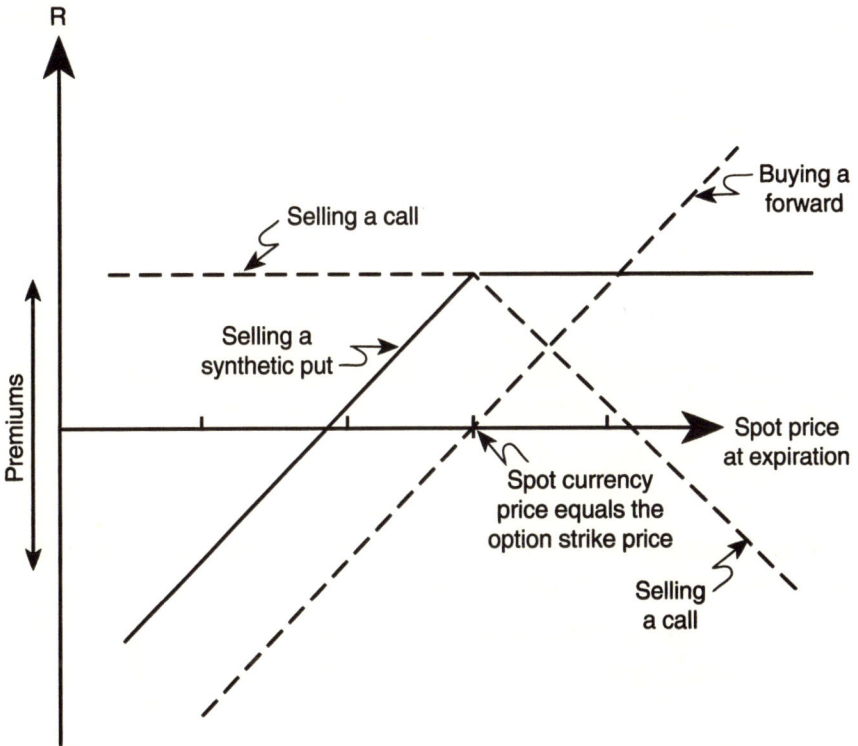

maintain through the use of stops, and using calls, which will produce a profit only if he is correct about the future direction of the
currency price.

Regarding the Call Spread. The call bought (E_2) has a far
greater delta, and therefore a far greater value, than the out-of-the-
money call sold. The profits in this spread depend entirely on the
increase in the value of the call bought in order to benefit from the
cash inflow produced by selling the call with a higher strike price.

Regarding the Put Spread. The put with a higher strike price
helps the spread due to its large cash inflow versus the lower cost
of the put with a lower strike price. It is important to realize that

the proper repurchase of the put sold is the key to the profitability of the put vertical spread.

A key factor regarding the put vertical spread is that it can be a good way to limit risk versus the outright selling of an in-the-money put.

The nature of the strategy resultant, R, can be best demonstrated with the two following examples:

1. A DM/$ December 63.50 call with a premium of 1.72 cents was bought and a DM/$ December 65.50 call with a premium of 0.82 cents was sold. An interest rate charge to expiration of 1.8 percent was incurred.

$$\text{Original conditions} = -1.72 + 0.82 = -0.90 \text{ cents}$$

Given a currency price below 63.50 cents at expiration and the 1.8 percent rate of interest, the maximum loss is

$$(-0.90) * (1.018) = -0.92 \text{ cents at expiration}$$

Given a currency price above the higher strike price of 65.50, the maximum profit is the difference between the two strike prices less the initial cost of the position:

$$65.50 - 63.50 - 0.92 = 2.00 - 0.92 = 1.08 \text{ cents}$$
$$\text{Death point of position} = 63.50 + 0.92 = 64.42$$
$$= E_1 + \text{Position cost}$$

2. In the put version of the bullish vertical spread, on October 2, a DM/$ December 63.50 put was purchased for 0.86 cents and a DM/$ December 65.50 put was sold for 1.89 cents, producing the following conditions:

$$\text{Original spread conditions} = 1.89 - 0.86 = 1.03 \text{ cents}$$

$S > 65.50$ and the 1.8 percent interest earned on the premiums produces the maximun gain, which equals

$$(1.03) * (1.018) = 1.05 \text{ cents}$$

$S < 63.50$ produces the maximum loss, which equals the difference between the two strike prices, increased by the initial positive cash flow:

$$(63.50 - 65.50) + 1.03 = -2.00 + 1.03 = -0.97 \text{ cents.}$$

FIGURE 5–20
Vertical Spread for a Rally Using Calls

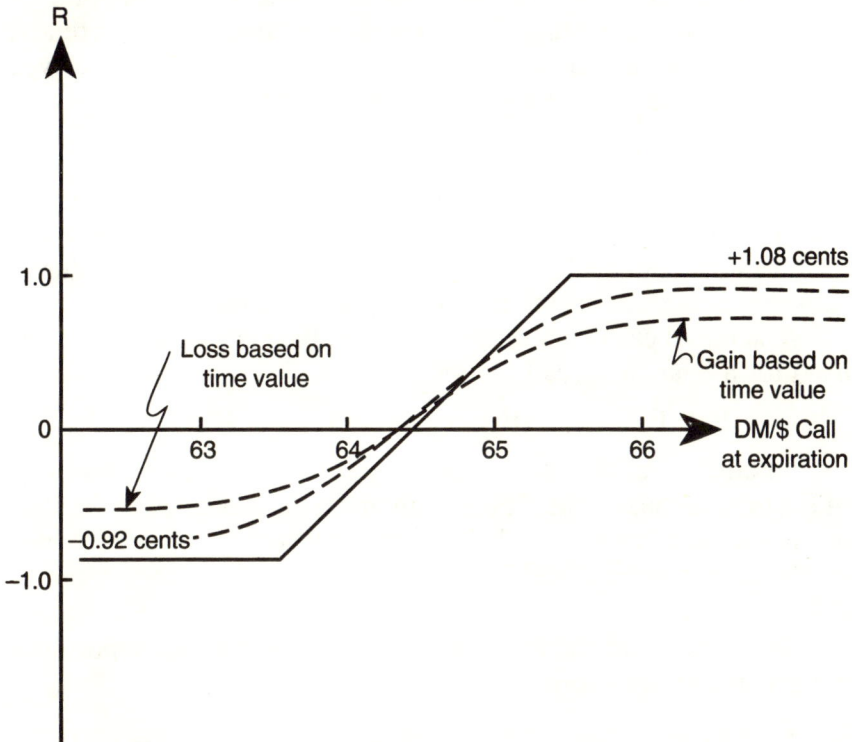

Evolution of Resultant over Time.
The profit profile evolves over time as the curves of the time values approach the higher strike price level at 65.50 and above. The loss of the spread is defined by subtracting from the upper strike price the difference between the two option strike prices and adding to that the option loss produced at an expiration below the lower strike price of 63.50, which is −0.97 cents.

A profile of the profits and losses over time is shown in Figure 5–20.

A Vertical Spread for a Decline
A vertical spread for a decline is created by selling an option at the lower strike price of the spread and buying an option of the same

type and with the same expiration date at the upper strike price of the spread.

A "bearish vertical spread," as the name indicates, is an attempt to profit from a drop in the price of the underlying currency.

The initial cash flow to the treasury office is a credit derived from the calls used to create the spread, as follows:

$$\text{Call } (E_2) < \text{Call } (E_1) \text{ or Call } (E_1) - \text{Call } (E_2) > 0$$

In effect, the price of Call (E_1), which is sold, is lower than the price of Call (E_2), which is purchased. The cash flow obtained when the position is established is the maximum obtainable, after interest gained is included, during the life of the position.

The initial cash flow to the treasury office is a debit if puts are used for a bearish spread, as follows:

$$\text{Put } (E_2) > \text{Put } (E_1) \text{ or Put } (E_1) - \text{Put } (E_2) < 0$$

In effect, Put (E_1) is sold at an exercise price lower than that of E_2, the purchased put. The maximum loss is produced at the start and is only increased by the lost interest that could have been earned on the cash being utilized.

Risk and Profit Expectations.   Two risks of equal importance are involved in the spread:

- One risk is that the price change in the underlying currency will be the opposite of what the spread trader desires, but the loss is at least limited.
- The other risk is that an exercise of the put sold will occur and thus that the spread will be involuntarily unwound.

The bearish spread is designed to gain as the spot currency drops in price.

For the Bearish Spread with Calls.   The call sold at E_1 has a delta greater than that of the call purchased at E_2. For this reason, the bearish spread appreciates in value based on the profits earned from the call sold.

The problem to be aware of is the possibility that the appreciation of the purchased call will exceed the premiums earned from the call that was sold. The logic of the call bear spread is that the behavior of the call sold is the one variable to follow.

For the Bearish Spread with Puts.   The delta of the put purchased at E_2 is higher than that of the put sold at E_1, and the attractiveness of the put depends on how little was obtained by selling the put at E_1. The profitability of the spread depends on the appreciation of the put purchased. If the spread has to be unwound, the gain obtained from selling E_2, the purchased put, must exceed the loss obtained by buying back E_1, the put sold.

The logic of the put spread forces one to mainly observe the performance of the put purchased.

The logic of the resultant, R, for the two cases follows:

1. For the call bear spread, one sells a DM/$ December 63.50 call at 1.79 cents and buys a DM/$ December 65.50 call at 0.82 cents, which defines the initial spread profit as $1.79 - 0.82 = 0.97$ cents.

With a currency spot price, S, below 63.50, the maximum spread is obtained, and interest increases the amount to $(0.97) * (1.018) = +0.99$ cents at expiration.

With $S > 65.50$, the maximum loss is obtained. It is the difference between the two strike prices plus the initial spread cash flow, shown as

$$63.50 - 65.50 + 0.97 = -2.00 + 0.97 = -1.03 \text{ cents.}$$
$$\text{Death point} = E_1 + \text{Initial cash gain}$$
$$= 63.50 + 0.97 = 64.47$$

2. For the put bear spread, one sells a DM/$ December 63.50 put at 0.86 cents and buys a DM/$ December 65.50 put at 1.89 cents.

$$\text{Initial cash flow} = 0.86 - 1.89 = -1.03 \text{ cents}$$

With $S < 63.50$, the maximum profit occurs. It is the difference between the strike price less the initial cash outflow:

$$65.50 - 63.50 - 1.03 = 2.00 - 1.03 = +0.97 \text{ cents}$$

With $S > 65.50$, the maximum loss is obtained. It occurs at expiration and includes interest cost:

$$(-1.03) * (1.018) = -1.05 \text{ cents}$$
$$\text{Death point} = E_2 + \text{Initial cash outflow}$$
$$= 65.50 - 1.03 = 64.47 \text{ cents}$$

Evolution of Resultant over Time

Both versions of the bearish spread have the same profile of the premium values across the price range for the DM from above 65.50

FIGURE 5–21
Bearish Spread Using Calls

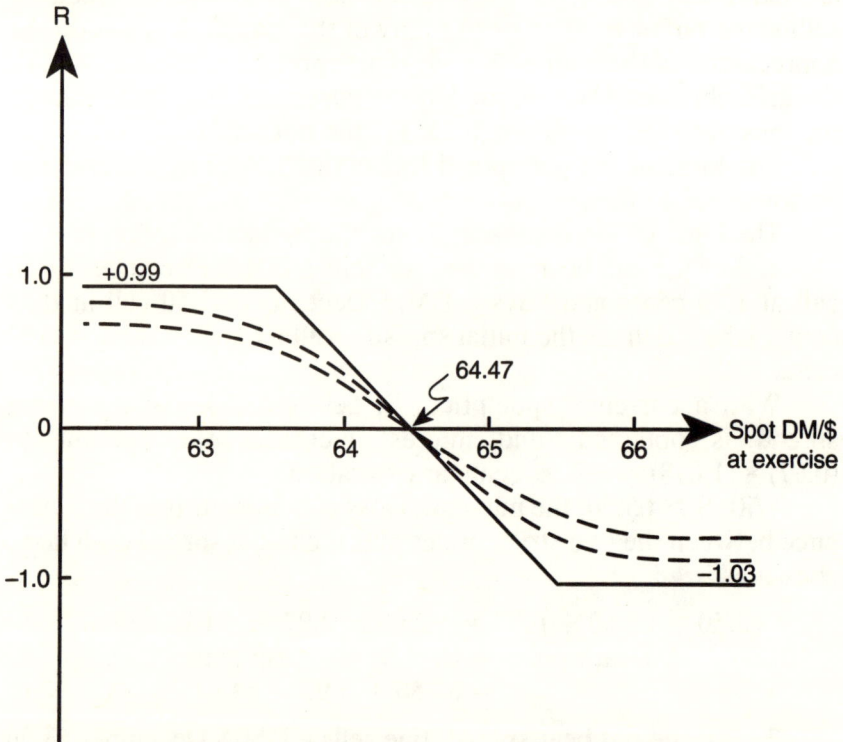

to below 63.50. Figure 5–21 shows the time values of the premiums for the call option case.

ANTICIPATION OF FUTURE VOLATILITY

Under certain circumstances traders have no opinions about the future direction of the marketplace and may find it difficult to foresee whether or not markets will be stable. Since options are dependent on volatility characteristics based on the behavior of the underlying currency, it is possible to have strategies that will benefit from both the stability and the instability of markets. If one can anticipate such market tendencies or, even better, simply monitor a moving

20-day window of the standard volatility measurements to detect changes in levels, which are often cyclical, there is money to be made.

A currently popular operation is analysis of such practical aspects of the marketplace. The key exercise is to constantly evaluate the fair value of puts and calls in order to buy "cheap" options and then to resell them when they achieve their fair value. The contrary exercise is to sell overvalued options in order to buy them back once they fall to their fair value. A great deal of option volume results from such exercises.

Although such intervention in the options markets by the professionals is a secondary aspect of option trading, its contribution to the liquidity of these markets is very important.

Most of the analysis for the strategies that follow is done to anticipate the new direction of volatility. The most obvious approaches evolve from recognizing when a given market is trading at either a high extreme or a low extreme. Movement away from an extreme and in the opposite direction is the only outcome for volatility. The only risk is how long a market can linger at such conditions. This is why measurement of the unfolding facts is the most sensible way to solve the problem. Don't guess; simply watch the facts unfold.

It should be borne in mind that a minimum evolving into a maximum is very different from a maximum evolving into a minimum. Minimum volatility can gradually become more extreme, but maximum volatility is characterized by extreme violence, and the crosscurrents can be devastating to trading positions. Gradual increase from a minimum is far safer from disappointments. As computer analysis becomes more sophisticated, market tendencies are becoming a time series that the better houses plot regularly.

Buying a Straddle: Anticipation of a Volatility Increase

Buying a Simple Straddle
Buying a straddle consists of simultaneously buying a call and a put with the same strike price and identical expiration dates.

- The straddle explained is known internationally as the "English approach" as opposed to the "French approach," which seeks to exercise the option whose exercise will take advantage of the currency price direction at the time of exercise.

- For practical reasons, the best choice is to purchase at-the-money options.

The cash flow at the treasurer's operation is a debit. This debit, which is also the maximum risk, is the sum of the premiums of the two purchased options.

Risk and Profit Expectations. The price of the currency spot is also the exercise price for either a rally or a decline, but, naturally, an exercise would destroy the straddle. Fortunately, early exercise rarely occurs in the American markets. The usual reason is that distant options must be exercised to alleviate cash stringencies resulting from extreme price behavior in expiring options. Although the problem rarely occurs, the damage done when it does occur can be so great that key stops should always be in place as insurance policies.

The maximum risk occurs only if expiration takes place at precisely the strike price, which is highly unlikely.

Example. The DM/$ spot price on October 2 was 64.47 cents. A DM/$ December 64.50 call was bought at 1.23 cents; a DM/$ December 64.50 put was bought at 1.30 cents.

The maximum loss is the sum of the two premiums (without including the cost of financing the debit):

$$-1.23 - 1.30 = -2.53 \text{ cents}$$

The death points for the straddle are

$$64.50 - 2.53 = 61.97 \text{ cents}$$

and

$$64.50 + 2.53 = 67.03 \text{ cents}$$

A gain occurs at $S < 61.97$ or $S > 67.03$. A loss occurs at $61.97 < S < 67.03$.

Evolution of Resultant over Time. For a straddle purchase, the maximum loss occurs in the unlikely circumstance that the

FIGURE 5–22
Purchasing a DM/$ December 64.50 Straddle

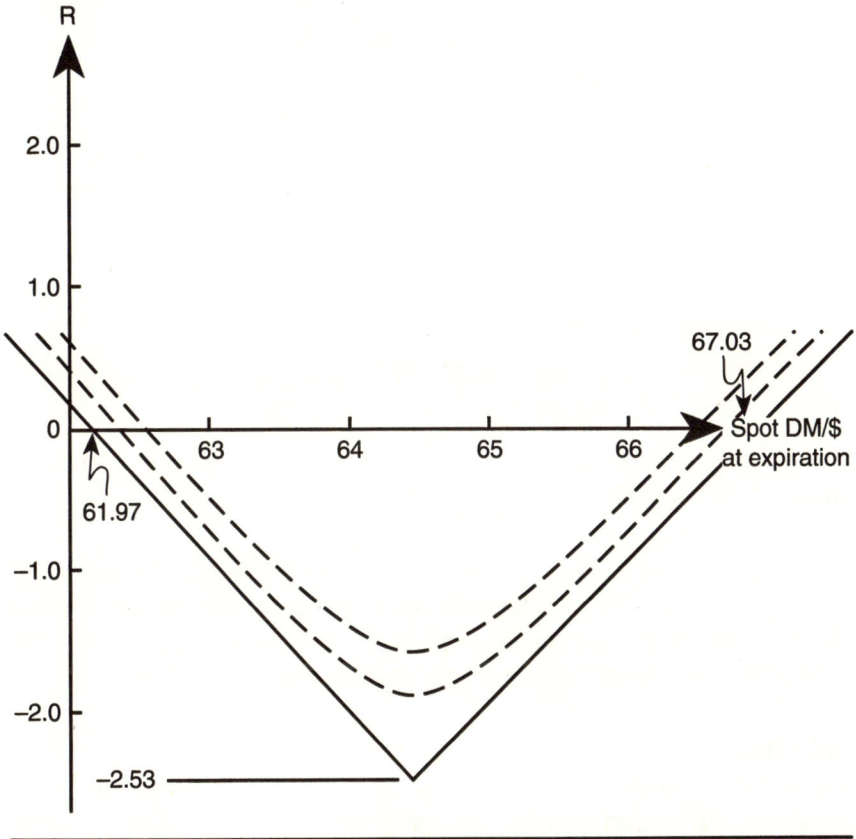

straddle expires at precisely the strike price and equals the sum cost of the two options purchased.

The straddle should obviously be sold prior to expiration.

Buying a Plateau Straddle (or Strangle)
One way to reduce the straddle cost is to buy a call and a put with the same expiration dates but different strike prices. The best way to reduce the straddle cost is to purchase two out-of-the-money options that equally bracket the current spot price for the currencies involved.

A trader purchases a strangle if he anticipates a significant increase in the volatility of the underlying currency. The strangle differs from the straddle in two major ways:

- The initial investment is considerably lower.
- The probability of a gain is lower.

Example.   A DM/$ December 63.50 put was bought for 0.86 cents; a DM/$ December 65.50 call was bought for 0.82 cents.

The maximum loss is the sum of the two premiums:

$$-0.86 - 0.82 = -1.68 \text{ cents}$$

The two death points are

$$65.50 + 1.68 = 67.15 \text{ cents}$$
$$63.50 - 1.68 = 61.82 \text{ cents}$$

A gain occurs at S < 61.82 or S > 67.15. A loss occurs at 61.82 < S < 67.15.

Evolution of Resultant over Time.   The best tactics regarding the straddle are to repurchase the position far enough before expiration to avoid suffering too large a loss of time value and also if signs of stability begin to appear in the marketplace.

Selecting the Exercise Prices

Buyers of straddles anticipate a strong increase in volatility and a new price direction in the underlying currency. Choosing between a straddle and a strangle usually depends on the degree of price change that the buyer expects. However, as Figures 5–22 and 5–23 indicate, it always pays to check out the cases because the price change needed to produce gains may be nearly the same for both a straddle and a strangle. In some cases, however, the strangle may offer a 33 percent reduction in the premiums paid.

A wise tactic is to monitor tendencies in the volatility trends, waiting for the first indication of an increase before making a commitment, since forecasting prices is an elusive art at best. Combining a fundamental hunch with factual evidence of change can be a wise way to operate.

The strike prices usually chosen are selected not because they are the outcome of guesses as to which way the market will move,

FIGURE 5—23
Buying a Plateau Straddle (a Strangle)

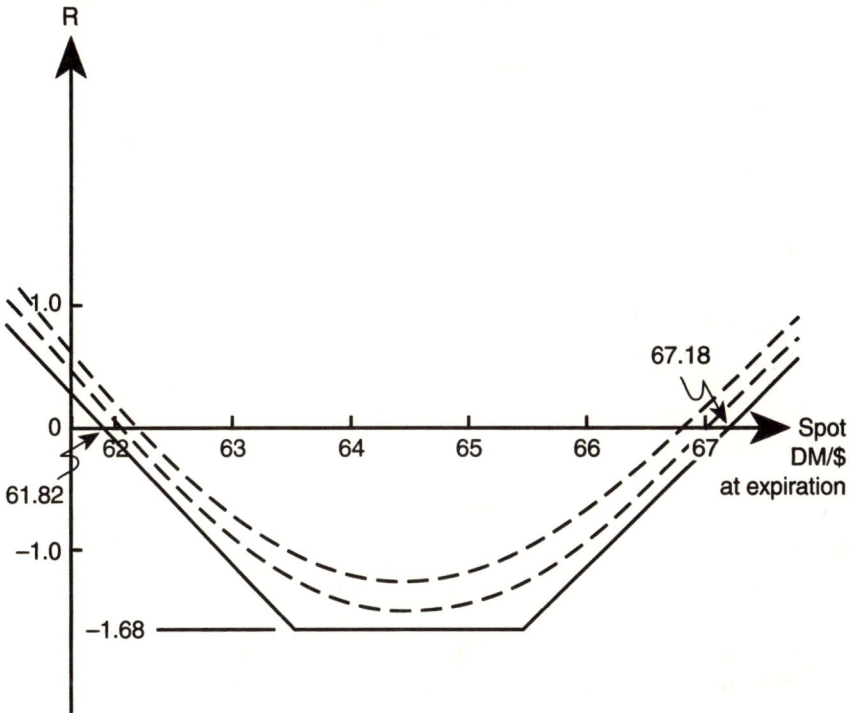

but because they are equally distant from the currency price. Some surprising insights are offered by using a computer to make the proper selection among the alternative choices. Successful options trading truly hinges on how thoroughly all of the reasonable alternatives have been examined.

Selling a Straddle: Anticipation of Stability in the Currency Price

Selling a Simple Straddle
Selling a straddle consists of simultaneously selling a call and a put with the same strike price and the same expiration. In general, the choice is at-the-money options.

The initial cash flow in the treasurer's operation is a credit equal to the sum of the two option premiums earned. That credit is also the maximum profit.

Risk and Profit Expectations. Profits are best achieved in a market that is heading toward or experiencing stability in the spot currency price, thus ensuring a decline in the time value of the two options sold. This occurs with the risk of early exercise, which is highly unlikely in the American markets.

The maximum risk is theoretically unlimited: it occurs beyond the death points if a strong rally or a severe decline occurs, as shown below.

Example. A DM/$ December 64.50 call was sold at 1.23 cents; a DM/$ December 64.50 put was sold at 1.30 cents.

The maximum gain is the sum of the two premiums:

$$1.23 + 1.30 = 2.53 \text{ cents}$$

The death points are the strike price plus and minus the sum of the two premiums:

$$64.50 + 2.53 = 67.03 \text{ cents}$$

and

$$64.50 - 2.53 = 61.97 \text{ cents}$$

A gain occurs at $61.97 < S < 67.03$; a loss occurs at $S < 61.97$ and $S > 67.03$.

Evolution of Resultant over Time. The seller of options benefits from the gradual loss in their time value, which can be measured as the position heads toward expiration. The profile of a straddle sale is shown in Figure 5–24.

Selling a Plateau Straddle (or Strangle)

Selling a plateau straddle is accomplished by selling two calls or two puts with the same expiration date but different strike prices. The profit profile obtained by the selling of a plateau straddle is symmetrical with the profit profile obtained by the buying of a plateau straddle. For practical purposes the strike prices chosen are out-of-the-money, and ideally they should be equidistant from the spot currency price. Another choice would be made only if one has a bias or if one is concerned about the possibility of a rally. In these cases, one would sell an out-of-the-money call that is further away from the spot than the opposite position.

FIGURE 5–24
Selling a Straddle

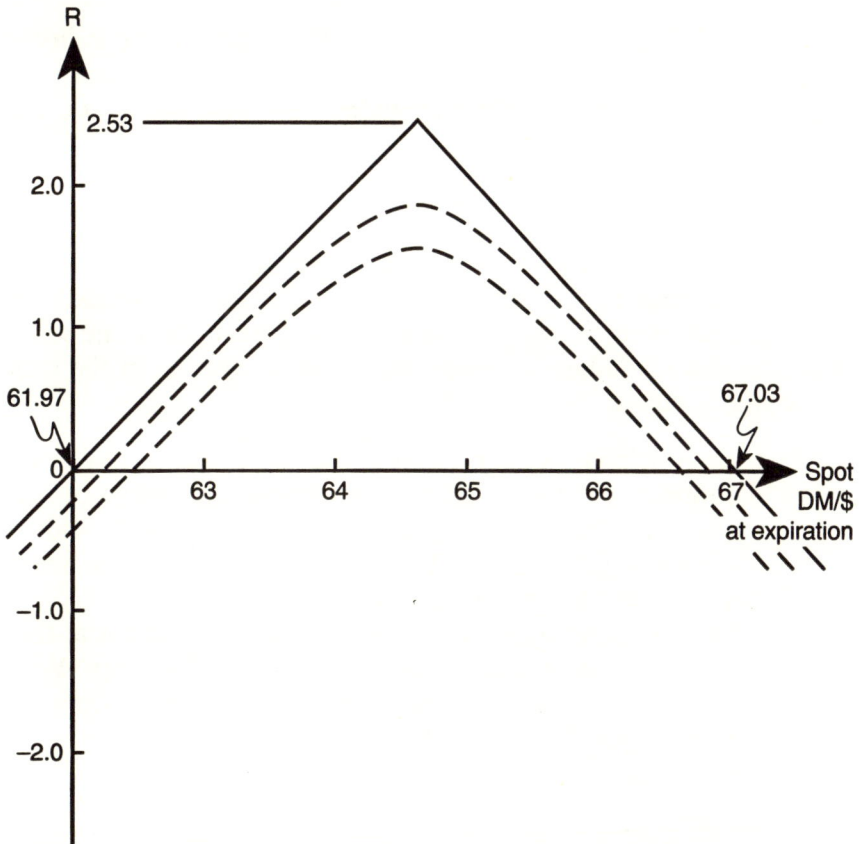

The plateau straddle anticipates stability within its profitable range, but it also offers a range within which profits can occur that is wider than the range offered by the simple straddle. Due to the lower premiums that the plateau straddle generates, it may be less profitable than the simple straddle, but it can be profitable over a wider range.

Example.   A DM/$ December 65.50 call was sold at 0.82 cents; a DM/$ December 63.50 put was sold at 0.86 cents.
The maximum gain is 0.82 + 0.86 = 1.68 cents.
The death points are 61.82 and 67.18.

Profits can be made at 61.82 < S < 67.18; losses can occur at S < 61.82 and S > 67.18.

Evolution of Resultant over Time.   The logic of profitability is simply to benefit from the loss in time value as long as the spot currency trades within the rather wide range from 61.82 to 67.18 during the option's life.

Choice of Exercise Price
As opposed to the buyer of a straddle or strangle, who anticipates a sizable change in the currency price, the seller of a straddle or strangle anticipates stability in the underlying currency. If the seller has a bias in his judgment about the future movement of the spot price, the required logic is as follows:

- If he anticipates a rally, he would sell an at-the-money or in-the-money put rather than an at-the-money or out-of-the-money call. With a strangle, the strike price of the call is further away from the spot price, or more out-of-the-money, than the strike price of the put.
- If he anticipates a decline, he would sell a call that is at-the-money or in-the-money rather than out-of-the-money. With a strangle, the strike price of the put is further away from the currency spot than the strike price of the call. The profile for selling a plateau straddle is shown in Figure 5–25.

Butterfly and Condor Spreads: Anticipations regarding Volatility
Certain brokers propose to their clientele combinations of vertical spreads with risk limitations that require the use of more than two options. Some analysts deem such strategies to be impractical, but they do offer some of the positive features of straddles and strangles, such as a rather wide range over which a profit can be made, and in addition they limit the maximum risk. Straddles and strangles have the serious disadvantage of unlimited risk. The disadvantages of the more complex strategies, as compared to straddles and strangles, are that these strategies have poorer profit capabilities, involve larger transaction costs, and are far more difficult to orchestrate.

FIGURE 5–25
Selling a Plateau Straddle (a Strangle)

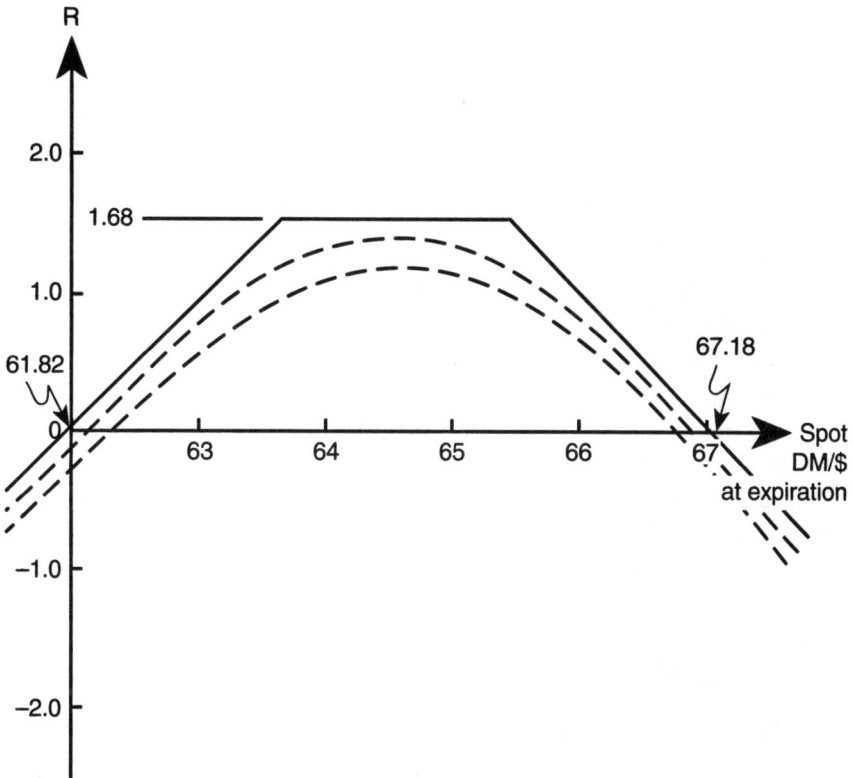

Buying a Butterfly and a Condor: Anticipation of Stability

Buying a Butterfly.   The butterfly is designed by combining a spread that anticipates a rally and uses strike prices E_1 and E_2 with a spread that anticipates a decline and uses strike prices E_2 and E_3, with $E_1 < E_2 < E_3$ and $E_2 - E_1 = E_3 - E_2$ (E_2 is at the midpoint between E_1 and E_3), while the maturities are identical.

Using calls to design the butterfly, one buys a call at E_1, sells two calls at E_2, and buys a call at E_3. Using puts to design the butterfly, one buys a put at E_1, sells two puts at E_2, and buys a put at E_3.

The initial cash flow at the treasurer's operation depends on the premiums available for the options chosen. If the premiums for the at-the-money options sold at the midpoint are greater than the premiums for the options bought at each of the extremes, a positive cash flow is possible, but it is marginal at best.

Risk and Profit Expectations.   The purchase of a butterfly indicates a hope on the trader's part that the underlying currency will be exceptionally stable during the course of the option's life. The major risk is either an increase in volatility or an important price change in the underlying currency. The maximum loss is equal to the cost of the initial debit.

The maximum profit is obtained if the spot currency is exactly at the mid-strike price of the butterfly at expiration, the odds of which are very low. The maximum profit is equal to E_3 minus E_2 (or E_2 minus E_1) minus the initial cash debit.

The death points are equal to E_1 plus the initial cash debit and E_3 minus the initial cash debit.

Figure 5–26 gives a rather detailed example of a butterfly designed on October 2. The attractiveness of the design is that the maximum loss (omitting transaction costs, which could be substantial) is only eight cents. To some, this has the appeal of a strategy in which it is hard to lose money.

The question that should be asked is: How often does such a strategy work out? Good money management strives for consistent results. For our example, the average gain over the 1.84-cent price range within which a profit can occur is $0.92/2 = 0.46$ cents. One may have a lot of fun in this way, but it is not a recommended way to build one's wealth. Bookkeeping is an important part of being a moneymaking options trader.

Some traders design an even more complex butterfly by combining a call butterfly and a put butterfly, using E_1, E_2, and E_3. Analyzing this more complex case is simply a matter of doing the type of bookkeeping that was demonstrated in Figure 5–26.

Buying a Condor Spread.   The condor is a variation of the butterfly that uses four strike prices instead of the three used for the butterfly. The two lowest strike prices are used to profit from a rally in the underlying currency, while the two highest strike prices are used to benefit from a drop in the underlying currency.

FIGURE 5–26
Buying a Butterfly Spread

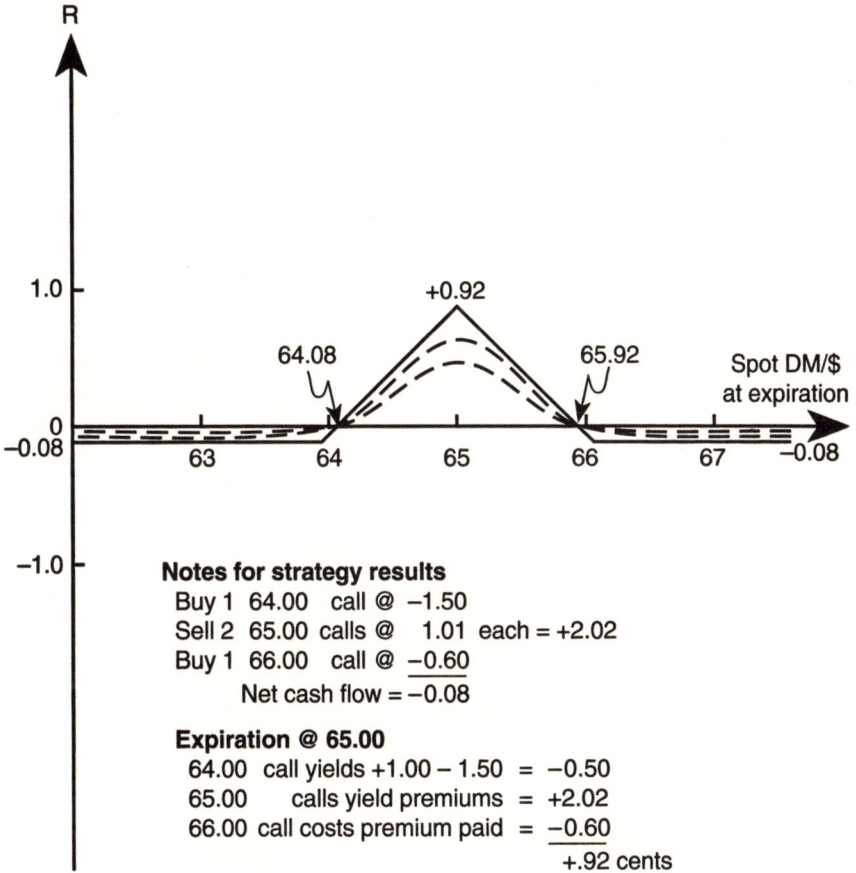

Notes for strategy results
Buy 1 64.00   call @ −1.50
Sell 2 65.00 calls @   1.01 each = +2.02
Buy 1 66.00   call @ −0.60
             Net cash flow = −0.08

Expiration @ 65.00
 64.00 call yields +1.00 − 1.50 = −0.50
 65.00   calls yield premiums = +2.02
 66.00 call costs premium paid = −0.60
                               +.92 cents

The design can be summarized as $E_1 < E_2 < E_3 < E_4$ and $E_2 < E_1 = E_3 - E_2 = E_4 - E_3$, with identical maturities.

The difference between the butterfly and the condor is that the condor has a plateau spread in its midrange and therefore offers a wider range over which a profit can be made at expiration. This profit, the maximum obtainable for the position, lies between E_2 and E_3. It is equal to $E_3 - E_2$ less the initial cash debit.

The death points lie above E_1 and below E_4.

The curves of the resultant are shown in Figure 5–27.

FIGURE 5–27
Buying a Condor Spread

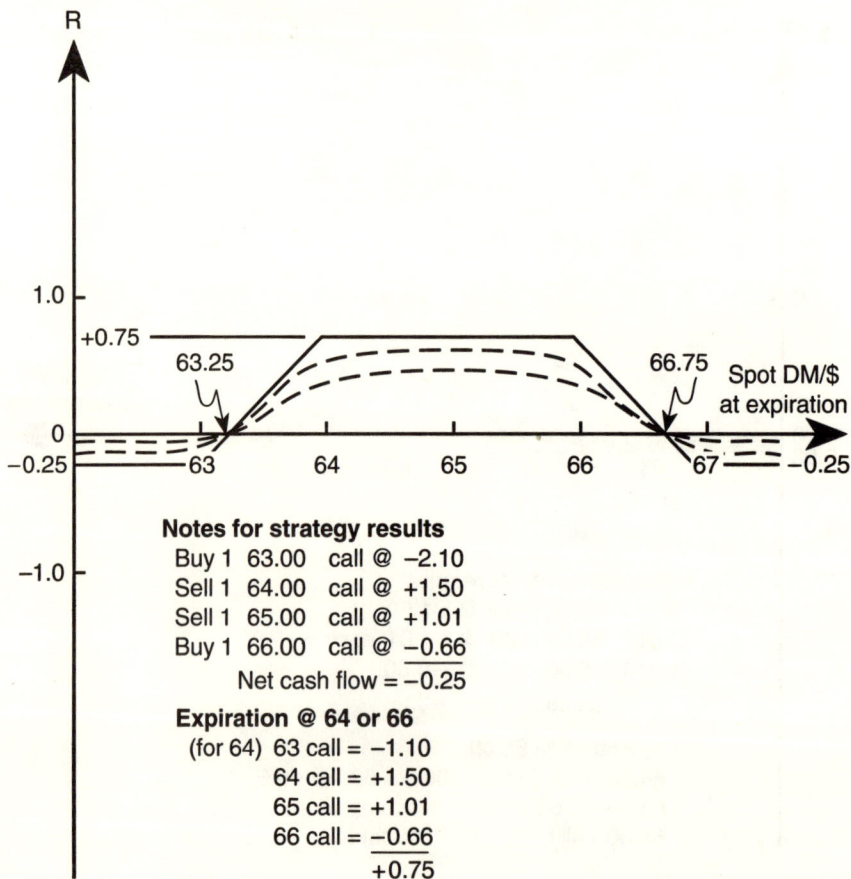

Notes for strategy results
Buy 1 63.00 call @ −2.10
Sell 1 64.00 call @ +1.50
Sell 1 65.00 call @ +1.01
Buy 1 66.00 call @ −0.66
Net cash flow = −0.25

Expiration @ 64 or 66
(for 64) 63 call = −1.10
64 call = +1.50
65 call = +1.01
66 call = −0.66
+0.75

Selling a Butterfly and a Condor: Anticipation of Volatility

Selling a Butterfly. The butterfly option combines a spread that anticipates a rally in the currency price and uses strike prices E_1 and E_2 with a spread that anticipates a drop in the currency price and uses strike prices E_2 and E_3, with $E_1 < E_2 < E_3$, $E_2 - E_1 = E_3 - E_2$, and identical maturities.

When using calls for the spread, one sells one E_1 call, buys two E_2 calls, and sells one E_3 call.

When using puts for the spread, one sells one E_1 put, buys two E_2 puts, and sells one E_3 put.

The initial cash flow to the treasurer's operation depends on the specific combination chosen. The results are mostly positive.

Risk and Profit Expectations.   The risk manifests itself if the spot currency price remains precisely at E_2, the mid-strike price.

The maximum profit equals the initial credit. This profit is enjoyed above E_3 and below E_1.

FIGURE 5–28
Selling a Butterfly Spread

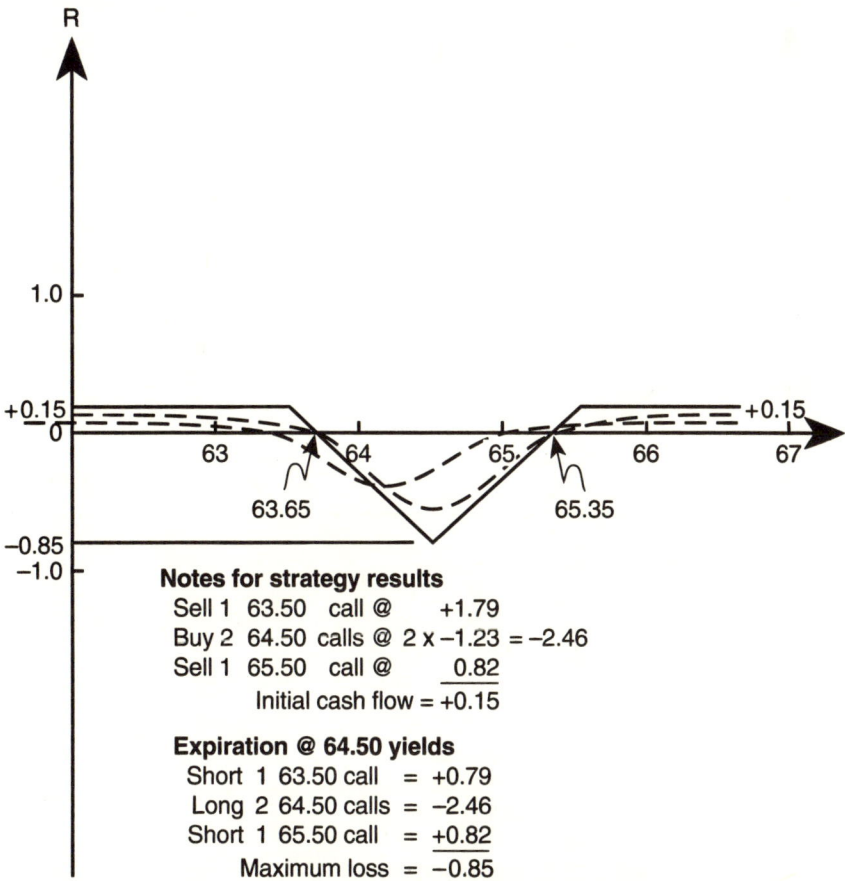

Notes for strategy results
Sell 1 63.50   call @   +1.79
Buy 2 64.50 calls @ 2 x –1.23 = –2.46
Sell 1 65.50   call @   0.82
          Initial cash flow = +0.15

Expiration @ 64.50 yields
Short 1 63.50 call   = +0.79
Long 2 64.50 calls   = –2.46
Short 1 65.50 call   = +0.82
          Maximum loss = –0.85

The death points are at E_1 plus the initial cash flow and at E_3 minus the initial cash flow credit.

Puts and calls are also combined in one spread. One approach is to combine selling a call at E_1 and buying a call at E_2 with buying a put at E_2 and selling a put at E_3.

The reverse is done as well; that is, selling a put at E_1 and buying a put at E_2 is combined with buying a call at E_2 and selling a call at E_3.

FIGURE 5–29
Selling a Condor Spread

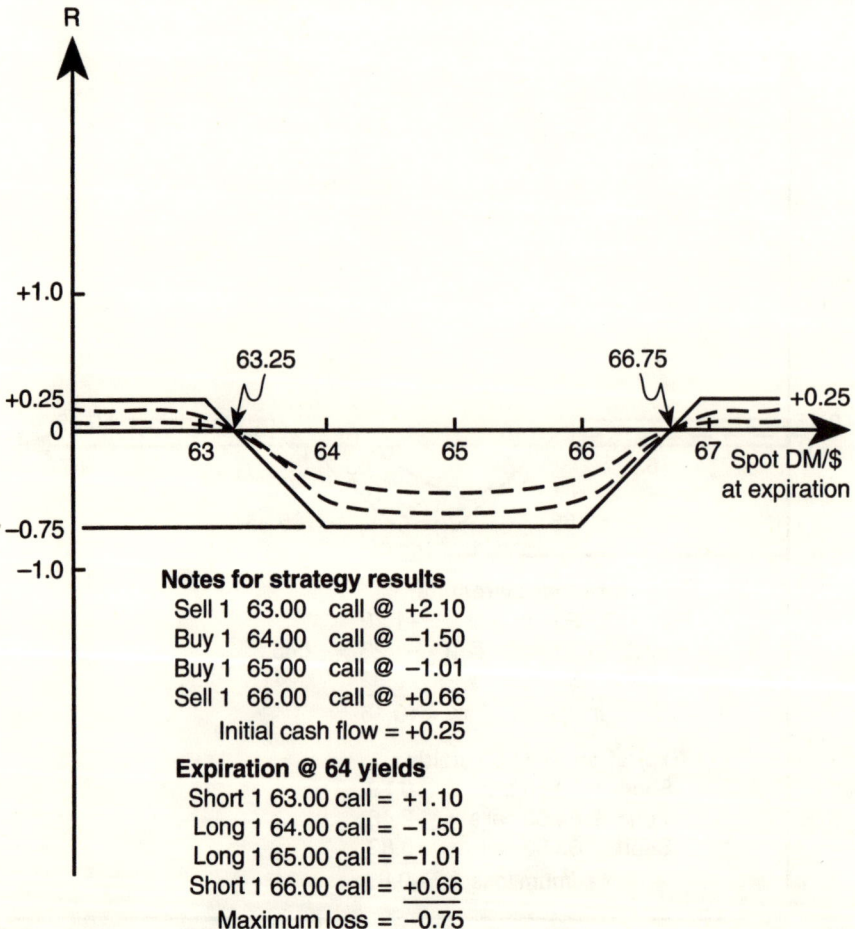

Notes for strategy results
Sell 1 63.00 call @ +2.10
Buy 1 64.00 call @ −1.50
Buy 1 65.00 call @ −1.01
Sell 1 66.00 call @ +0.66
Initial cash flow = +0.25

Expiration @ 64 yields
Short 1 63.00 call = +1.10
Long 1 64.00 call = −1.50
Long 1 65.00 call = −1.01
Short 1 66.00 call = +0.66
Maximum loss = −0.75

Naturally, the initial cash flow depends on the exact version of the many varieties that exist not only in the types but in the strike prices and premiums that are available in the marketplace. The profile for selling a butterfly spread is shown in Figure 5–28.

Selling a Condor.   The condor is a variation of the butterfly that uses four strike prices. These strike prices combine a spread at E_1 and E_2, designed to profit from a rally, with a bearish spread at E_3 and E_4, with $E_1 < E_2 < E_3 < E_4$, $E_2 - E_1 = E_3 - E_2 = E_4 - E_3$, and identical maturities.

The comments that have been made with regard to the sale of the butterfly also apply to the sale of the condor.

The maximum profit, which equals the initial cash flow, is attained at expiration below E_1 and above E_4. The death points are at E_1 plus the initial cash flow and at E_4 minus the initial cash flow. The profile for the sale of a condor is shown in Figure 5–29.

MIXED STRATEGIES

The richness of the option concept is proven by the grand variety of the possible strategies. Up to this point, multiple strike prices and a variety of premium values have been considered with a view to taking advantage of changes in the direction of the spot price, changes in the volatility, and the simple passage of time.

It is impossible to cover all of the possible mixed strategies, but the two used most commonly by options traders will be presented, namely vertical spreads using ratios of options and calendar spreads. A mixed strategy that combines two strike prices, termed a *diagonal spread,* will also be presented.

Vertical Spreads Using a Ratio of Options

In this case, options with the same expiration and different strike prices are sold and bought simultaneously, but the ratios between the number of options bought and sold are different from those considered so far. The most common current ratio between the options is 2 to 1.

Vertical Spread Using a Ratio of Calls: Anticipation of Stability in the Spot Price Allowing for a Rally in the Currency as Defined by the Two Strike Prices Used

A ratio spread in which one call is bought and two are sold consists of buying a call at strike price E_1 while simultaneously selling two calls at a higher strike price. The call purchased at E_1 is generally at-the-money, while the two calls sold at E_2 are generally out-of-the-money.

The initial cash flow that the treasurer's operation obtains from the positive credit of the two calls sold is usually greater than the cost of the call purchased, producing a positive amount.

Risk and Profit Expectations.   The greatest risk of the strategy is a strong rally that exceeds the upper death point. Due to the risk of an unwanted exercise, such a rally would force the repurchase of the two calls sold.

With the spot trading at the level of the call option purchased at E_1, a moderate rally that would increase the spot in the vicinity of the upper strike price to E_2 is anticipated. If more were anticipated, a call more in-the-money could be chosen. The maximum profit of the strategy is realized at the strike price at which the two calls are sold. Ideally, the two options sold expire unexercised and the expiration is between E_1 and E_2. If the options expire with the spot below E_1, the profit is the initial cash flow.

Example.   On October 2, the spot DM/$ was 64.47 cents. One DM/$ December 64.50 call was bought for 1.23; two DM/$ December 65.50 calls were sold for 0.82 each, or 1.64.

$$\text{Initial credit} = 1.64 - 1.23 = 0.41 \text{ cents}$$
$$\text{Maximum gain} = \text{Difference between the two strike prices}$$
$$+ \text{ Initial cash credit} = 1 + 0.41 = 1.41 \text{ cents}$$

Death points at exercise:

1. In the case of an initial cash debit, the death point is equal to the lower strike price less the initial debit.
2. In the case of a strong rally in the currency spot, the death point is equal to

$$E_2 + \text{Difference between } E_2 \text{ and } E_1 + \text{Initial cash credit}$$
$$= 65.50 + 1 + 0.41 = 66.91 \text{ cents}$$

The time value of the options sold at E_2 decreases to the benefit of the spreader. The profit obtained in this way is decreased by the cost of the option purchased at E_1. If the spot occurs at a value below E_1, the profit diminishes with the loss in the time value. The best situation is a position between E_1 and E_2.

If the spot is higher than E_2 as the position approaches expiration, the profitability of the position is determined by the profits obtained from the repurchase of the calls sold less the cost of the call originally purchased. The profile for a ratio spread using calls is shown in Figure 5–30.

FIGURE 5–30
Ratio Spread Using Calls

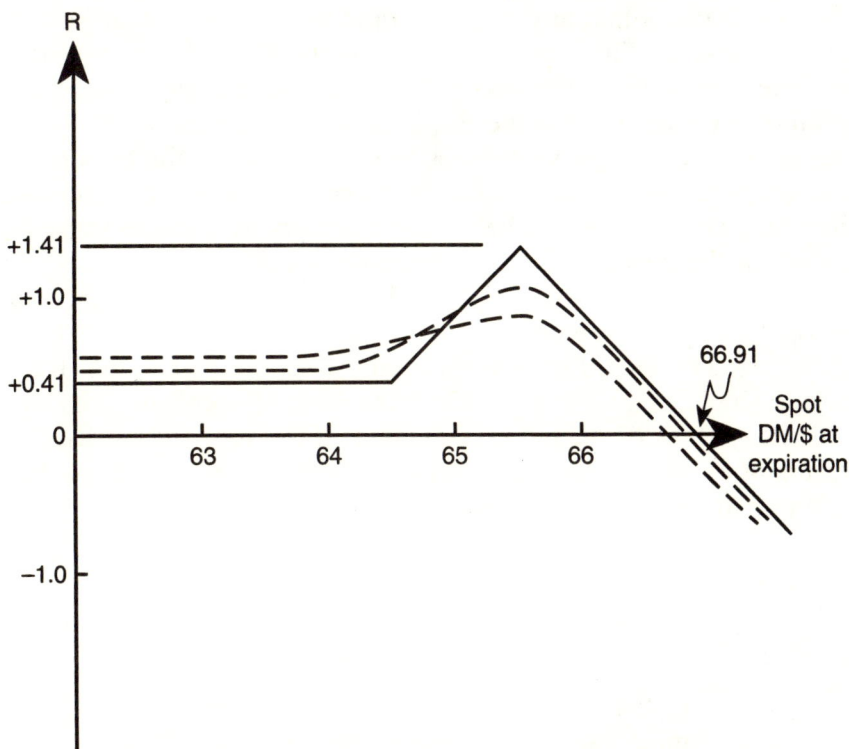

Vertical Spread Using a Ratio of Puts: Anticipation of Stability in the Spot Price or of a Decline in the Spot Price Limited to the Extent of the Lower Strike Price

A ratio spread in which one put is bought and two are sold consists of selling two puts at a strike price of E_1 and buying one put at E_2, a higher strike price. The put purchased at the higher strike price is usually at-the-money, while the two puts sold are out-of-the-money.

The initial cash flow is usually done with the credit produced by selling the two puts, which usually exceeds the debit produced by buying the one put. A position in which the cash flow is done with a debit would not be following the same design rules.

Risk and Profit Expectations. The risk of the strategy is that a sizable decline and an exercise of the puts sold will occur.

The spread is originally established at E_2, which is selected in the expectations that any decline would be to an area near E_1 and that a worse decline would cause the repurchase of the puts sold and the sale of the purchased put. In the case of a more moderate decline in the area of E_2, the E_2 put is more in-the-money than the puts sold at E_1. If the spot drops to the area of E_1, the options at E_2, which are not in-the-money, run the risk of being exercised. Since the risk is unlimited below the death point, it makes sense to close out the position if exercise becomes likely.

The maximum profit occurs at E_1 at expiration. The puts sold at E_1 expire without value, and the value of the put bought at E_2 is determined by the difference between the spot price and the strike price, which is equal to $E_2 - E_1$. The resultant is enhanced by the initial cash flow or the initial cash debit. If the spot ends at E_2, the resultant is limited to the initial cash flow, since the out-of-the-money put expires without value.

Example. On October 2, the spot DM/$ was 64.47 cents. Two DM/$ December 63.50 puts were sold at 0.86 cents = 1.72 cents; one DM/$ December 64.50 put was bought at 1.30 cents.

$$\text{Initial credit} = 1.72 - 1.30 = 0.42 \text{ cents}$$
$$\text{Maximum gain} = \text{Difference between strike prices}$$
$$+ \text{ Initial credit} = 1 + 0.42 = 1.42 \text{ cents}$$

Death points at expiration:

- For a rally, the death point occurs only with an initial debit.

    Death point = Strike price E_2 − the Initial debit

- For a decline, Death point = Strike price E_1 − Difference $(E_2 − E_1)$ − Initial cash flow = 63.50 − 1 − 0.42 = 62.08 cents

Evolution of Resultant over Time.   With the spot price at strike price E_2, the resultant diminishes with the passage of time. With the spot between E_1 and E_2, the resultant improves with the passage of time. With the spot less than E_1, the death point declines with the passage of time and is finally determined by the number of options sold versus the number purchased.

The profile of the ratio spread using puts is shown in Figure 5–31.

Backspread Using a Ratio of Calls: Anticipation of an Increase in Volatility and a Tendency toward a Decline in the Spot Price

The spread is constructed with a ratio of one call sold and two calls purchased. It consists of selling a call at E_1 and purchasing two calls at E_2, a higher strike price. The calls purchased are generally out-of-the-money or at-the-money, while the call sold is generally in-the-money.

The initial cash flow to the treasury is usually a credit as long as the premiums of the two calls purchased are less than the premium of the one call sold. If a debit is produced, then the logic rules for the spread are not being closely followed.

Risk and Profit Expectations.   The risk is limited by the curve of the resultant that evolves around the debit formed about the maximum loss defined at E_2, the upper strike price. The upper strike price, E_2, is where the maximum loss occurs (see Figure 5–32).

The currency spot at the origination of the spread is less than, or at best equal to, E_2. A large rally is anticipated. If it occurs, the two calls purchased at-the-money or out-of-the-money will appreciate considerably and their sale will produce a large profit. The logic of the spread's construction is to have the increase in the intrinsic

FIGURE 5–31
Ratio Spread Using Puts

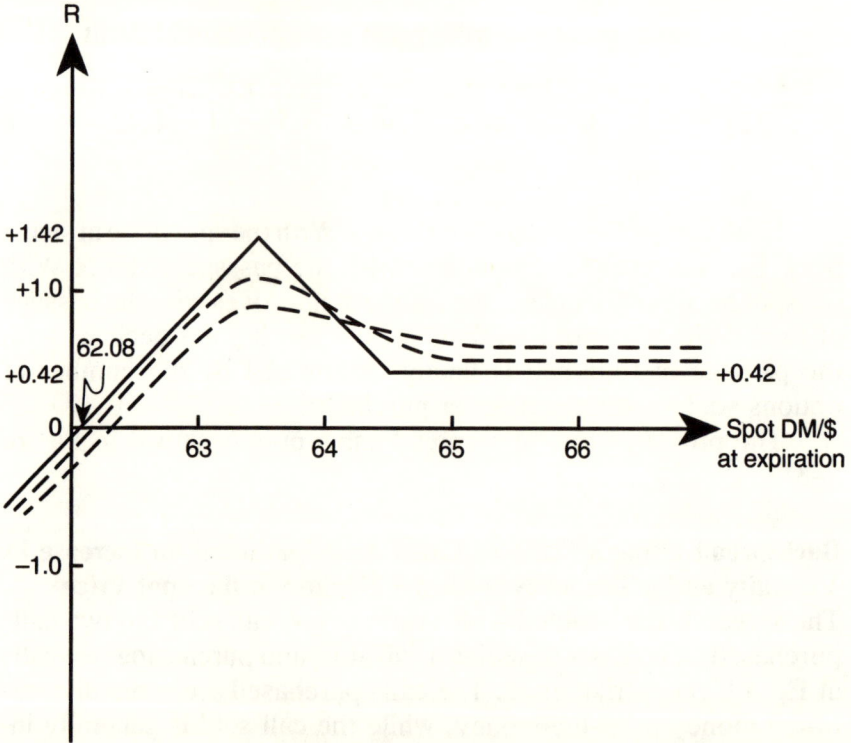

value of the two calls purchased exceed the loss in the one call sold.
If the rally is only to E_2, the purchased calls expire worthless, while
the call sold is exercised at a two-point setback. That is the case of
the maximum loss.

If the spot is less than or equal to E_1, the calls are out-of-the-
money and the only profit earned is the initial cash flow.

Example. Two DM/$ December 66.00 calls were bought at
0.66 each $= -1.32$ cents; one DM/$ December 64.00 call was sold
at $1.50 = +1.50$ cents.

Initial cash flow $= 1.50 - 1.32 = 0.18$ cents

FIGURE 5–32
Inverse Ratio Call Spread (Backspread)

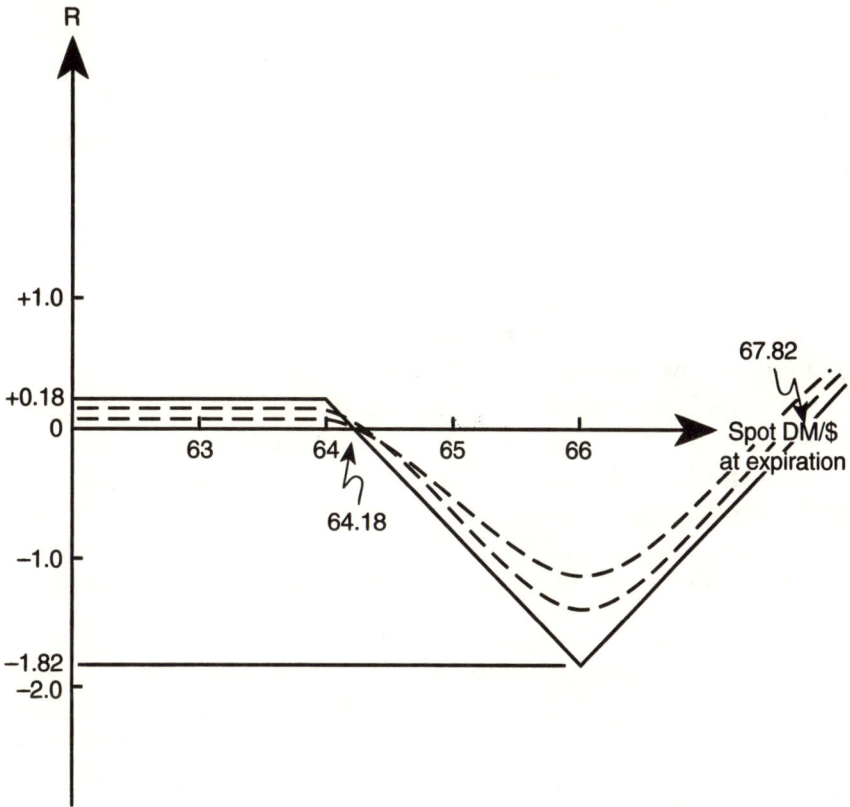

Maximum loss = Difference between the two strike prices + Initial cash flow = 64 − 66 + 0.18 = −2 + 0.18 = −1.82 cents

Death points at expiration:

- With a decline:

Lower strike price + Initial cash flow = 64 + 0.18 = 64.18

- With a rally:

Upper strike price + Difference between the two strike prices − Initial cash flow = 66 + (66 − 64) − 0.18
= 68 − 0.18 = 67.82 cents

Evolution of Resultant over Time.   If the spot ends at or below the lower strike price, with no time value, the profit is simply the initial cash flow.

Above 66 to the upper death point at 67.82, the positive value depends on the time value in existence at the moment. If a rally is strong enough to rise above the upper death point, an open-ended profit can result. The profile of a "backspread" is shown in Figure 5–32.

Inverse Ratio Spread Using Puts (Backspread): Anticipation of a Strong Rally for the Spot Currency

This spread is constructed by selling one put at a higher strike price and buying two puts at a lower strike price.

The puts purchased at E_1 are generally out-of-the-money or at-the-money and the put sold at E_2 is generally in-the-money.

The initial cash flow to the treasury is a credit, which is accomplished by seeing that the cost of the two puts purchased is less than the premium raised from the one put sold. A debit is evidence that the logic of the backspread is not being closely followed.

Risk and Profit Expectations.   The risk is limited by the worst case for the profit curve, which is to have the spot remain at E_1, the lower strike price. At the origination of the spread, the spot is above or equal to E_1 and a serious decline is anticipated. It is expected that the puts bought at E_1 will be repurchased and that a loss will be suffered on the put sold at E_2, which would then be in-the-money. The objective is to have the intrinsic value of the two puts purchased at E_1 exceed the intrinsic value of the put sold at E_2.

If the spot simply stays at E_1, the put sold at E_2 would be exercised at expiration and the puts purchased at E_1 would expire worthless. This is the case for the maximum loss.

If the spot is more than or equal to E_2, the two puts purchased would be worthless and only the initial cash flow would be earned.

Example.   Two DM/$ December 63.50 puts were bought at 0.86 cents each = −1.72; one DM/$ December 65.50 put was sold at 1.89 cents = +1.89.

$$\text{Initial cash flow} = 1.89 - 1.72 = +0.17 \text{ cents}$$

Maximum loss = Difference between the two strike prices
$$+ \text{ Initial cash flow} = 63.50 - 65.50 + 0.17$$
$$= -2 + 0.17 = -1.83 \text{ cents}$$

Death points at exercise:

- With a decline:

Strike price E_1 − Difference between the two strike prices
$$+ \text{ Initial cash flow} = 63.50 - 2 + 0.17 = 61.50 + 0.17$$
$$= 61.67 \text{ cents}$$

FIGURE 5–33
Inverse Ratio Put Spread (Backspread)

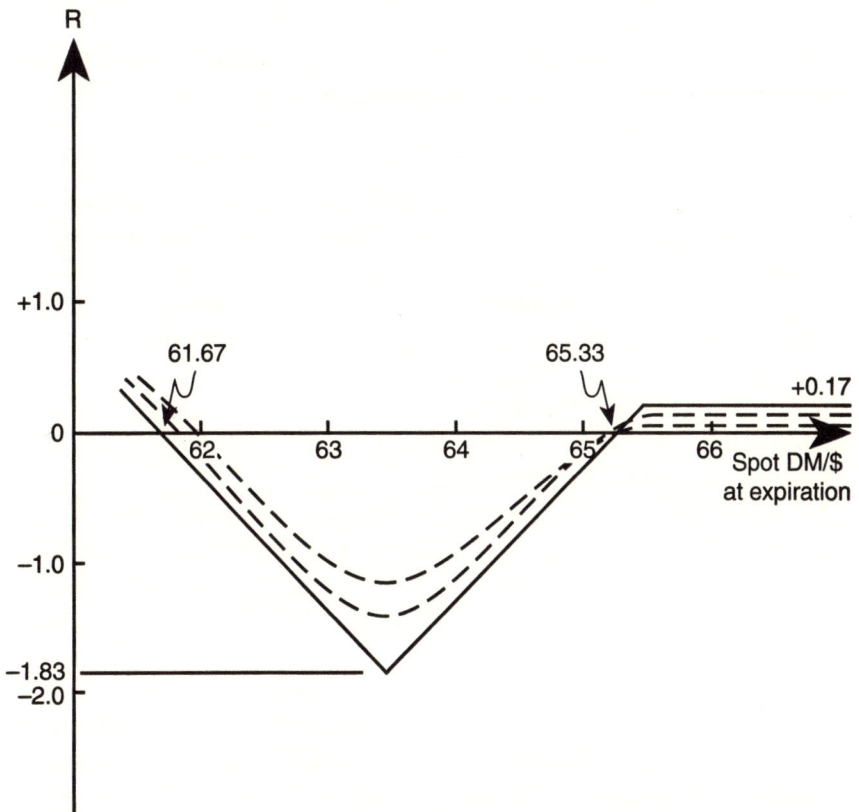

- With a rally:

  Strike price E_2 + Difference between the two strike prices − Initial cash flow = 65.50 − 0.17 = 65.33 cents

With a rally above 65.33, the profit gradually approaches the upper value of +0.17, the net positive cash flow.

Evolution of Resultant over Time. Above E_2 the resultant builds with time. Below E_2 the value drops as one passes the death point and heads toward the maximum loss point at E_1. As the spot continues below E_1, the loss decreases until the lower death point has been passed. With a strong enough decline, the gain obtained from the two puts bought easily surpasses the loss incurred by the one put sold and the profit is unlimited. The profile of the put version of the "backspread" is shown in Figure 5–33.

Calendar and Diagonal Spreads: Anticipation of Volatility and the Rhythm of the Loss in the Time Value

Calendar Spreads

A calendar spread is the simultaneous buying and selling of two puts or two calls with the same exercise price but different expiration dates.

In general, a calendar spread is created by buying an option with a long-term expiration while selling the same option with a near-term expiration. Most important, the time value of the near-term option declines more rapidly than the time value of the long-term option, and the profit is provided by this difference in the rates at which the time values decline.

The premium of the long-term option is not necessarily proportionately higher than the premium of the near-term option. The price of the long-term option can be somewhat less sensitive to changes in the underlying spot price than the price of the near-term option.

With a calendar spread, one assumes that the intrinsic values of the two options evolve identically. The way in which an American-style option responds to the underlying spot depends on whether it is tied to a currency future or to a currency forward contract. The relationship between a forward contract and a long-term option can be different from the relationship between a forward contract and a short-term option, and that difference, whether positive or negative, will be reflected in the marketplace.

The risk of the calendar spread can be affected by interest rate changes whose impact on the intrinsic values of the options is independent of the forces that generally govern those values.

Since, given identical strike prices, more is realized by buying the long-term option than by selling the short-term option, the initial cash flow to the treasury is ordinarily negative.

Risk and Profit Expectations.   Risk is established immediately in the sense that the calendar strategy depends highly on good executions of buying and selling in the marketplace. Usually, the best calendar spreads are produced by experienced traders in the option pit who can take immediate advantage of good momentary situations. Interest rate changes can have both negative and positive effects on risk.

The most realistic approach to the strategy is to seize opportunities as they appear randomly in the trading pit. An approach in which theoretical models are used, constant interest rates are assumed, and trades are performed at a distance from the trading floor is not recommended. To quote Albert Einstein, "It takes all of man's knowledge to create a theory, yet it does not work; the practical works, but no one can explain why."

The maximum profit occurs at expiration if the spot is trading at the exercise price. Unfortunately, the near-term option is subject to exercise, while the long-term option is not. Realizing a profit in the calendar spread thus requires a good execution in unwinding the spread to close it out. This point also demonstrates the desirability of having an experienced trader perform the spread in the pit.

The following example does not give a complete representation of the results of the calendar spread, since the options chosen expire after the time period analyzed. However, it does illustrate the main points of the strategy.

Example.   In December, a DM/$ June 34 call was bought at 0.89 cents; also in December, a DM/$ March 34 call, with expiration on March 15, was sold at 0.40 cents.

Initial cash flow $= -0.89 + 0.40 = -0.49$

The maximum gain occurs on March 15 if the spot DM/$ $= 34$ at that time. This resultant can be written as $-0.89 + 0.40 +$ Time value for call purchased.

Death points:

• With a decline (Spot < 34)

The resultant for the March call is equal to its premium when it is sold, or $+0.40$.

The resultant for the June call is equal to 0.89 cents, its time value less the cost of buying it.

The death point of the sum of the two options is zero:

$R = 0 = 0.40 +$ Time value $- 0.89$, therefore $R = 0$
$=$ Time value $- 0.49$, leading to time value
$= 0.49$ at death point

According to the option valuation model, the spot price should be 33.61 cents.

• With a rally (Spot > 34):

The resultant for the June call equals the value of the call on March 15 less the cost of the call, as follows:

$$S - 34 + \text{Time value} - 0.89 \text{ cents}$$

For the total position, $R = 0$:

$$-S + 34 + 0.40 + S - 34 + \text{Time value} - 0.89 \text{ cents} = 0$$

or

Time value $= 0.89 - 0.40 = 0.49 = -$Initial cash flow

The option price model for the June option with the spot at 34 is 34.41. The difference between 34.41 for the June option and the 33.61 fair value for the March option is 0.80 cents. If this estimate is accurate, the spread could have been closed immediately, giving a profit of

$0.80 - 0.49$ (initial cash flow) $= 0.31$ cents profit prior to transaction costs

Several approaches to the calendar spread seem to be very logical but prove impractical if attempts are made to apply them. One such approach is the design of calendar spreads in which the time between the near-term and the far-term options is increased. This approach does not seem to improve results, and it may also force the trader to seek executions in less liquid markets. Another approach is to select out-of-the-money calls that anticipate a large rally, rather than at-the-money calls. The odds of overcoming the initial debit are low if this is done, and in addition the greater time values of at-the-money options, which are the source of spread profits, are forgone.

For general conditions, the resultant of the near-term option at expiration is as follows:

R = Initial cash flow + Time value residual of the purchased call

The effects of the currency spot price on the near-term option can be summarized as follows:

- If the currency spot price is below the strike price:

Resultant for the call sold = Option premium
Resultant for the call bought = Residual time value
          − Option premium
Resultant for the position = Residual time value
          + Initial cash flow

- If the currency spot price is above the strike price:

Resultant for the call sold = 34 − S + Option premium
Resultant for the call bought = S − 34 + Residual time value
          − Option premium
Resultant for the position = Residual time value
          + Initial cash flow

If the spot price remains the same, the death points are elongated due to the higher premiums that occur at-the-money. In effect, as with any option, whether out-of-the-money or in-the-money, the expiration of an option at the strike price means that the premium is headed toward zero. As a result, the maximum loss of the position is limited to the initial cash debit.

The use of a calendar spread is based on the anticipation that the volatility, and therefore the risk and the profits, will be limited.

FIGURE 5–34
Calendar Spread for Calls

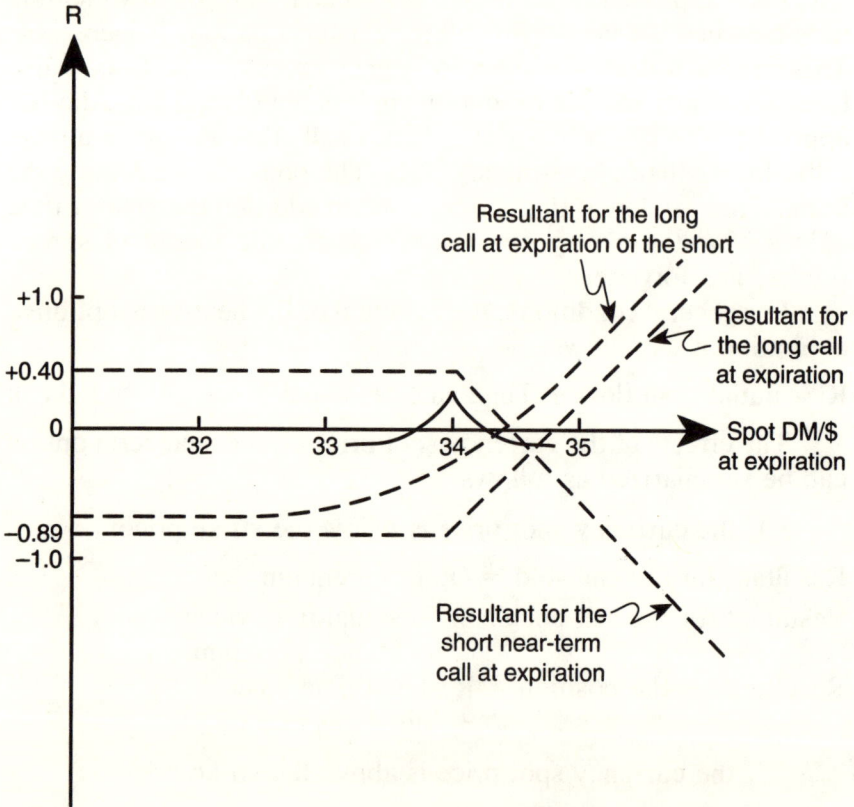

A variation of the calendar spread that should be at least mentioned is the inverse of buying the near-term option and selling the far-term option. Here a profit cannot be derived from the natural erosion of the option time values. Thus, the inverse calendar spread anticipates, not the stability of the currency spot, but a change in the currency spot to levels beyond the death points computed for the standard calendar spread. The profile for a calendar spread is shown in Figure 5–34.

Diagonal Spreads
Like vertical spreads using ratios of options and calendar spreads, diagonal spreads are a mixed strategy. In this strategy, options of the

same type, but with different strike prices and different expiration dates, are bought and sold.

As with calendar spreads, the variations in the possible applications of diagonal spreads are nearly infinite in number and the spreads are best executed by the professionals on the exchange floor. Based on their fair valuation models, these professionals can continuously monitor and take advantage of momentary variations from fair value. Capitalizing on such variations is the key to producing the liquidity that has enabled the marketplace to perform all of the functions that have given options their helpful status in the securities markets.

CONCLUSION: THE PRACTICAL ASPECTS OF DESIGNING OPTIONS POSITIONS

Merely explaining the principal strategies for designing options positions does not constitute a practical guide to options trading. In addition, a practical guide must cover three important considerations.

First, and most important, the transaction costs must be considered in designing positions and appraising the risks and the resultant. In Chicago, the transaction cost of a spread is one or two centimes per cent. In Philadelphia, that cost is limited to four cents. In the over-the-counter market, the transaction cost of a spread ranges from 10 percent of the premiums to more than 40 percent. The commissions are sometimes negotiable, especially for larger orders and for customers who trade large amounts of capital. Major traders always negotiate the best deal they can get before establishing relationships with a trading organization. If transaction costs are neglected, profits from options positions can become severely limited.

Second, it is important to know the specifics of the trading rules and the available types of orders of the various option exchanges. In dealing with any exchange, the key to preserving capital and to limiting the risk of strategies is to work with people who have practical experience and can provide good execution of orders.

Third, it is essential that the loss and gain potentials associated with strategy be evaluated beforehand. In designing a position, it is

FIGURE 5–35

Security Position	Premium Curve	Vectors
Buying a call		$\begin{pmatrix} 1 \\ 0 \end{pmatrix}$
Selling a call		$\begin{pmatrix} -1 \\ 0 \end{pmatrix}$
Buying a put		$\begin{pmatrix} 0 \\ -1 \end{pmatrix}$
Selling a put		$\begin{pmatrix} 0 \\ 1 \end{pmatrix}$
Buying a currency		$\begin{pmatrix} 1 \\ 1 \end{pmatrix}$
Selling a currency		$\begin{pmatrix} -1 \\ -1 \end{pmatrix}$

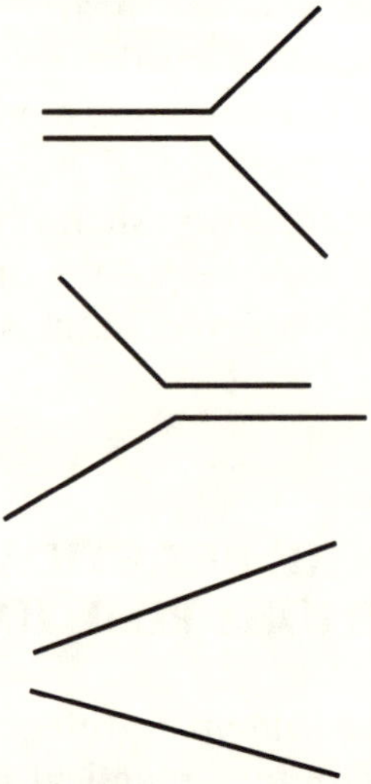

advisable to analyze all of the logical questions involved in its success. This task includes the computation of the fair price of the option to make certain that the best possible position is being established. Always looking and asking is the essence of successful options trading. As in other spheres, the greatest opportunities in the marketplace are happy accidents. If one stops looking, those opportunities are missed. It is as simple as that.

In order to offer a rapid way of seeing the logic that underlies the performance of options, ignoring their value for the moment, we code a profit $+1$, a loss -1, and no return 0 in the following exercise. The exercise is structured to show the outcome if the currency spot is above the strike price (the upper number) or below the strike price (the lower number).

Some of the major option postures are shown in Figure 5–35.

The vector approach of the exercise makes it easy to provide an overview of options and option-currency combinations. For example:

$$\text{Buying a call and selling a currency} = \begin{pmatrix} 1 \\ 0 \end{pmatrix} + \begin{pmatrix} -1 \\ -1 \end{pmatrix} = \begin{pmatrix} 0 \\ -1 \end{pmatrix}$$
$$= \text{Buying a put}$$

$$\text{Buying a straddle} = \begin{pmatrix} 1 \\ 0 \end{pmatrix} + \begin{pmatrix} 0 \\ -1 \end{pmatrix} = \begin{pmatrix} 1 \\ -1 \end{pmatrix}$$
$$= \text{Buying a call and a put}$$

$$\text{Selling a straddle} = \begin{pmatrix} -1 \\ 0 \end{pmatrix} + \begin{pmatrix} 0 \\ 1 \end{pmatrix} = \begin{pmatrix} -1 \\ 1 \end{pmatrix} = \text{Selling a call and a put}$$

$$\text{Selling two calls and buying a currency} = 2\begin{pmatrix} -1 \\ 0 \end{pmatrix} + \begin{pmatrix} 1 \\ 1 \end{pmatrix} = \begin{pmatrix} -1 \\ 1 \end{pmatrix}$$
$$= \text{Selling a straddle}$$

$$\text{Buying a straddle and buying a currency} = \begin{pmatrix} 1 \\ -1 \end{pmatrix} + \begin{pmatrix} 1 \\ 1 \end{pmatrix} = \begin{pmatrix} 2 \\ 0 \end{pmatrix}$$
$$= 2\begin{pmatrix} 1 \\ 0 \end{pmatrix} = \text{Buying two calls}$$

The vector approach has offered a rapid way to design strategies that is limited only by the constraint of having the same expiration or the same strike price.

Vector notations other than those provided here can be developed to portray more complex positions. A logic specialist working for an investment operation could certainly produce far more complex and complete designs.

CHAPTER 6

COVERING CURRENCY RISK USING OPTIONS

Foreign currency options were originally introduced in France to cover the conditional risk of French manufacturers and were later integrated into French business operations to the point where they were advertised as a feature in sales catalogs. Since their introduction, the application of currency options has now become so extensive that they are now used to provide French manufacturers protection against total risk. Also, in France and elsewhere, importers, exporters, and lenders and borrowers of currencies have begun to use them as a new means of risk protection.

The increasing use of currency options stems mainly from the realization that they permit far greater flexibility in managing the risk of change. The treasurer can construct profiles of the risk resultant to his choice of exercise prices. The profiles depend on the cost of the option premiums. By constructing such profiles, the treasurer can weigh between the amount of risk he is willing to take and the amount of money he is willing to spend on risk protection.

The examples presented in this chapter are meant to give an overview of the available risk protection strategies.

EXAMPLES OF PROTECTION FROM CERTAIN RISK

Protection for Exporting

The General Principle of Protection
Let's take the case of an American exporter who, on June 6, 199X, receives a payment in pounds sterling that must be repaid on October 25, 199X.

On June 6, he obtains the following information: currency spot £/$ = 1.6882; forward price £/$ October 25 = 1.6465.

The exporter can choose among three strategies:

1. *Maintain his long position in pounds sterling.* This strategy, which provides no protection against risk, allows the exporter to participate completely in any appreciation in the pound between June 6 and October 25. The exporter's business, which he is usually attempting to protect from unexpected setbacks, must absorb any drop in the value of the pound.

2. *Use the forward market.* In this market, the exporter can achieve the 141 days of protection he needs by selling a forward contract deliverable on October 25 at a cost of 1.6465. In choosing this strategy, the exporter protects his firm against a drop in the pound. His choice may reflect his own expectation that the pound is likely to lose ground relative to the dollar.

3. *Buy a December, 199X, pound sterling put at the Philadelphia Currency Option Market.* The organized options markets limit the number of expiration dates and the December expiration date comes closest to meeting his needs. Through the OTC market, the international banks that deal in options can offer clients negotiated options that meet the client's specific delivery needs. Such a bank could create a pound sterling put that expires on October 25. However, our example will work with the conditions of the organized markets. Our exporter buys a December 170 put that an exchange broker quotes at 8.38 asked. Taking the strike price of 170 and subtracting the cost of the premium yields $1.7000 - 0.838 = 1.6162 £/\$$, which is lower than the forward price of 1.6465. If the dollar depreciates and the pound gains, so that the exporter no longer needs the protection offered by the option, he can always sell the option.

By October 25, 199X, the pound had appreciated relative to the dollar. On that date British interest rates were more than 4 percentage points higher than American interest rates. This made the pound a more attractive vehicle for storing cash than the dollar. The facts at the option exchange on October 25 were as follows:

Price for spot £/\$: 1.9537.

The pound December 170 put: 0.05.

Studying the results of the three strategies shows the following:

Maintaining the Currency Position.   The exporter received a spot £/\$ quote of 1.9537. He obtained a profit because of the drop in the dollar during the holding period, but he could have incurred a loss. Thus, maintaining the currency position cannot be defended as a sound commercial approach.

Using the Forward Market.   Our exporter's forward contract obligated him to deliver the pound at a price of 1.6465. Thus, his use of the forward contract caused him to incur a setback relative to the spot rate of 1.9537 − 1.6465 = 0.3072 $/£.

Buying the Put Option.   At a 10 percent prime rate, the total cost of our exporter's put is 8.38 * (1 + 0.0386) = 8.70. Thus, the effective delivery price on October 25 would be 1.7000 − 0.0870 = 1.6130 £/$. Since the pound appreciated relative to the dollar well beyond the 170 level, the exporter was able to sell the pound in the currency option market at a spot price of 1.9537. The cost of the risk insurance can be computed as follows:

Cost of the spot £/$	1.9537
− Premium of the option purchased	−0.0838
+ Premium of the option when sold	+0.0005
Effective price using insurance	1.8704

The exporter received 1.8704 for the pound he sold on October 25, which was superior to the forward alternative of 1.8704 − 1.6465 = 0.2239 £/$. Purchasing a put option enabled him to realize the appreciation of the pound relative to the dollar. At the same time it gave him the assurance that if the pound dropped in price relative to the dollar, the lowest price he would receive for it would be 1.6162 £/$. The put option allowed him to realize a nice profit in his pounds position while affording him risk protection.

When the exporter was considering the purchase of the put, he could have constructed a curve to determine the guarantee that the put offered and the price that would be obtainable if the option position were liquidated. He could have done this by determining the logical relationships that existed given the available put options. Figures 6–1 and 6–2 show separately the logical relationships of the forward and the put.

Accepting the hypothesis that the currency option markets are theoretically efficient, the exporter was able to benefit from two

FIGURE 6–1
Effective Spot without Risk Control

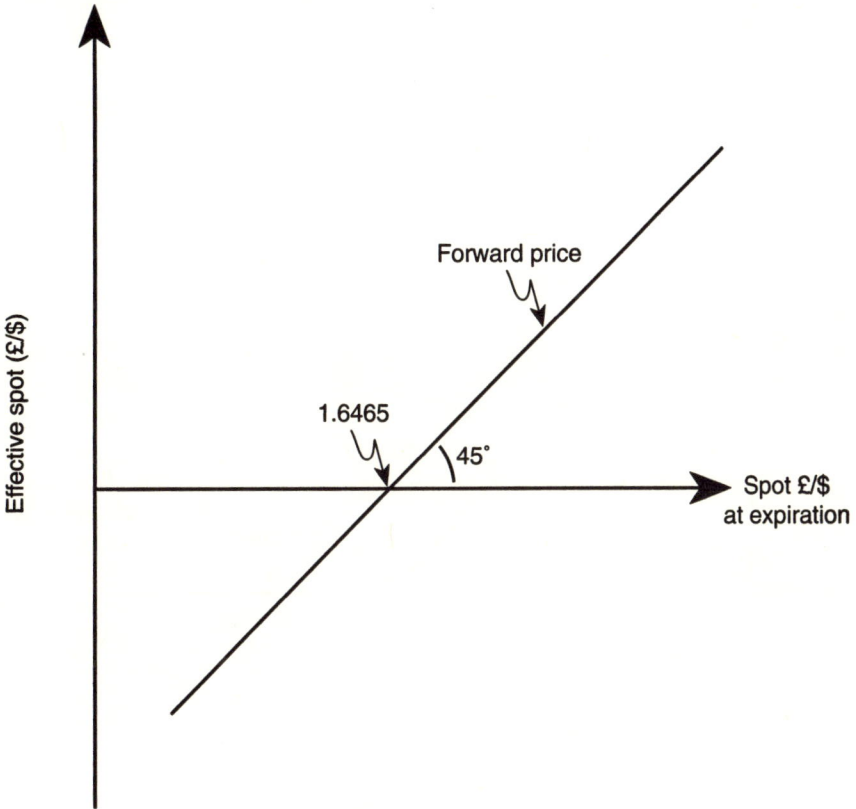

advantages that the options market offered over the forward market, namely an opportunity to profit from a rally in the currency market and protection against a drop in the currency. Given such a drop, the exporter simply delivers his currency position at the option's exercise price.

If the currency is delivered at the option's expiration, the resultant for the put purchased is as follows:

R = Strike price of put − Currency spot price − Option premium

or

$$R = E - S - P$$

FIGURE 6–2
Loss and Gain Potential with a Long Put Position

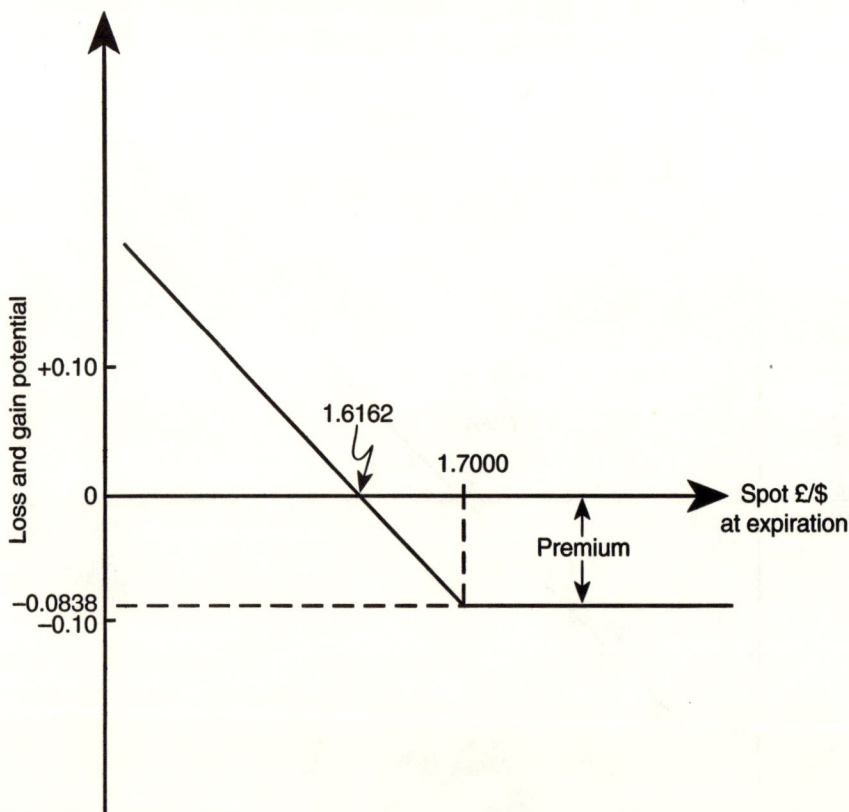

If the exporter does not exercise the option (because the currency spot is greater than the exercise price), he sells it at whatever price it is trading for in the marketplace or, at worst, he absorbs the entire amount he paid for it as a cost of purchasing sensible protection.

In this example, if the spot sterling at exercise is less than 1.7000, at which point the vector equation for option logic would be -1, the resultant equation crosses the x-axis where $R = 0$, which can be expressed as $S = E - P$ or as $1.7000 - 0.0838 = 1.6162$ £/$.

That point is the death point of the option position. The profile for protecting the currency position in this manner is shown in Figure 6–3.

FIGURE 6–3
Profile of Currency Value with Protection

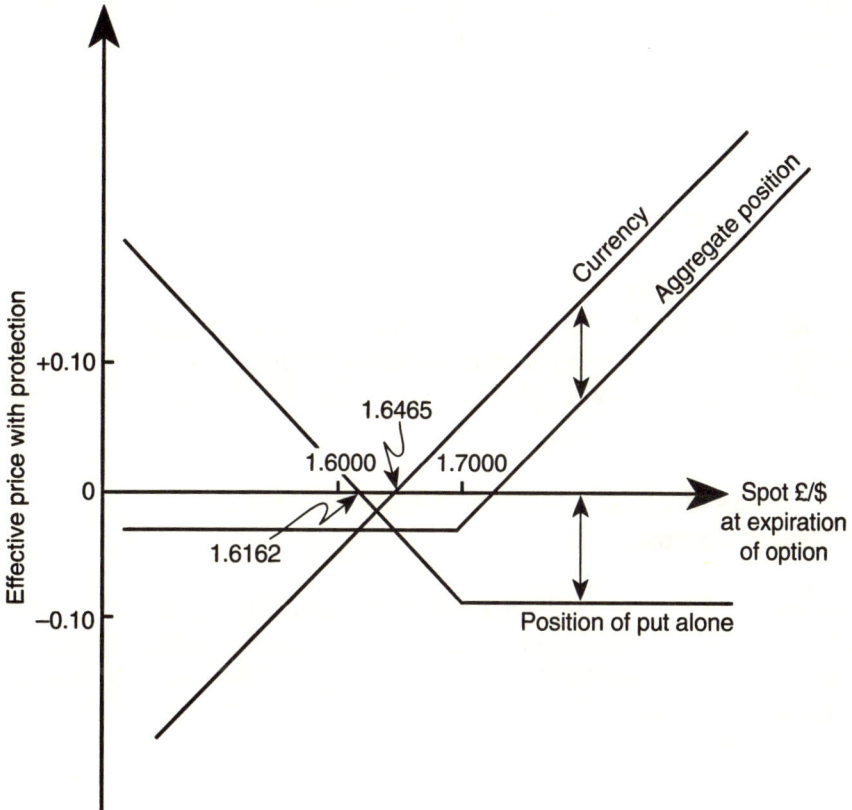

The preceding example deals with a situation that occurs regularly in the import/export business. Had a different situation been selected, the example could have also shown the protection against losses that options afford. The important concept to understand is that before entering into an important shipping transaction a profile showing the combined effects of owning a currency and using an option for insurance purposes can easily be drawn to study the costs involved and the available protection. The following examples all look at the option expiration to see how the protection would resolve itself.

• The currency spot at expiration of the option, 1.9537, is higher than the exercise price (the strike price), 1.7000. The value of the put is zero (the option ended out-of-the-money). The value for the spot currency that takes into account the cost of the option protection is $1.9537 - 0.0838 = 1.8699$ £/$, which is greater than the forward alternative of 1.6465. If the spot currency at expiration had been at 1.7838, then only the cost of the option protection would have been covered.

• The currency spot at expiration, 1.7000, equals the option exercise price. Allowing for the cost of the option protection, 0.0838, that results in a level of 1.6162, which is less than 1.6465, the forward alternative.

• The currency spot at expiration is less than the strike price of 1.7000. If the spot is below 1.6162 (the strike price minus the option cost), it pays for the exporter to exercise the put, since the price he would receive is higher than the price obtainable in the forward market.

Protecting the Management of Capital for a Foreign Company

A German firm decided on June 6, 199X, to increase the capital of an American affiliate by $2 million on an autumn date that had not yet been fixed. On June 6, the spot $/DM was trading at 1.6906. Translating that into $2 million equals $2 \times 1.6906 = 3.38$ million DM.

The treasurer did not want to risk the appreciation of the dollar into autumn, so he decided to cover his position by purchasing DM puts. He wanted to cover the entire $2 million, but he also wanted to allow for the fact that the DM could appreciate.

Since the treasurer anticipated a drop in the dollar, he chose out-of-the-money options to reduce the cost of the premiums. Because of the uncertainty regarding the precise date on which the funds would be transferred, he decided to work with December options.

He estimated that a final exercise price of 56 cents, or $1/0.56 = 1.79$ DM/$, would be appropriate. He determined the number of puts to purchase as follows:

$$\frac{2,000,000}{62,500/1.79} = 57 \text{ contracts}$$

The premium for the put was 0.55 cents per DM, so that the cost per contract, 0.55 × 625, was $343.75. Thus, the cost of the option protection was 343.75 × 57 = $19,593.75.

The cost of the interest for the period was 4.8 percent. The date set for the arrival of the funds was October 25.

The drop that the treasurer anticipated in the dollar actually occurred, and he exercised his put options at the strike price of .62 cents.

The gain realized from the treasurer's program was as follows:

2,000,000 × (1.69 − 1.61)	160,000 DM
Cost of the option protection: 19,593.75× 1.69	−33,113 DM
Gain from the option protection	126,887 DM

The German firm paid nearly $20,000 not only to obtain protection but also to enable the treasurer, in case his currency forecast was in error, to acquire strong rather than weak dollars in the currency markets on October 25 and then to exchange them for more rather than fewer DM. The treasurer's anticipation proved correct, and on October 25, the DM was actually trading at 1.52 DM/$. The total profit with no protection, the unbusiness-like way of operating, would have been (1.69 − 1.52) × 2,000,000 = 340,000 DM. With protection and the flexibility to operate sensibly, 37 percent of that amount was gained.

Protection for Importing

A certain U.S. firm imports goods from Switzerland. Unless it purchases Swiss francs and sells dollars, it faces a currency risk when the goods it imports are put up for sale in the United States.

Example.   On June 6, the firm decides to cover its currency risk of being short Swiss francs. It has to be able to cover $4 million in liabilities that are due on October 25. It obtains the following facts:

Swiss franc/$ spot = 69.71 ($/Swiss franc = 1.43)
Swiss franc/$ October 25 = 69.45 ($/Swiss franc = 1.44)

The treasurer of the firm buys December Swiss franc calls at the Philadelphia Currency Option Market. Anticipating a rally in the dollar, he selects a strike price of 72 cents, which is out-of-the-money. However, the actual outcome turns out to be a catastrophic drop in the dollar.

The quantity of Swiss francs covered by the option contract is 62,500, so that the number of contracts purchased by the treasurer is $4,000,000/62,500 = 64 contracts.

The total cost of the protection strategy, is the cost of the 64 contracts plus the premium cost of 1.11 cents for the December 72 calls = (64 × 62,500 × 1.11)/100 = $44,400.

Possible scenarios for October 25:

• The Swiss franc appreciates contra the dollar, contrary to the treasurer's expectations. The Swiss franc actually rallies to 78.09 on October 25, well above the 72 strike price. The treasurer exercises his call contract and delivers his Swiss francs, originally valued at $4 million, for $4,131,401 (69.71 to 72.00) less the protection cost of $44,400, or 63,692 Swiss francs, for a gain of 67,709 Swiss francs.

• The Swiss franc remains the same or drops contra the dollar. The treasurer sells the calls he purchased for protection and buys the Swiss francs he needs in the currency market. The cost of the purchase must be below 69.71 − 1.11 = 68.60 for him to cover the cost of the protection (assuming that the calls sold are virtually worthless on October 25).

Table 6–1 summarizes the various outcomes that can occur in the financial markets.

THE CHOICE OF THE EXERCISE PRICE: SELECTING APPROPRIATE RISK

The choice of the exercise price is at the heart of using options as a businesslike means of dealing with currency risk. The exercise price determines, in effect, the risk profile and reflects the degree of the treasurer's aversion to risk.

Should the change in a currency price over time be unfavorable, currency options limit the risk of their purchases through what is

TABLE 6–1
Case for an American Importer Factoring with Swiss Francs

Strategy \ Swiss Franc	Rally	Decline
No protection	Loss in Swiss franc rally, less to carry forward (more to ship)	Gain equal to loss in Swiss franc, less to ship (more to carry forward)
Protection with a forward	0	0
Protection with options	Loss equal to currency guarantee less the forward cost	Gain equal to loss in Swiss franc less the premium, less to ship (more to carry forward)

termed the *effective guarantee price*. This price is defined by the obligation that the exercise of an option assures. In the case of a call, it is equal to the exercise price plus the premiums paid; in the case of a put, it is equal to the exercise price minus the premiums paid.

The price of the effective guarantee approaches the behavior of a forward contract if an in-the-money exercise is selected; if a distant relationship with the underlying currency is desired, an out-of-the-money exercise is selected. The two extremes differ mainly in the time value of the options. The intermediate approach is an at-the-money option.

The choice of an effective guarantee that approaches the behavior of the forward implies a willingness to forgo any gain in the underlying currency. In this case, the option buyer believes it is difficult to appraise the direction of the currency or that any change in the currency will at best be rather feeble during the option-holding period. Inversely, the choice of out-of-the-money options implies a lack of interest in the guarantee of following the spot currency. The buyer of such options either regards currency change as acceptable or anticipates a catastrophic change and prefers an opportunity to realize an immediate profit in his currency position. The choice of the exercise price is essentially an arbitrage against risk.

The graph in Figure 6–4 shows how the three exercise prices serve as vehicles that offer a range of guarantee prices. In this

FIGURE 6–4
Protection (£/$Puts)

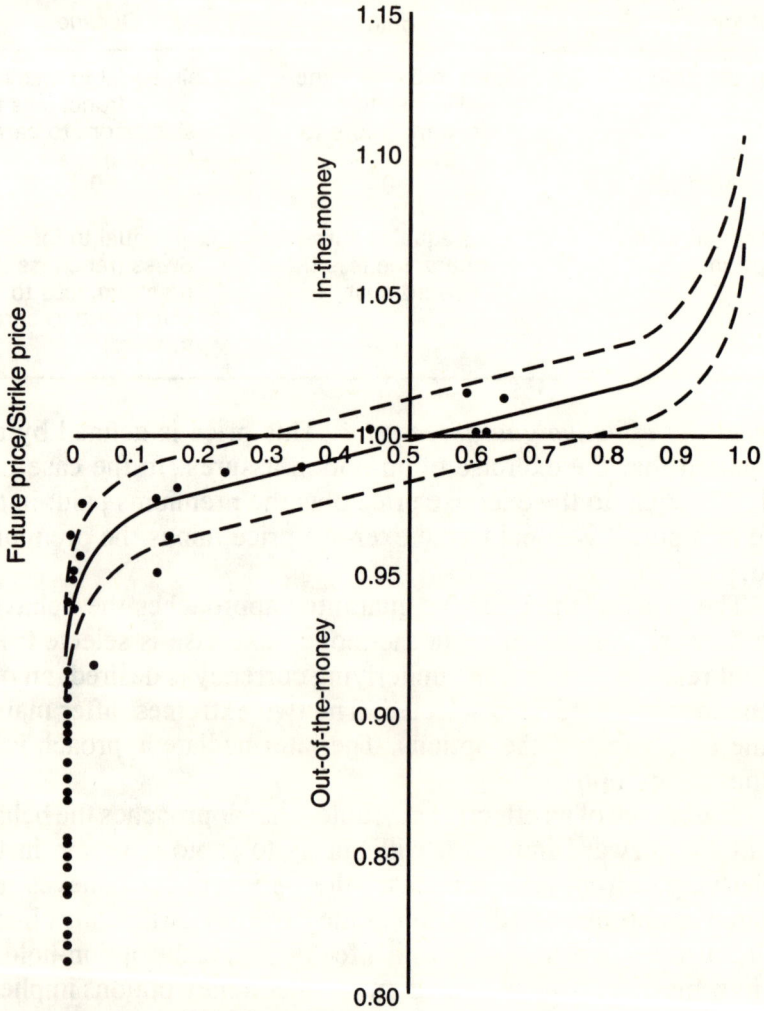

Since the diagram is expressed in terms of pounds, the curves shown are in inverse to the curves of the standard put diagram.

graph, put options are shown in their inverse form (the curves behave like call options since they deal with the pound price instead of the dollar price, using an option that offers £/$). The options are for December as quoted on October 25, 199X.

The profile of the effective price for the in-the-money option approaches the price curve for a forward. The probability of exercise for such an option approaches 1, while the logic conditions for the contract are such that the time value approaches 0.

In contrast, the profile of the effective price curve for the out-of-the-money option approaches the value of a simple currency. Very little of the curvature of an option that is severely out-of-the-money is related to its time value. Since the probability of exercise of such options approaches zero, the buyers of those options pay for time values that are close to zero.

Figure 6–4 demonstrates the flexibility of option choices which can range from an unprotected currency to a forward. The purchaser of options has at his disposal a near-infinite range of choices through which he can optimize his own arbitrage with the risk he chooses to take.

RESPONSES TO THE FALSE PROBLEM OF THE COST OF CONVERSION WITH OPTIONS

A False Problem

Efforts to introduce the use of options are impeded by both psychological and organizational obstacles. The introduction of any new product that is based on a high degree of mathematical and computer-oriented logic will be resisted by people who lack the education needed to easily understand the concepts underlying the product. The organizational obstacles stem in part from the somewhat complex way in which currency options are handled in the United States. Chicago Mercantile Exchange options, for example, expire into currency futures contracts, which are then deliverable into currencies. The more positive features of options were presented in the preceding section, in which it was shown that options offer the treasurer a near-infinite choice in the handling of his firm's exposure to currency risk.

An opinion commonly expressed by those who resist the use of options is that "currency options are too expensive as compared to forward contracts." Anyone who expresses this opinion lacks an understanding of the logic that underlies options. The most important point to be understood about options is that they represent obligations to perform a helpful service in the financial community. A look at the basic economics of forwards versus options should demonstrate that they are far from being identical and that options offer far greater flexibility than forwards.

The price of an option is a subject that must be analyzed in terms of the option's cost as an investment. At equilibrium, option premiums are an adjustable mathematical expression of the probabilities for a gain or for no gain. The logic that must be analyzed is the goals of a position, and it can be determined mathematically whether or not those goals can be achieved. Options are neither a long-term solution nor an instant solution, but—like forward positions and outright positions in a currency—an intermediate solution. The arbitrage aspect of forward positions, outright positions, and options is not so much a forecasting approach as an expression of the aversion to risk among decision makers:

• Using a forward contract gives the treasurer a 100 percent chance that he will benefit from the forward's expiration price. If there is a loss in the underlying currency, his loss is zero; if there is a gain in the underlying currency, his gain is zero.

• Having a currency on its own, the chances are 1 in 2 that the treasurer will experience either an increase or a decrease in the currency's value. The treasurer who does not use any form of protection is handling himself as if he simply wants to "maintain his position." However, his posture exposes his firm to all the risks of changes in the value of currencies.

• Having options gives the treasurer a choice among a variety of potential gains and possible losses. In-the-money options cost more than the other types of options, but they offer a greater potential for profiting from an important currency change.

For example, on June 6, 199X, when the spot DM was at 0.5915, an in-the-money 57 call for September was quoted at 3.15. Since an in-the-money call tracks the underlying currency with a delta that approaches 1, the call could at any time be sold for a profit close to the gain made in the currency and the currency position could be sold as well. The point of loss on the purchase of the in-the-money call was 0.6015 (0.5700 + 0.0315), which was not far from the spot price when the option was purchased.

On June 6, 199X, an out-of-the-money 61 call for September could have been purchased for 0.97 cents, but that option would have tracked the currency level at only 30 percent, so the point of loss would have been 0.6197, 282 ticks away from the 0.5915 spot.

The options market has a pricing mechanism that takes such risk/reward realities into account. If one wants to track the currency closely, the appropriate price must be paid. The out-of-the-money approach makes it possible to achieve a large gain at a minimal cost, but it also results in the greatest setbacks if one is wrong in having chosen to use it.

The premiums of the option alternatives are the costs of the desired levels of risk, as expressed in the option valuation models. In this sense, options are not "expensive." They are simply an appraisal of the risk at hand, an expression of the "fair value" of the conditions that exist in the marketplace.

The treasurer may have to justify his choice of a protection strategy using options to top management, but it is certainly a defendable choice.

Strategies to Minimize the Cost of Options

Treasurers who desire to purchase options to provide protection, but at reduced costs, employ two main strategies:

- Purchase out-of-the-money options.
- Reduce the cost of the option purchased by simultaneously selling the opposite type of option.

Such strategies, known as *low-premium strategies,* guarantee the exporter (importer) a minimum (maximum) cost by selling (buying) the currency without limiting the gain that might otherwise occur in the currency market.

Strategies to Buy Options Out-of-the-Money: Extending the Death Point

An American importer decided on June 6, 199X, to cover his short pound sterling position with an expected expiration (delivery of the sterling) on September 4. On June 6, the spot pound was 1.6882 and a forward expiring on September 4 was trading at 1.6790. Desiring to minimize the cost of his strategy, the importer purchased out-of-the-money calls with a strike price of 1.7000. He had to pay 2.02 cents for a September call expiring on September 15, the third Saturday prior to the third Wednesday of the month. He did not want to pay the 2.02 cents, but his protégé, who was concerned about the possibility of a "currency disaster," convinced him that buying the calls would enable him to profit from a rally in the pound as well as offer him a protection point with the options at 1.6588 and a strike price of 1.7000. The profile for using the protection of owning a call option is shown in Figure 6–5.

Figure 6–6 demonstrates the strategy of providing protection by buying in-the-money options. The differences between this strategy and the out-of-the-money strategy are as follows:

• With the in-the-money strategy, as opposed to the out-of-the-money alternative, the price of the effective guarantee is much closer to the price of the forward. While the price of protection is higher for the in-the-money strategy, the degree of protection provided by the strategy is much closer to the price of the spot currency when the position is originated.

• Since in-the-money options closely track the value of the underlying currency, as the value of the currency appreciates, the in-the-money strategy offers the possibility of selling the options to realize the benefit of the appreciation. If the treasurer is pessimistic regarding the pound, he can avoid paying the high premium of in-the-money options and select the out-of-the-money alternative.

The preceding example confirms our contention that the choice of the exercise price reflects one's point of view about currency behavior and about the extent to which options should reduce risk. In a sense, recourse to the at-the-money strategy is not a neutral approach but the expression of an aversion to risk that lies between the aversion to risk manifested by recourse to the extreme alternatives. A profile for using the protection on an in-the-money call is shown in Figure 6–6.

Strategies to Reduce the Premium Cost
A treasurer who desires to reduce the cost of protection with currency options puts in place a guarantee of a maximum price at which

FIGURE 6–5
Hypothesis—Buying an Out-of-the-Money Call (Exercise Price = 1.70)

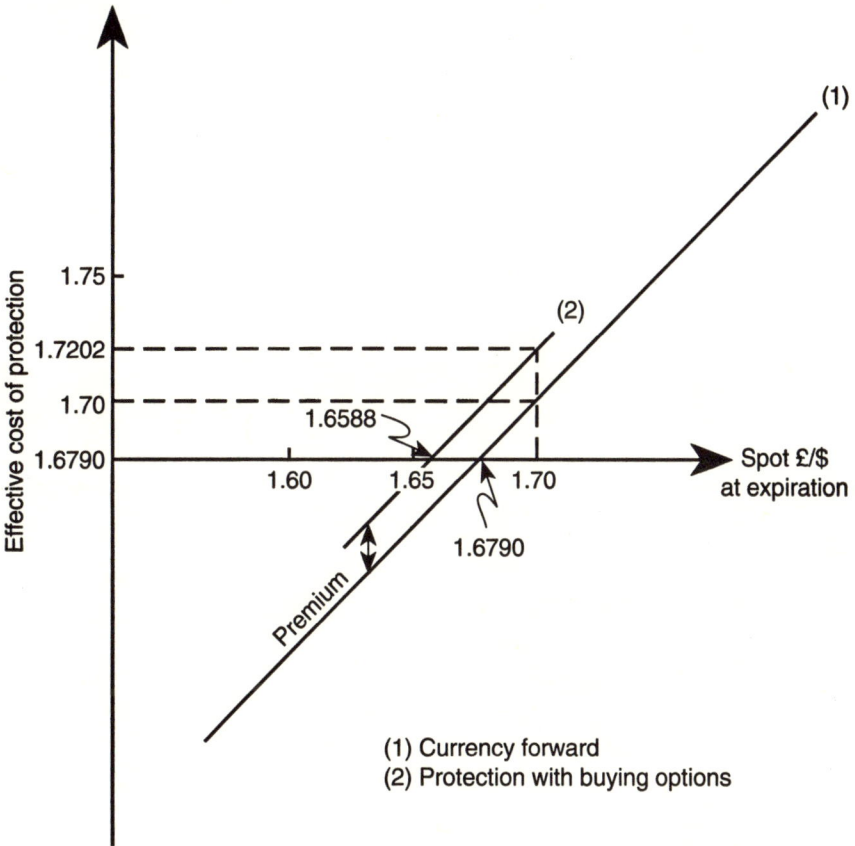

(1) Currency forward
(2) Protection with buying options

to buy options (or a minimum price at which to sell them) that limits to some degree the benefits that can be enjoyed from favorable changes in the marketplace currency price. The treasurer defines the marketplace rally or decline that would make him want to liquidate his option's positions. The profile of the effective price is similar to that of a spread, in which the treasurer constructs a level that defines his anticipation regarding the underlying currency. In much the same way, a "strategy of zero premiums" can be designed through the proper choice of exercise prices.

FIGURE 6–6
Hypothesis—Using an In-the-Money £/$ Call (Exercise Price = 1.60)

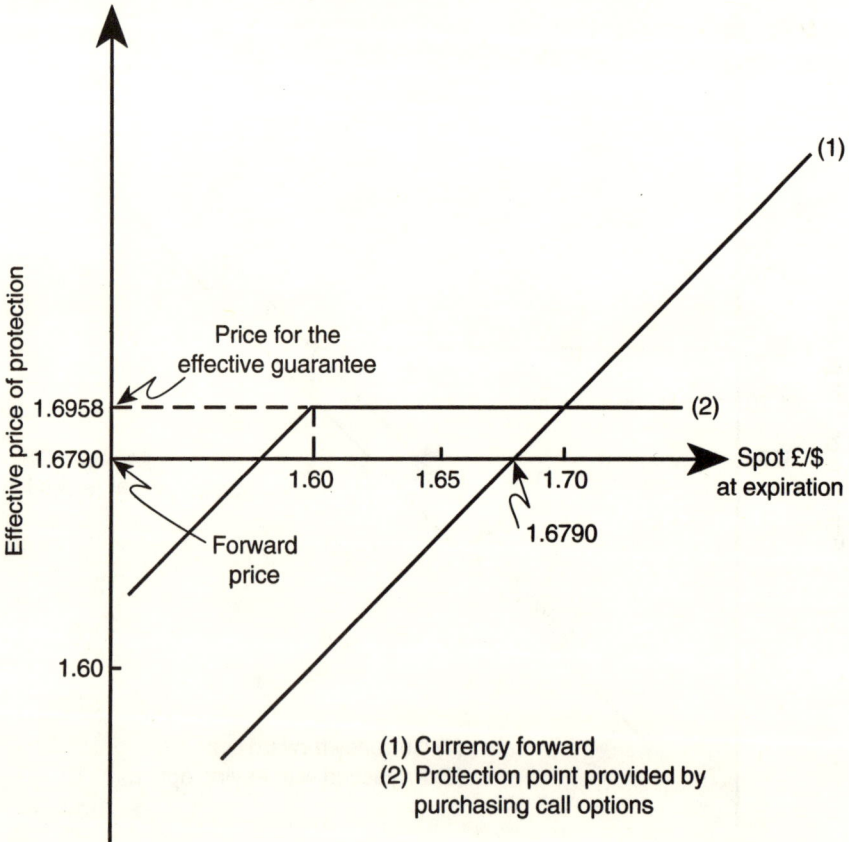

(1) Currency forward
(2) Protection point provided by purchasing call options

The Principle of Protection with Cost Reduction

We will now show how an American importer who is currently short pounds sterling can protect his position by establishing a maximum price for the purchase of pounds sterling while limiting the cost of the premiums he pays. He purchases an out-of-the-money call, and to reduce the expense of this purchase, he sells an out-of-the-money put. The spread he enters into consists of a call whose exercise price is higher than that of the currency forward and a put whose exercise price is lower than that of the call. The time value of the call purchased is less than the premium of the put sold.

The treasurer's approach is to protect himself against the risk of a rally in the pound by buying a call that has a high enough exercise price. To obtain a spot price that is far enough above the price of the currency forward, the treasurer buys a call that is more out-of-the-money than the put is. The following example will demonstrate how he accomplishes this.

On June 6, 199X, an American importer buys a September 1.70 pound call and sells a September 1.60 pound put. The cost of the two simultaneous operations is as follows:

$$\text{Premium cost} = 2.02 - 1.30 = 0.72 \text{ cents}$$

The effective cost of liquidating the options position relative to the currency spot at expiration can be calculated as follows:

• If the spot £/$ at expiration is lower than the lower exercise price, 1.60, the buyer exercises his put and the importer purchases his pounds at 1.60. The effective cost of the purchase is $1.60 + 0.0072 = 1.6072$. This is the minimum cost of the pound, given the strategy used.

• If the spot £/$ at expiration is higher than the upper exercise price, 1.70, the importer exercises his call and procures his pounds at an effective price of $1.70 + 0.0072 = 1.7072$. This is the maximum cost of the pound, given the strategy used.

• If the spot £/$ at exercise is between the two exercise prices, neither option is exercised, and the effective liquidation price lies somewhere between the exercise prices at a point that depends on where the spot is at the moment. The profile of this combined posture is shown in Figure 6–7.

The profile of the effective costs is a result of these two lines of reasoning:

• Determining the profile of the risk and the resultant of the options position.

• Determining the position in the options for the exchange where one is short and the effective maximum and minimum spot prices for the currency as established by the options position. The curve for the effective costs is shown in Figure 6–8.

The Strategy of Zero Premiums: The Indospread

The strategy of zero premiums—the "Indospread"—is aimed mainly at reducing the cost of option premiums. The use of this

FIGURE 6–7
Profile of the Risk and the Resultant for the Options Position

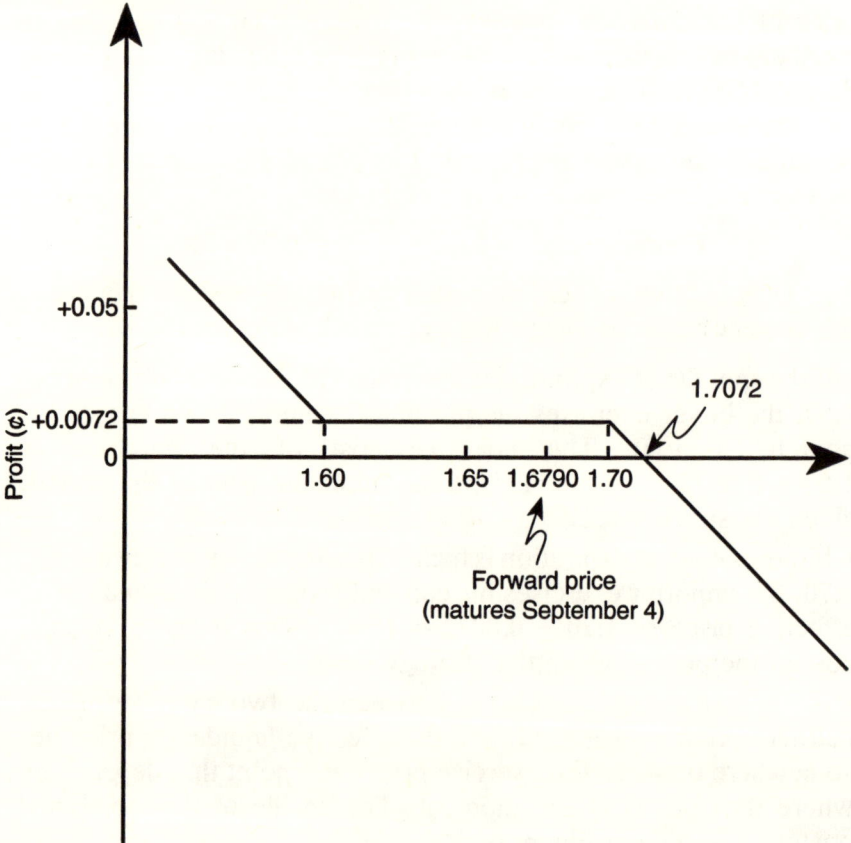

strategy implies the absence of a particular bias regarding the performance of the underlying currency. In the strategy of zero premiums,
the premium paid for the option purchased exactly equals the income produced by the option sold. This is accomplished by having
the strike prices of the options equidistant from the currency spot
when the position is established. Out-of-the-money options whose
premiums consist of the time value are of necessity chosen. Given
the symmetrical nature of the position, the probability of exercise
is equal for the call and the put. For this reason, the time value of

FIGURE 6–8
Profile of the Effective Costs with the Strategy of Reducing the Cost of the Premiums

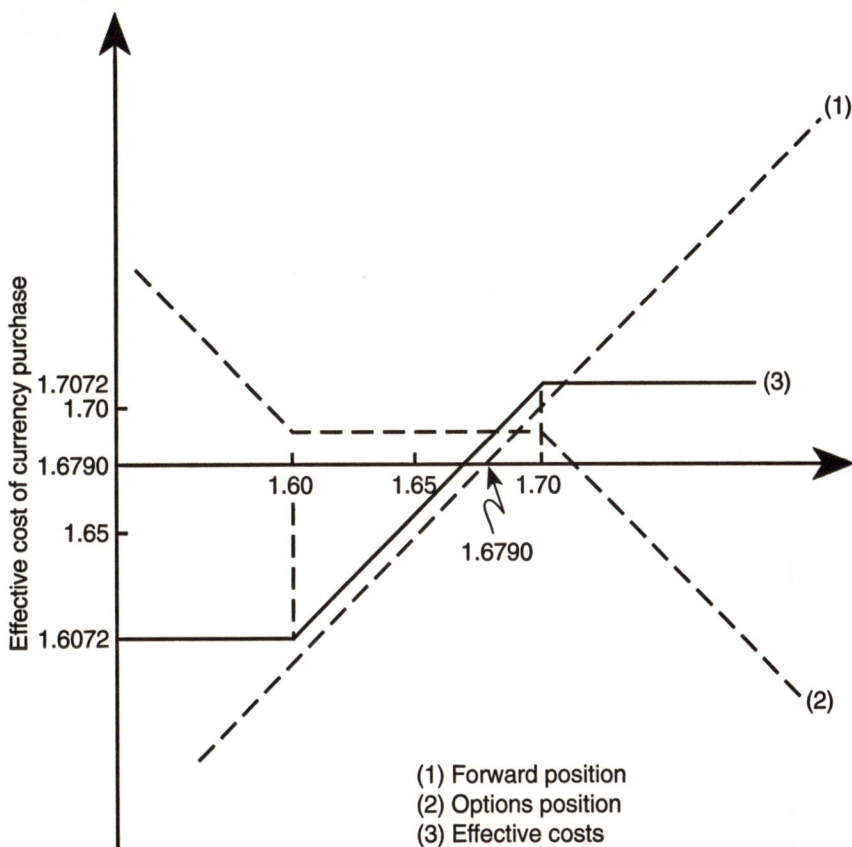

(1) Forward position
(2) Options position
(3) Effective costs

the call must be equal to the time value of the put. The theory behind the strategy of zero premiums is discussed in Chapter 5.

An American importer decides to enter into an Indospread as follows: On September 23, he buys a December £/$ 1.50 call for 2.55 cents and sells a December £/$ 135.60 put for 2.55 cents. (He does this in the OTC market, which is the only one in which a call and a put equidistant from the spot currency can always be obtained.) The forward is trading at 142.80. The cost of the options position is zero. The profile for the zero-cost Indospread is shown in Figure 6–9.

Interpretation of Risk Profile and Resultant.   If, at expiration, the spot £/$ is below 135.60, the put owner exercises the put, incurring a loss on his position, which can be written as follows:

$$R = -S + 135.60$$

The vector logic for this result is −1.

FIGURE 6–9
Profile of the Risk and the Resultant for the Indospread

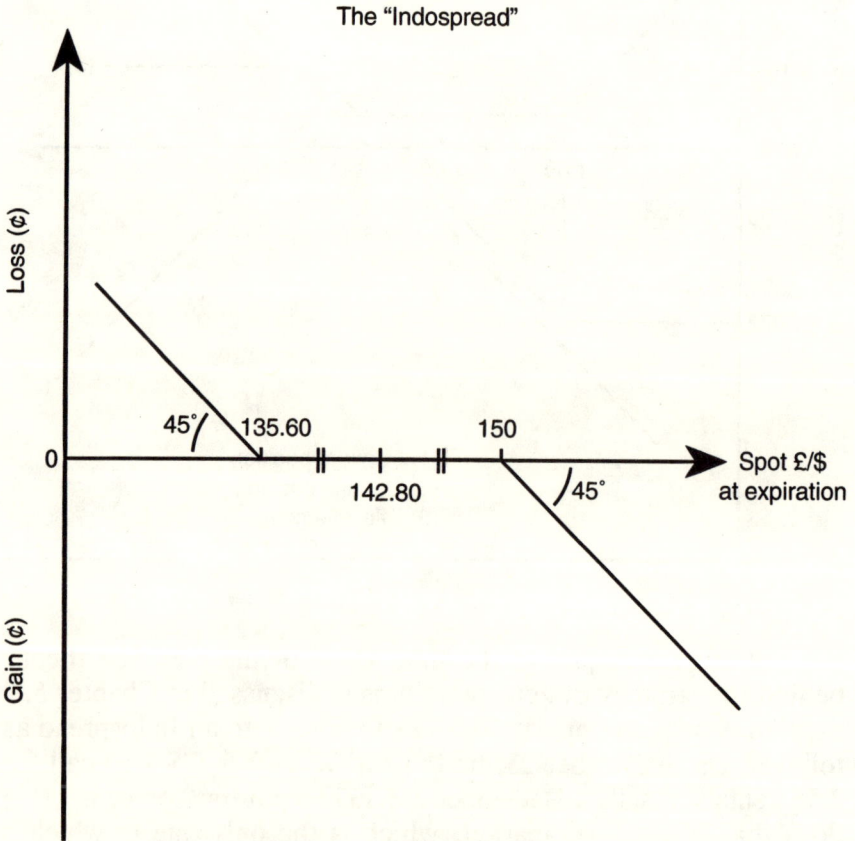

The "Indospread"

If, at expiration, the spot £/$ is above 1.50, the importer exercises his call option and, based on the equation for the profile, realizes the following profit:

$$R = -S + 150$$

The vector logic for this result is -1.

If, at expiration, the spot £/$ is between 135.6 and 150, neither option is exercised and the resultant for the options is zero.

The profile of the resultant is shown in Figure 6–10.

FIGURE 6–10
Profile of the Effective Prices for the Indospread

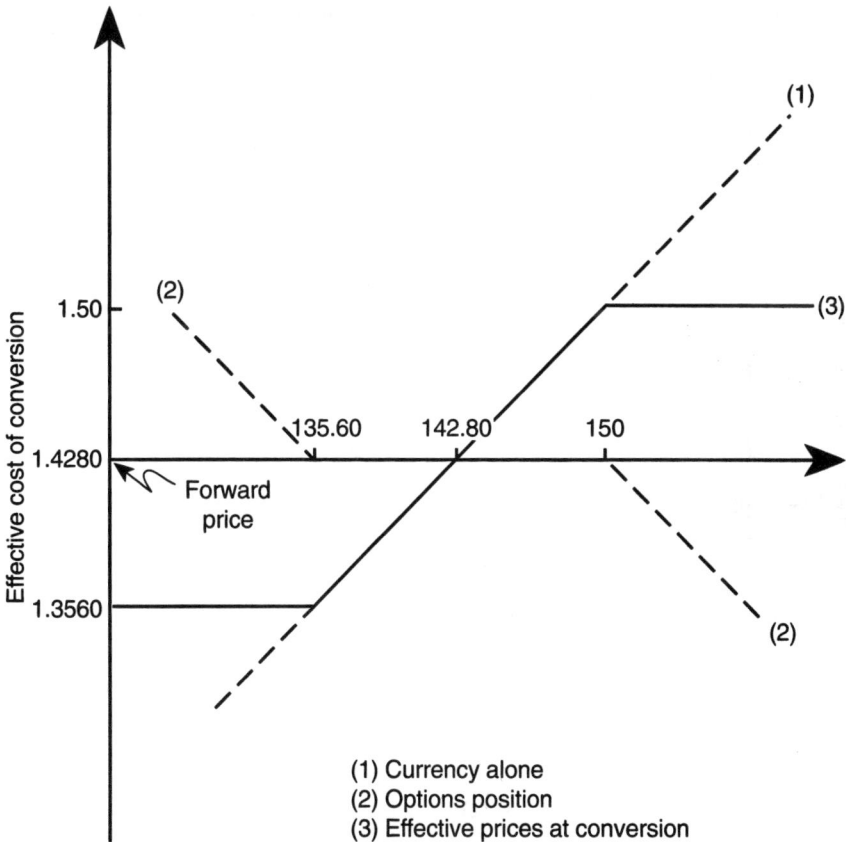

(1) Currency alone
(2) Options position
(3) Effective prices at conversion

In designing the Indospread, the treasurer selects a spot minimum and a spot maximum at which to purchase the pound, which he must ultimately do, with the conversion points equidistant from the conversion value of the forward contract. The treasurer could select a distance that is far out-of-the-money. Given the likelihood that such options will not be exercised, this is similar to a currency position. If a call is purchased and a put sold at the forward price, the two options act as a forward.

In assessing the contention that option premiums are too expensive, one should consider Figure 6–11, in which the Indospread is

FIGURE 6–11
The Indospread versus Standard Call Buying

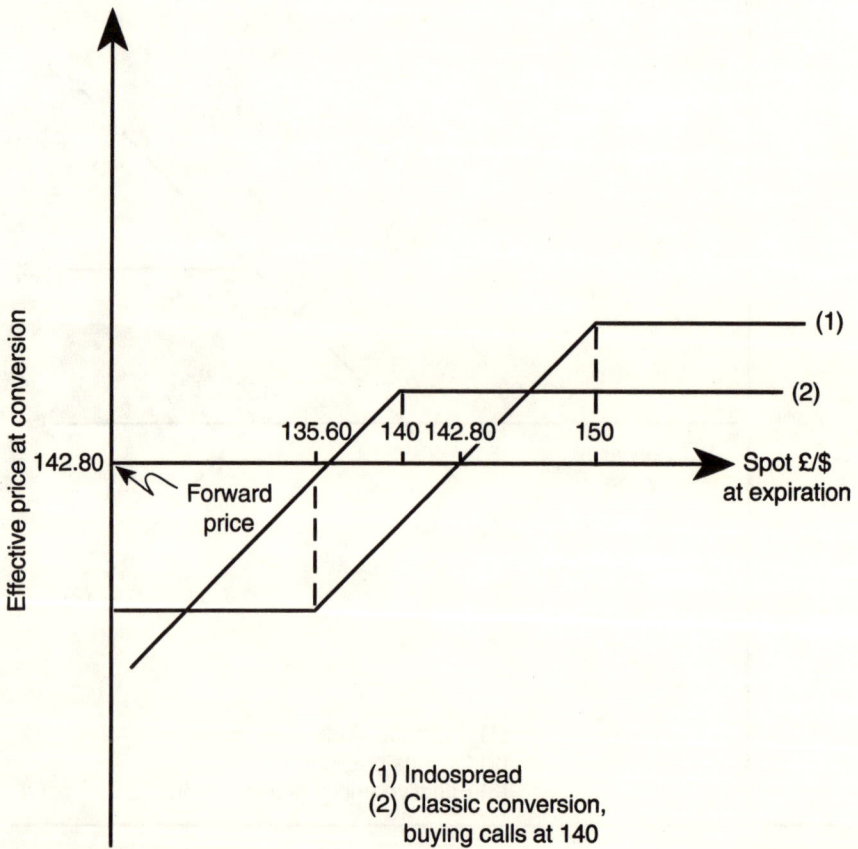

(1) Indospread
(2) Classic conversion, buying calls at 140

compared with the standard approach to buying a call. As mentioned, the Indospread is done at no cost. The call strategy shown provides no downside protection and carries the bias that a strong pound is needed to have it work out well. The Indospread has no bias. It provides protection against extreme price movement in either direction, and it offers a comfortable range over which a profitable move in the underlying currency can be enjoyed.

In designing any option strategy, the most important thing to bear in mind is that the details must be investigated before a decision is made. The Indospread offers a good balance of the advantages obtainable from all of the available alternatives. It is an excellent approach, and a treasurer should reject it only if he is quite confident about the direction that the currency markets will take. But predicting the direction of the currency markets is rarely done consistently well, and where corporate financial survival is at stake, a balanced approach is more likely to succeed in the long run.

CHAPTER 7

DEVELOPING THE HEDGE PROGRAM

"Outside of typical manufacturing expenses, foreign currency is probably one of the largest risk components a multinational organization has," says Stanley Yabroff, an NYU professor and the foreign exchange (FX) specialist of Gerald Incorporated. As firms attempt to increase their market shares, reduce manufacturing costs, and still realize a profit by exploring opportunities abroad, changes in the value of foreign currencies can have a disastrous effect not only on a specific product or service but on the entire organization. Yabroff continues by saying, "Hedging is risk management, and if you're not hedging, you're speculating in the physical market, and that's unacceptable to most businesses." What many businesses *have* found acceptable, however, is their ignorance with respect to protecting themselves against exchange rate risks. In order to combat that ignorance, a clear understanding of the framework for a foreign exchange hedge program must be developed.

The flowchart in Figure 7–1 presents the six basic segments of such a program: (1) planning, (2) development, (3) approval, (4) implementation, (5) execution, and (6) post-execution evaluation and control. The decision to use option contracts as a vehicle in foreign exchange risk management must be authorized by the company board of directors and/or senior management personnel. Before work on a hedge program gets started, it is important that senior management adopts a corporate resolution stating that the company will be using commodity futures and options as hedging devices. In general, this corporate resolution should:

- Recognize that futures and options contracts can be effective tools for hedging the company's foreign exchange rate risks.
- Authorize the company's officers and employees to engage only in futures, options, and hedging activities that are consistent with prudent risk management practices, that correlate

FIGURE 7-1
Developing the Hedge Program

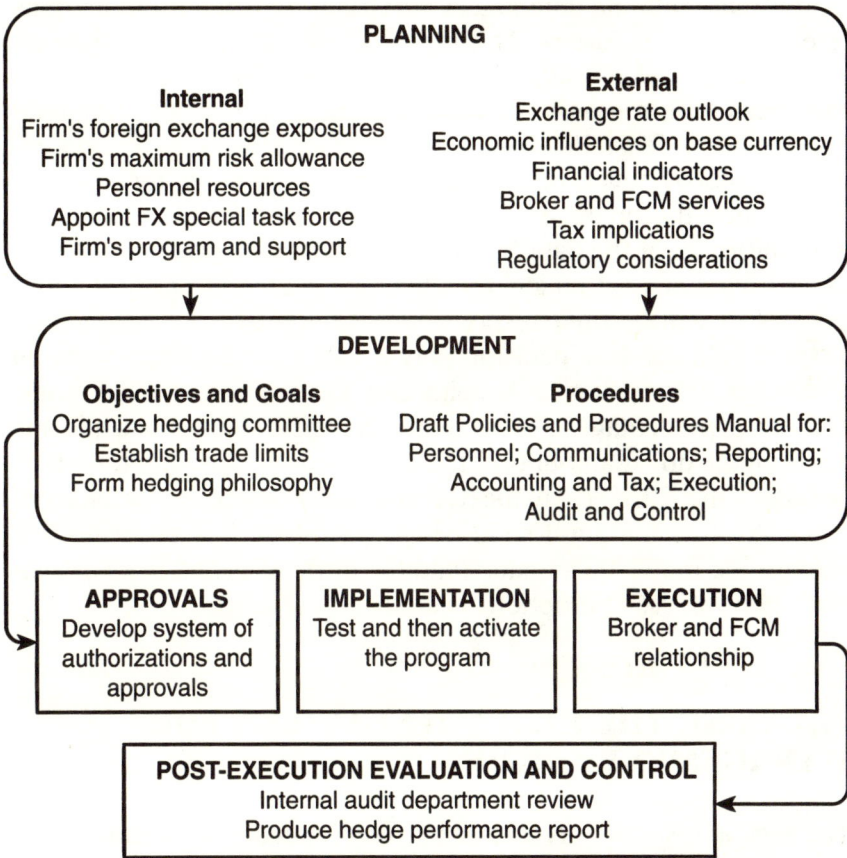

PLANNING

Internal
Firm's foreign exchange exposures
Firm's maximum risk allowance
Personnel resources
Appoint FX special task force
Firm's program and support

External
Exchange rate outlook
Economic influences on base currency
Financial indicators
Broker and FCM services
Tax implications
Regulatory considerations

↓   ↓

DEVELOPMENT

Objectives and Goals
Organize hedging committee
Establish trade limits
Form hedging philosophy

Procedures
Draft Policies and Procedures Manual for:
Personnel; Communications; Reporting;
Accounting and Tax; Execution;
Audit and Control

APPROVALS
Develop system of
authorizations and
approvals

IMPLEMENTATION
Test and then activate
the program

EXECUTION
Broker and FCM
relationship

POST-EXECUTION EVALUATION AND CONTROL
Internal audit department review
Produce hedge performance report

---

with the company's business needs and abilities, and that are
used to satisfy the company's commitments.

- Base the hedge program and its implementation on a comprehensive study of the company's foreign exchange rate exposure.

In addition to adopting such a corporate resolution, senior
management should assemble a special task force to prepare an
in-depth report of the company's operations to determine where
exchange rate exposures exist. For instance, exchange rate fluctua-

tions inconsistent with the rates quoted in pricing orders may cause manufacturing companies that use just-in-time delivery practices for raw materials and component purchases to forfeit profit margins or even to suffer losses. The report should therefore include an analysis that begins with the proposal and closing of sales and concludes with the delivery of and payment for goods. It should also include a feasibility study on the management of foreign exchange risks by means of currency futures, options, or their derivatives. Once the board of directors and senior management have been informed of the dangers of volatile currency prices and of the alternative available means for obtaining protection against those dangers, it will be their responsibility to approve the appropriate hedging vehicle. This decision may involve certain limitations on contract activities, such as hedging only existing assets or liabilities, hedging a percentage of anticipated material needs, and placing limits on the dollar amounts of the underlying commodity for which hedging is used. Critical to the decision and its successful implementation are formulating a solid hedging strategy and ensuring that responsible individuals understand the intricacies and risks associated with futures and options trading.

PLANNING THE HEDGING STRATEGY FOR MANAGEMENT APPROVAL

The special task force recruited by senior management should present a well-designed strategy for managing foreign exchange risk *that answers questions before they're asked.* This strategy should include details on trade and hedge research, operations and trade execution, control and audit systems, and accounting and tax-reporting procedures. An accountant who specializes in foreign exchange hedging should be retained to assist the special task force in presenting the tax and reporting requirements since as yet there are no clear Financial Accounting Standards Board guidelines or standard practices for documenting such transactions (see Appendix A). In addition, many software products have been developed that can assist the special task force in planning the FX program and, later, in operating the program and monitoring its usefulness to the organization (see Appendix B). A well-designed strategy helps management understand hedging transactions before the company enters the futures or options markets.

As stated, the company's senior management should pass a corporate resolution expressing its desire that the company hedge in futures and options. To avoid the lure of speculation, that resolution should set specific limits on the dollar amount of open positions based on the underlying currency. However, arbitrary limits should not be set, since that may defeat the entire purpose of the hedging strategy. Instead, the resolution should authorize buying or selling enough contracts to hedge the specific dollar amount of the exchange rate exposure. In situations in which the specifics cannot be known until after the risk already exists, an approximation should be made on the basis of historical product data coupled with a reasonable allowance for time and price variances. No more contracts should be bought or sold than are required by the needs of the specific situation. Otherwise, the position is *overhedged*, which can be viewed as speculation and thus is prohibited by the corporate resolution.

THE HEDGING COMMITTEE AND ITS RESPONSIBILITIES

Once the special task force has conducted its evaluation and management has approved the concept of hedging and the hedging strategy, a hedging committee should be formed that oversees implementation of the hedging strategy and is responsible for monitoring the hedge program. This committee will define where exchange rate exposures exist within the company operations and will decide how to implement the hedging strategy. It will also delegate responsibilities for

- Implementing the hedging strategy.
- Analyzing the effectiveness of the risk reduction strategies that are to be used.
- Coordinating all new accounts and original margins with the broker or FCM.

- Introducing the persons from whom the FCM can accept orders.
- Structuring reliable monitoring and control procedures for routinely reviewing the hedge program and reporting the results to an internal audit department.
- Producing monthly or weekly performance reports in which each trade is evaluated.
- Reviewing contract position limits and recommending changes where necessary.
- Implementing a hedge-tracking system that values hedge positions against hedged items and the opportunity costs of maintaining margin.

The gross and net financial results of the hedging should be analyzed daily by a hedging committee appointee, and reviewed periodically by senior management and the board of directors.

DETERMINING THE HEDGING NEEDS OF THE ORGANIZATION

Oliver Bajor, director of Toronto-based Wood Gundy, Inc., explains that "the primary objective of the hedge program is to decouple . . . cash flow, or revenues, or earnings, from the foreign exchange volatility" and that "if you are certain of cash flows, you are probably well off by being *hedge neutral* or exactly hedged. But if you are uncertain of your future cash flows, then your firm must set policies for decision making as to how much of your FX exposure you wish to hedge." Therefore, senior management must dictate to the hedging committee the risk allowances it is willing to accept when the cost of *insuring* the firm's exposure to foreign exchange fluctuations is being weighed. Stan Yabroff suggests that the firm "initiate the [foreign exchange] position fully hedged (100 percent), and steadily decrease [its] position as the time frame warrants or delta moves. A position does not have to be held static." The delta he is referring to is the correlation between an option's premium and the value of the underlying currency (as discussed in Chapter 2). Ultimately, corporate policy will determine the organization's hedging needs and set standards accordingly.

SELECTING A BROKER AND AN FCM

Even the best foreign exchange hedge programs employed by man-agement's finest personnel can be tainted by unorganized or careless brokers to whom the responsibility of transacting hedge orders is entrusted. All too often, the deciding factor in choosing a futures commission merchant (FCM) is cost and cost alone. Although cost certainly plays a significant part in this decision, the importance of developing a rapport with a broker that understands the business and will help the special task force to uncover areas of exposure to foreign exchange risks should also be taken into account. Other factors that should be taken into account include the following:

- The financial strength of the FCM (review its latest annual report and its current balance sheets).
- How the FCM organizes its accounting and control departments.
- The FCM's procedures for position accountability and auditing.
- How many institutional hedge clients the FCM currently serves (references).
- The experience of the FCM's floor brokers, clerks, and account executives.
- The FCM's financial and business integrity as evidenced in its dealings with the National Futures Association (NFA), the Commodity Futures Trading Commission (CFTC), and the Securities and Exchange Commission (SEC).
- Whether the FCM or broker has had any major customer complaints, and, if so, why.

Sid Jones, a financial consultant and vice president of Merrill Lynch, a well-known FCM, suggests that you "find a firm with good pricing and compare [it] with others" and that you "get comfortable with an individual that will spend time with you and truly learn your needs, [as hedging] doesn't have to be complex—the more unsophisticated the better." Jones also says that a pitfall of hedging is "hiring a broker that is not on top of the market."

Finally, the ways in which hedges are initiated or removed can be confusing and difficult to understand. Table 7–1 defines only a

TABLE 7–1
Commodity Futures and Options Contracts: Types of Orders

---

day order   An order that, if not executed during the trading day it is entered, automatically expires at the end of that trading day.

limit order   An order in which a customer specifies a price; the order can be executed only if the market reaches or betters that price.

market order   An order for immediate execution given to a broker to buy or sell at the best obtainable price.

　market on open   A qualifier to an order indicating that the order is to be executed only during the opening period of the market, if possible. Also called *on-the-open*.

　market on close   A qualifier to an order indicating that the order is to be executed during the closing range of the session.

open order   An order that remains in force until it has been canceled or until the futures (or options) contract expires.

stop order   An order that becomes a market order when a particular price level has been reached.

　stop-limit order   A variation of a stop order that can be filled only at the specified price or better.

　stop-loss order   An order that becomes a market order to buy only if the market advances to a specified level or to sell only if the market declines to a specified level. As soon as the specified level has been traded, the order is executed at the next obtainable price. There is no guarantee as to price. Stop-loss orders are used to prevent or minimize losses on either a long or a short position.

Source: *The CME English/Japanese Dictionary of Futures and Options Terms* (Chicago: Chicago Mercantile Exchange, 1991). Terms used by permission.

few of the types of orders that are used in hedge transactions. Make sure that the broker or FCM account executive thoroughly explains the various types of orders and that no order is executed unless the individual designated by the organization clearly understands the transaction. Any wrong assumptions can be costly.

MARGIN REQUIREMENTS

FCMs are required to deposit margin or cash reserves with the clearinghouse, and therefore customers are required to deposit with their FCMs margin based on their hedging activity. Unlike securities trading, in which margin constitutes equity, in futures trading margin is referred to as *good faith money* because the margin requirements in futures trading are generally far lower than the margin requirements in securities trading. However, minimum margin requirements are set by the exchanges for both FCMs and their customers. FCMs occasionally require higher margins from their clients, and they may also change the margin they require for each type of contract from time to time. Margin requirements for option contracts vary even more, as the total risk for the option buyer is the premium he pays for the option, whereas the option writer or seller must have sufficient margin to cover any losses resulting from adverse moves in the currency. Put plainly, the option buyer has the right to exercise his option at any time, and the option writer must make delivery of the underlying currency, which may have become more expensive for him to acquire.

FCMs and their customers are obliged to furnish both initial and variance margin (known as *maintenance margin*). Initial margin is required when the customer establishes a new position or increases an existing position. Maintenance margin is required when the value of a customer's position declines (determined at the day's end by calculating, based on the day's settlement prices, the net loss on all liquidated contracts and the net loss on all open contracts). The customer must then make a cash deposit to restore the initial margin level of his account. Failure to do so could result in the liquidation of all of the customer's positions and the termination of the customer's account.

POLICIES AND PROCEDURES MANUAL

The hedging committee must develop a written policies and procedures manual consistent with the hedging strategy formulated by the special task force and approved by senior management. This manual is used as a guide by the individuals responsible for operating the hedge program. In addition to providing general policy statements and position limit guidelines, the manual must establish procedures for the execution of trades, trade verification controls, and postexecution accounting. Policies and procedure are necessary to ensure that hedging activities are properly documented and that the hedge program is in compliance with accounting, tax, and regulatory requirements and practices.

The policies and procedures manual should also outline policies for supervising and training all of the employees involved in the hedge program to ensure their thorough familiarity with the concept of hedging, the terminology of hedging, and the risks associated with the trading of futures and options. Software packages are available that can help the hedging committee to inform employees about standard operating procedures, various control measures, and precautionary practices that reduce the threat of errors.

INTERNAL CONTROL

Once exchange rate exposures have been revealed by the special task force and management has approved the use of hedging and the hedging strategy, the hedging committee implements the hedge program and introduces its most critical segment—control. After a trade has been executed and recorded, the open position should be maintained and monitored until the risk has been neutralized and the hedge transaction closed. During the life of the hedge transaction, changes in the contract value and related maintenance margin cash flows must be properly documented for internal management reporting and financial accounting purposes. An internal accounting control system and an internal audit department should ensure that

- Only relevant hedge transactions are approved, executed, and documented.
- These transactions are initiated and processed on a timely basis.
- Any errors in execution or recording are detected and corrected immediately.

Developing Control Objectives

As in multinational firms that practice a decentralized management style, the internal audit department must be segregated from operating personnel. This promotes efficiency and reduces the risks of misappropriation, fraud, and other difficulties. Furthermore, records maintained by employees independent of the trading operation should contain all of the information needed to

- Verify positions with the firm's broker and FCM.
- Provide accurate records for all ledger and accounting entries relating to maintenance margin, realized and unrealized gains or losses, and the like.
- Monitor all open positions.

Vitally important to the success of the internal audit department is its ability to communicate with the FCM and to understand the FCM's accounting records. Oliver Bajor stressed this point when he said, "Even if you know what you are doing, if the [control] departments are not getting good information, you are not going to do the right thing." Figure 7–2 shows the makeup of the control environment.

Listed below are specific control objectives with suggestions on which persons within the organization should perform certain functions. The entire control effort is subject to senior management review and should be monitored by the firm's internal audit department.

- All transactions and open positions are appropriate for hedging and can be justified, given the firm's existing or anticipated exchange rate exposures.
- The number of contracts, long or short, used in a hedge transaction represents the amount of a given foreign currency needed to offset any exchange rate risk.
- The delivery month or months selected in the hedge transaction are consistent with company policy as to the month in which the exchange rate exposure ceases. (For certain option hedge strategies, back month contracts are used to avoid negatively affecting the hedge by time decay.)
- The hedge order is executed in a timely fashion.
- The executed price is consistent with the desired limit price imposed by the company's trader.
- The trade is accurately recorded before and after the transaction.

FIGURE 7–2
Makeup of the Control Environment

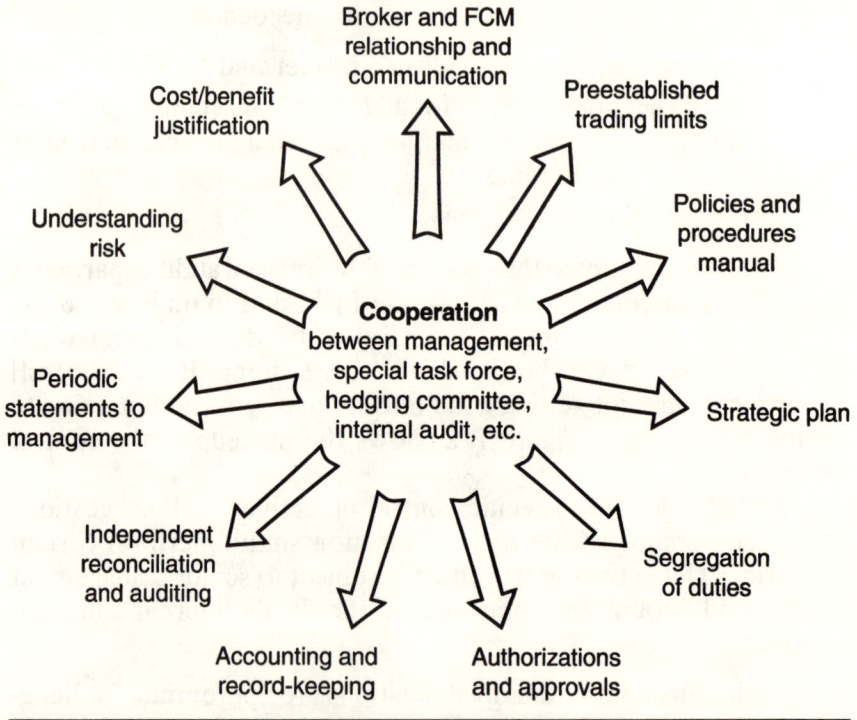

- All trading is consistent with the hedging strategy and management approval.
- Trading strategies are constantly reviewed and updated.
- Position values are recorded daily on the company's books.
- Increases or decreases in the firm's original margin deposits are documented in a timely fashion.
- The company verifies changes in the value of positions before variation margin deposits, made by wire transfer or check, are approved.

The above control objectives can be implemented by the following procedures. All of these procedures are subject to senior management review and should be monitored by the internal audit department.

- Board of directors, senior management, and hedging committee policies are documented and incorporated into the hedging strategy.
- The hedging strategy is documented.
- The broker and FCM are chosen on the basis of specific criteria.
- Company traders are specifically authorized in writing to enter into transactions with the broker and/or FCM.
- The broker and/or FCM has written authorization to accept orders from designated company traders.
- Preestablished trading limits are documented.
- Procedures are written describing how original margin deposits and subsequent changes in position values are recorded and monitored.
- Control and monitoring systems are developed and implemented before the first hedge transaction is executed.
- Employees independent of trading operations should receive broker or FCM trade confirmations and should verify them against the internal trade tickets prepared by the company's trader.
- Any differences between postings in the internal trade log and broker confirmations should be resolved by the company's trader and approved by senior management.
- Daily buy and sell activities along with updates on open positions and their contract settlement prices should be documented separately and reviewed by the internal audit department.
- Month-end open positions and money balances must be reconciled with the statements received from the broker or FCM.
- Any changes in maintenance margin deposits or withdrawals must be verified by an employee independent of bookkeeping responsibilities.
- Reinvestments of excess margin deposits due to favorable contract price changes are authorized and approved by the company's treasurer.
- An accurate report of the company gross and net financial performance is provided daily to the hedging committee, re-

FIGURE 7–3
Policies and Procedures Paper Trail

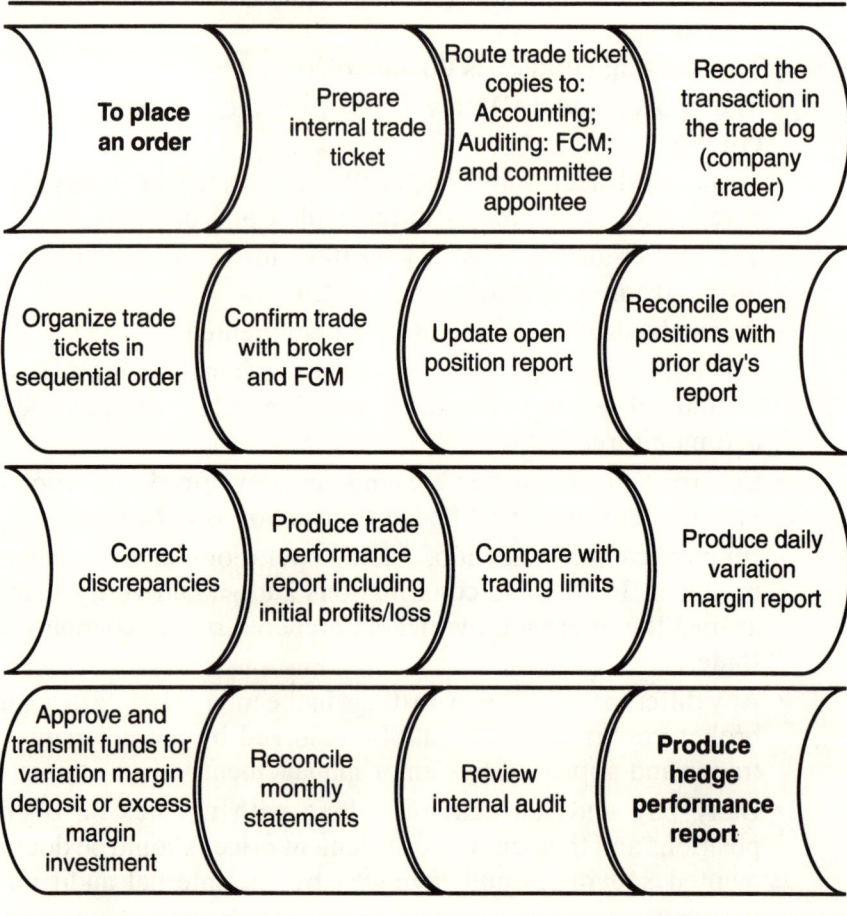

To place an order	Prepare internal trade ticket	Route trade ticket copies to: Accounting; Auditing: FCM; and committee appointee	Record the transaction in the trade log (company trader)
Organize trade tickets in sequential order	Confirm trade with broker and FCM	Update open position report	Reconcile open positions with prior day's report
Correct discrepancies	Produce trade performance report including initial profits/loss	Compare with trading limits	Produce daily variation margin report
Approve and transmit funds for variation margin deposit or excess margin investment	Reconcile monthly statements	Review internal audit	**Produce hedge performance report**

viewed periodically by senior management, and routinely examined by the internal audit department.

• Internal audit reviews of the entire hedging operation are conducted to help ensure compliance with company policies and procedures.

By promoting open communication links among senior management, the hedging committee, and all of those involved in the hedge program and by following the above procedures on a timely basis, it should be possible to identify errors early, minimize their costs, and optimize the effectiveness of the hedging operation. An overview of trade control policies and procedures and the related paper trail is provided in Figure 7–3.

Unauthorized Trading Control

Prior to initiating a foreign exchange hedge program, company executives frequently express fears about the possibility of unauthorized trading by company employees. As mentioned earlier, delegating various duties to responsible persons independent of the trading function makes it easy to detect and deal with company traders who speculate on their own. In addition, the company's trading policies and procedures should be considered a part of any of its authorization agreements with its FCM and broker. In this way, the broker will become involved in the company's control process and will report any perceived inconsistencies in its trading orders.

Reporting Controls and Getting Started

The first step in launching a foreign exchange hedge program is to make the initial margin deposit with an FCM to activate the account. This cash deposit would be entered on the company's books through the cash disbursements register, and all subsequent margin activity concerning open contract positions due to changes in their value would be posted to the original margin deposit account in the general ledger, with the offset posted either to a balance sheet hedge valuation account or through the income statement as an unrealized gain or loss.

The source document for posting executed trades is typically the internal trade ticket, which is prepared at the trader's desk. The internal trade ticket (an example is shown in Figure 7–4) should contain information similar to that of any standard company purchase or sales order for a cash market transaction. After executing the trade, the company's trader should manually prepare a log indicating all of the information on the internal trade ticket along with the actual execution price and time. Copies of the internal trade ticket should be sent to the internal audit and accounting departments, to the FCM that actually executes the order, and to the hedging director who approves all trades.

FIGURE 7–4
Internal Trade Ticket

Company Name	**No. 91-00001**

Time: _____ A.M. P.M.   Date: _____ _____ 199___

Currency: _____   Delivery mo. _____

Contracts: _____   Price unit: _____

Buy _____ Sell _____   FCM Acount # _____

Authorized by: _____

Trader: _____

	Hedge Information
Filled at: _____	Company job no. _____
Time: _____	Exposure amount: _____
Date: _____	Exposure dates: _____

Monitoring Contract Values and Position Limits

It is necessary to verify and analyze the daily change in the value
of the contracts that the company holds. Each day's settlement
prices are entered into the open positions ledger, and the difference

between the original contract price and the settlement price is calculated. After the per contract and total position gain or loss has been determined and has been compared with the previous day's results, appropriate action should be taken on variation margin deposits or investment of the available equity. The open positions ledger should have extra columns for the posting of margin deposit requirements and round-turn commission expenses.

In addition to preparing the trade log, the company's trader should monitor and document all of the positions in the open positions report and should periodically check its entries with the broker and FCM. This report can help the trader determine whether a position is exceeding the contract limit and can also serve as the basis for verifying daily variation margin calculations. Again, an employee independent of the trading function should analyze the data compiled by the trader and the final report should be reviewed by the company's treasurer. The treasurer can then authorize the transfer of additional funds for maintenance margin deposits or the investment of increases in equity with the FCM.

The Hedge Performance Report

A *perfect* hedge occurs when any loss in the currency's cash position is equal to the gain in the options position, or vice versa. For various reasons, though, this relationship or *basis* between the currency's spot and futures prices will vary over the life of the hedge and should be monitored closely. Similarly, currency option premiums are based on their futures price, which ultimately influences the basis between the option value and the currency's spot price. The hedging committee should introduce a hedge performance ledger to track changes in these values, and the data contained in the ledger should be analyzed daily. This ledger is critical to the assessment of variation margin requirements and the overall effectiveness of the hedge position.

The hedge performance ledger is the final chapter of the hedge program. It focuses attention on the economic results of open hedges and of hedges that have already been offset. Information drawn from this ledger can be useful in the evaluation of hedging strategies and procedural compliance.

THE PSYCHOLOGICAL EFFECTS OF TRADING

A frequently overlooked aspect of the hedging process is the psychological effects of commodities trading on particular individuals. Choosing the *best* among many qualified candidates should involve more than just reviewing résumés. How do the candidates manage stress? Financial responsibilities? Losses? Dr. Van K. Tharp, a well-respected psychologist and futures industry consultant specializing in peak performance trading, has devoted eight years to researching and analyzing this topic. His suggestions for firms poised to implement a foreign currency hedging program are presented below.

• *First, find the right people to begin with.* Trading performance is human performance. Managers can save themselves a lot of time and grief by selecting traders who will produce optimal performance with as little training as possible. If the traders have psychological blocks to success, no amount of training in technique will overcome those blocks. Dr. Tharp says that the hedging committee should look for two characteristics: (1) high self-esteem and (2) the desire to work as part of a team.

• *Second, develop high self-esteem and the desire to work as part of a team in people who are already in the hedging department and part of the trading function.* Developing high self-esteem often requires psychological coaching. For example, Dr. Tharp suggests that the hedging committee determine how to most effectively praise traders (by asking them) and to do so as much as possible. Bonuses for a job well done can pay big dividends for a successful foreign currency hedging operation.

• *Third, maintain an atmosphere that supports traders by minimizing stress and advancing their best interests.* Dr. Tharp suggests that (1) traders be encouraged to take breaks several times a day to meditate, relax, or exercise; (2) a smoke-free working environment be maintained; and (3) the phones used by the traders be elevated above eye level. Most trading departments put their telephones down low and often on the right side. According to Dr. Tharp, this encourages eye movements that frequently promote fear, anger, and other stressful emotions.

• *Fourth, develop a supportive management team.* Dr. Tharp's suggestions for the hedging committee include the following:

(1) make sure that trader/supervisor relationships are supportive rather than antagonistic; (2) determine the comfort level and optimal trading environment of each trader; and (3) make sure that trading supervisors understand trading and hedging.

• *Finally, foster a better understanding of the concept of risk.* Company hedging committees often do not define their policies concerning risk, and traders are therefore often left wondering what losses are *too high*. Specific control limits as to the number of contracts and the total financial risk that a position can allow are necessary. However, the skills of each trader should be considered when those limits are established.

APPENDIX A

TAX AND REPORTING ISSUES

In the March 1991 issue of Risk Management *magazine, an article by Michael S. Joseph, a partner at Ernst & Young and a member of the AICPA Options Task Force, addressed questions concerning tax and reporting practices for foreign currency options. The article appears below and is reprinted by permission.*

Generally accepted accounting principles (GAAP) are frequently criticized for not reflecting the results of economically hedging risks that arise from operations or foreign currency–denominated transactions. Real and perceived inconsistencies between economic substance and accounting treatment for hedging have impeded management from hedging these risks.

The Emerging Issues Task Force (EITF) of the Financial Accounting Standards Board (FASB) recently clarified some ambiguity regarding the use of foreign currency options contracts to hedge foreign currency exposure.

This clarification, which established a recognized source of GAAP, should increase the ability to treat options contracts as hedges of certain foreign currency–denominated transactions.

At the same time, the EITF reaffirmed other existing authoritative guidance relating to hedging, including foreign currency risks. Although further discussions are planned, clarification provided by the EITF to date goes a long way toward alleviating perceived accounting limitations to using currency options as hedges. Here is how the November 8 and January 10 EITF consensus clarifies the use of currency options.

Statement of Financial Accounting Standards (FAS) 52, *Foreign Currency Translation,* was issued in late 1981. It provides the authoritative GAAP relating to the translation of foreign currency transactions and financial statements. Generally speaking, FAS 52 provides that

- Transactions denominated in a foreign currency should be "remeasured" into a company's functional currency using exchange rates in effect at the reporting date. Gains and losses from the remeasurement process are reflected in income.

- If the foreign subsidiary's functional currency is different from the reporting currency (the parent company's functional currency), the financial statements must be translated as follows: Assets and liabilities are translated at current exchange rates, while income and expense items generally should be translated at average exchange rates that were in effect during the period. The gain or loss arising from translating the assets and liabilities of a foreign subsidiary should be included as a component of equity.

FAS 52 also offers a guide to accounting for hedging certain foreign currency risks. It indicates that gains or losses from transactions in foreign currencies meeting the criteria to be treated as a hedge should be included in the measurement of the hedged item instead of reflected in income like other remeasurement gains or losses.

This statement requires the hedge instrument to be *designated* as a hedge and be an *effective* hedge. FAS 52 specifically includes foreign currency forward exchange contracts, swaps, and similar instruments. Exchange-traded futures contracts also are considered to fall within the scope of FAS 52, a practice confirmed by their exclusion from the scope of FAS 80, *Accounting for Futures Contracts.*

FAS 80 generally provides similar hedge accounting criteria for futures contracts used to hedge risks other than foreign exchange risks.

Not surprisingly, neither FAS 52 nor FAS 80 addressed options contracts. The market for options other than equity options had not yet developed. Thus, the need to establish accounting principles to deal with them was not great.

The Accounting Standards Executive Committee of the American Institute of Certified Public Accountants (AICPA) responded to this void in accounting principles for options by forming a task force in 1984. The committee and task force spent approximately two years developing the AICPA Options Issues Paper to address and recommend guidance relating to options transactions.

The AICPA included all types of options contracts (on fungible items) in its paper. While the AICPA Options Issues Paper has gained acceptance in practice, and the Securities and Exchange Commission (SEC) generally has required registrants to follow its provisions, it has not been fully embraced by FASB. FASB is studying options as a part of its financial instruments project. Therefore, the paper is not the highest level of authoritative literature within GAAP.

As a result, questions have arisen about the authority of its conclusions, particularly those not agreeing with FAS 52 or 80.

A most significant conceptual difference between FAS 52 and 80 is in their definitions of the nature of risks arising in future transactions that can be hedged.

Further, an appreciation for the one-sided risk/reward characteristics of options contracts has led some to argue that hedge criteria need not be as stringent as for futures contracts where the participant will incur losses as well as gains. Those arguments have persuaded some to conclude that options are an appropriate vehicle to hedge the expected future net income of a foreign subsidiary. That view is inconsistent with the principles of FAS 52 and 80.

The AICPA Options Task Force attempted to address the accounting treatment of foreign currency as well as other kinds of option transactions. It did so within the framework of FAS 52 and 80.

However, where the statements were inconsistent, the task force selected the alternative it saw as most appropriate—usually following the guidance of FAS 80.

These conditions have caused different practices in using foreign currency options as hedges. The EITF's November 8 action clarifies the proper treatment of options used as hedges of foreign currency exposures.

One of the first questions to be addressed under either FAS 52 or 80 is what constitutes an exposure to risk that qualifies for hedging. FAS 52 and 80 provide differing guidance on this.

Both statements establish a precedent of a risk assessment to determine that a position intended to be hedged has risk. However, FAS 52 requires only that a particular transaction have exposure to risk, while FAS 80 requires that it contribute to the risk of the enterprise as a whole.

For example, a commitment by a dollar-based company to purchase a piece of equipment at a future date in yen would be viewed by the guidance in FAS 52 to have exposure to the yen-dollar exchange rate. This exposure would be viewed to exist even if an expected inflow of yen that could be used to satisfy the yen obligation existed. Although not applicable to foreign currency transactions, the hedge principles of FAS 80 would conclude that the purchase commitment does not constitute a risk exposure because of the expected inflow that would provide the yen to meet the company's obligation.

The statements also differ on risk exposures that are eligible to be hedged. Both permit a company to hedge assets or liabilities. FAS 52 even allows hedging of a net investment in a foreign subsidiary.

For future transactions, FAS 52 permits only firm commitments to be hedged. FAS 80 allows firm commitments and anticipated transactions to be hedged. FAS 80 does not impose the firm commitment requirement embodied in FAS 52 to transactions whose interest rate or noncurrency risk is to be hedged with futures contracts.

The difference between a firm commitment as described in FAS 52 and the anticipated transaction allowable under FAS 80 can be significant.

Firm commitments have been interpreted only to include legally enforceable agreements whose terms are subject to reasonable estimation. Anticipated transactions, on the other hand, are transactions for which management can identify the significant characteristics and terms and which probably will occur.

For most well-established companies, some portion of future revenues or expenses can often be considered to meet the anticipated transaction criteria even though they are not contractually committed. As such, revenues or expenses associated with these anticipated transactions could be considered to be hedgeable risks under the criteria established in FAS 80 but not under those established by FAS 52.

Both FAS 52 and 80 are transaction focused. That is, they require the identification of specific assets, liabilities, or future transactions to be hedged. Although in practice, groups of assets, liabilities, or future transactions are hedged, they tend to be homogeneous groups of items. The hedge result is then allocated to the individual items comprising the group.

Neither of the statements permits aggregation of dissimilar (but related) items into a hedgeable group of assets, liabilities, or future transactions. Accordingly, neither supports the concept of hedging expected net income, for net income is the result of numerous dissimilar transactions and not itself a hedgeable transaction.

The AICPA Options Task Force, among its many conclusions, adopted a transaction (rather than enterprise-wide) risk exposure approach. FAS 80 is specifically referred to in the AICPA Options Issues Paper as providing the anticipated transaction criteria that should be applied when hedging future transactions with options.

The failure of FASB to endorse the conclusions of the issues paper has led to uncertainty about the applicability and the authority of the paper. Some see it as a useful guide to accounting for options positions. Others see it as an inappropriate circumvention of the criteria in FAS 52.

Many companies with well-established foreign revenue sources can satisfy the anticipated transaction criteria of the AICPA Options Issues Paper, even though the revenues are not firm commitments. They wish to hedge the foreign currency risks of part of these future revenues with options contracts. Others even want to go as far as designating the expected net income of a foreign operation as an anticipated transaction that could be hedged with foreign currency options.

By August 1989, a diversity in the application of the principles was becoming apparent. The SEC observer to the EITF provided his staff's views on several issues in an effort to offer some clarification. His statement at the August 19, 1989, EITF meeting contained three major points:

- Hedge accounting requires identifying specific assets, liabilities, or transactions to be hedged. Therefore, hedging future net income is inappropriate.
- Transactions denominated in a foreign subsidiary's own reporting currency do not expose either the subsidiary or the parent to a foreign currency risk that is capable of being hedged.
- Foreign currency options that do not qualify as hedges should be carried at their market value.

The SEC observer's statement addressed only these narrow issues. It did not address when and how foreign currency options contracts could be used as hedges. It also left largely unresolved the questions of the authority of the AICPA Options Issues Paper.

The EITF addressed these issues at its meetings, indicating that the AICPA Options Issues Paper is the appropriate authoritative guide to accounting for all types of options contracts. As such, it clarified that the criteria of the issues paper, rather than the more restrictive criteria of FAS 52, can generally be applied to foreign currency options as hedges.

Thus, the EITF discussions confirm the practice some companies follow in viewing future currency revenues as qualifying for hedge accounting according to the more practical anticipated transaction criteria of FAS 80. The discussion also confirms that future net income may not be hedged because it does not represent a transaction.

Nonetheless, the ability to hedge a portion of revenues that meet the rigorous probability tests of FAS 80 should provide significant flexibility to companies desiring to hedge risks resulting from transactions denominated in a foreign currency.

Additional discussions of related topics are planned, including the appropriateness of hedging intercompany transactions. However, EITF discussions to date greatly clarify the GAAP applicable to hedging with options contracts. Companies wanting to hedge the risk of expected foreign currency transactions that meet the anticipated transaction criteria can now do so without significant questions about the relevant financial reporting literature.

APPENDIX B

SOFTWARE DIRECTORY

The following directory for foreign currency option software products and associated databases and option valuation programs is designed to help companies locate computer support appropriate to their needs and their strategic hedging plan. The information presented below is based on the vendors' responses to a mailing. Due to the large number of products covered, no attempt has been made to verify it. Prospective users should investigate each vendor individually and should ask for demonstrations and references as well as detailed descriptions of the listed services or software.

AIQ Systems—MarketExpert, StockExpert, IndexExpert, and OptionExpert

Each of the systems is designed to assist the trader/hedger in deciding what to buy or sell and when. All of the systems utilize the "Expert" subfield of artificial intelligence. In the AIQ systems the knowledge and insight of experts in the field of market analysis culminate in a series of rules. The rules are then combined with time-proven technical indicators that work together to analyze market data to develop buy and sell signals. The user can query the knowledge base for justification of signals. The technical indicators being used for analysis can be altered for in-depth analysis and signal confirmation.

Each of the systems has been developed for a specific investment mechanism: StockExpert—for individual equities; MarketExpert—for general market direction; IndexExpert—for index option trading; and OptionExpert—for use with equity options. A communications package is built into each system for automatic data retrieval.

AIQ is currently creating a system for the professional arena. It is also performing research to determine the feasibility of designing expert systems for FX operations, bonds, etc. For more information: **AIQ Systems, Inc.,** 916 Southwood Boulevard, Suite 2–C, Incline Village, NV 89450, (702) 831-2999.

Aspen Research Group—Aspen Graphics

Aspen Graphics is a PC- and/or network-based decision support system providing power, clarity, and flexibility for the serious currency trader and hedger. The system's highlights include graphics on thousands of instruments with no user maintenance of symbol lists; unique windowing abilities; comprehensive traditional analytics plus profiles, tic by tic, point and figure, candlesticks, and more; unlimited custom pages; multiple independent screens; real-time P&L; a large historical database; ASCII import/export; and single-user and LAN configurations. The system is currently available on the following data feeds: Comstock, Signal, and Knight Ridder/Unicom worldwide.

For more information: **Aspen Research Group, Inc.,** 201 Centennial Street, Suite 209, Glenwood Springs, CO 81602, (303) 945-2921.

Black River Systems—Macro*World Forecaster

Macro*World Forecaster is an expert forecasting system with a self-contained database. It automatically completes a variety of sophisticated analyses to provide forecasts for up to five years ahead, turning points, exceptional events, a composite outlook for sectors, and the best leading indicators. It comes with 10–25 years of historical data for over 120 U.S. and international business and financial indicators, including business and financial indicators for Canada, Japan, Germany, and the UK. Macro*World Forecaster easily exchanges historical data and forecasts with other systems to allow users to include additional data for the same complete analyses. An update service keeps the system's database current for users with a monthly diskette of new data, historical revisions, bulletins, and telephone support.

The primary categories for this product are financial planning and long-term hedging, analysis, and forecasting. For more information: **Black River Systems Corporation,** 4680 Brownsboro Road, Building C, Winston-Salem, NC 27106, (919) 759-0600.

Bonneville Market Information—Ensign III

Ensign III is a comprehensive, customized real-time commodity, currency, stock, and option quote system.

Traders consider Ensign III a masterpiece in financial trading software because it delivers crisp, colorful graphics and more than 40 comprehensive technical tools and studies.

Ensign III's customizing flexibility enables traders to create their own tools for detailed financial analysis. Ensign III also simplifies options trading with the Black-Scholes model, which when used with the technical tools, enables traders to manage their foreign currency, options, and other instruments. More than 300 intraday, daily, weekly, and monthly charts can be monitored with Ensign III's screens.

Combining Ensign III with Bonneville's elaborate data system offers more than 100,000 symbols on stocks, futures, bonds, and options, delivered at 19,200 baud.

For more information: **Bonneville Market Information, Inc.,** 19 West South Temple, Salt Lake City, UT 84101, (801) 532-3400.

Coast Investment Software—CIS Trading Package

The CIS Trading Package is a graphically oriented technical analysis tool. It provides the trader with quality graphics and user-friendly studies. In addition to the usual trend line studies, RSI, stochastics, MACD, moving averages, and oscillators, CIS has added DEMA, Hurst Cycle Projection capability, displacement of moving averages, a volume and open interest study, and CIS's proprietary Oscillator Predictor, which indicates a day ahead of time the prices that will produce overbought and oversold conditions in the marketplace. This information is highly applicable to option valuation in general and currency hedging in particular.

The CIS Trading Package also contains the Timesaver, a tabular printout of support and resistance levels, as well as a series of user-defined charts. The process is fully automatic. The hardware requirements are EGA and IBM or compatible with 512K hard drive. Additional tutorials and teaching information are available.

For more information: **Coast Investment Software,** 86 Cobia Street, Destin, FL 32541, (904) 654-5999.

Coast Investment Software—Fibnodes

Fibnodes, a computerized Fibonacci retracement and objective calculator, is especially designed for hectic, high-pressure, intraday trading and option valuation strategies, particularly in currencies and cross-rate operations, where a knowledge of support and resistance levels can be known ahead of market action. Fibnodes

- Calculates the two major nodes, or up to 58 combined nodes per market swing.
- Recalculates up to 58 nodes within 10 seconds of a new market high or low.
- Has been engineered to measure volatile market moves, such as those in the currencies, into bite-size, recognizable, tradable pieces.
- Highlights user-selected nodes for instant recognition.
- Comes with a complete "where and how" operation manual that includes many specific examples.
- Has minimal system requirements—single floppy or diskette drive, 256 memory, IBM or compatible hardware.

For more information: **Coast Investment Software,** 86 Cobia Street, Destin, FL 32541, (904) 654-5999.

Computrac (a Telerate Company)—Computrac

Computrac is a spreadsheet-based technical analysis charting program used by traders and hedgers to perform price trend analysis, cycle analysis, overbought/oversold analysis, chart pattern analysis, and more, using technical methods included in the program. Computrac's features include a module to create proprietary analysis methods; a module to create and test trading strategies for specific markets, using price conditions, technical signals, broker variables, filters, etc.; and a module to calculate option values using the Black-Scholes model. The spreadsheet structure allows the user the flexibility to better use market data by creating spreads, ratios, and derivatives, such as a proprietary index created by combining various studies or markets in the spreadsheet. Computrac includes virtually every type of charting and technical method. It is available in PC and Macintosh versions. An on-line program is currently being developed.

For more information: **Computrac Software, Inc.,** 1017 Pleasant Street, New Orleans, LA 70175-5951, (800) 535-7990.

Data Transmission Network—DTN Wall Street

DTN Wall Street is a low-cost electronic financial market information and market quote service that uses satellite (Ku-band and C-band) and cable television delivery technology. The service provides

- Quotes delayed 15 minutes on the NYSE, Amex, and NASDAQ exchanges.
- Continuous quotes on all of the major indexes.
- Coverage of foreign exchanges.
- Commentary on U.S., Asian, and European markets.
- Futures and cash quotes on precious metals, currencies, Treasuries, mortgage-backed securities, commercial paper, LIBOR, and others.
- The latest worldwide, national, and regional business news.
- Time-sensitive economic reports from the U.S. government and from the Federal Reserve System and other government agencies.
- A comprehensive record of the U.S. economy's performance.

The charge for DTN Wall Street is $34.95 per month for satellite delivery (or for cable TV delivery in a few selected areas) plus a onetime $295 service installation fee.

DTN Wall Street is easy to install and simple to operate—no keyboard, no modem, no phone line charges, and no exchange fees. Data Transmission Network provides all of the equipment—there's absolutely no equipment to buy. DTN Wall Street can operate as a stand-alone system or tied to a PC or printer to support compatible portfolio management and technical analysis software.

For more information: **Data Transmission Network,** 9110 West Dodge Road, Suite 200, Omaha, NE 68114, (800) 779-5000 or (402) 390-2328.

L. A. Ehrhart—WINdoTRADEr

Help in timing the market entry of hedging operations in real-time trading is provided by WINdoTRADEr's market profiles, bar charts, technical studies, long-term activity reports, Dalton Capital's PRI, daily "value area" charts, market facilitation index, and TicBars.

WINdoTRADEr's market profiles have real-time value areas, easy scaling, and TPO counts, and they cover multiple days. Unique features of WINdoTRADEr include cumulative market Profiles; TicCars, a distribution of tic volume; TicBars, a count of tics at each price of each bar; Point 'n Time, a "time stamp" for point and figure charts; a Dalton LTA and PRI index; and extensive "running" market profiles.

Designed by a trader, WINdoTRADEr has a sophisticated bad price filter, bar chart frequencies that do not need to be predefined, and the ability to "replay" days tic by tic. Twenty pages, with up to eight windows each, display up to 45 commodities/options, depending on the hardware. WINdoTRADEr is IBM compatible.

For more information: **L. A. Ehrhart,** 3700 North Lake Shore Drive, Suite 709, Chicago, IL 60613, (312) 871-4687.

Ensign Software—Ensign III

Ensign III is a financial trading software program featuring real-time commodity, stock, and option quotes, technical studies, charts, and news. Ensign III includes the following features:

- Black-Scholes option model analysis.
- Directory of 10,000 symbols showing last and net.
- 16 portfolio pages showing high, low, bid, ask, volume, etc.
- Intraday, daily, weekly, and monthly charts.
- Library of 50+ technical studies and tools.
- Japanese candlesticks, market portfolio, point and figure.
- 1,000 on-line news stories.
- Open position equity for 20 portfolios.
- User-defined macro keys providing customized program control.
- Programming language to create tools and studies.
- Data file manager for editing, copying, deleting files.

- CSI, Computrac, Tick Data, and ASCII file support.
- Print charts and tabular listings.
- Multiuser configuration.
- Multitasking with Desqview 386.
- Logical menus and mouse interface that make it simple to use.

A free evaluation disk presenting the capabilities of Ensign III is available. For more information: Call **Ensign Software** at (800) 255-7374.

Equis International—Metastock Professional 2.5

Metastock Professional 2.5 is a comprehensive technical analysis charting program that studies the relationships between the price movements of securities and past price and volume information.

Metastock comes ready-made with more than 60 preprogrammed technical indicators and studies to help analyze virtually any futures contract, futures option, currency option, stock, bond, commodity, index, or mutual fund. In addition, Metastock's enhanced formula builder contains over 75 math and statistics functions for creating custom indicators and formulas.

Metastock can display as many as 36 charts simultaneously for quick comparison of securities, indexes, and studies. Each chart can display up to 1,000 days, weeks, or months of data.

Traders can create expert system formulas that illustrate a currency's technical merit based on whether multiple preprogrammed indicators are bullish or bearish. The trader determines the ranges, weighting, and indicators. Metastock is compatible with more than 25 national and international data services for charting historical and end-of-day prices.

This is for IBM and true IBM compatibles. For more information: **Equis International, Inc.,** P.O. Box 26743, Salt Lake City, UT 84126, (801) 974-5115.

Euromoney Axxess—Spectracap

Spectracap is a software computer program for the pricing of interest rate caps, floors, and collars for all currency options. It is a menu-driven system, with user-configured defaults and a simple, easy-to-use interface. Its users include traders, corporate treasurers, brokers, auditors, and risk managers dealing with interest rate risks. The program was developed by Spectrasoft, Inc., a New York-based financial software developer.

The software handles caps, floors, collars, and corridors for each currency, and uses the Black-Scholes model for pricing. The pricing methodology used is suitable for transactions with maturities of up to five years. Spectracap's capabilities include the option premium, net position, implied volatility, implied strike, delta, gamma, theta, and vega, and special custom features allow the user to compare the premiums of up to 40 options with different bids and offers. The grid design is flexible and easy to use.

Detailed position and transaction reports can be generated from the database. Within each input field, Spectracap features extensive context-sensitive help, describing in detail the required input.

For more information: **Euromoney Axxess,** 84 Vincente Road, Berkeley, CA 94705, (415) 540-6252.

Financial Research Company—F/Xpert

Financial Research Company's F/Xpert will help in selecting the strategies and products that are ideally suited for an exposure situation. F/Xpert records the decision rules used by experienced foreign exchange specialists to reach conclusions on managing currency exposures.

F/Xpert offers efficient trade decision review; an expert's assessment of the degree of confidence for specific hedge decisions; customization based on corporate policies, guidelines, or restrictions, alteration to accept data feed; employment on most Treasury Department computer systems; a cost-effective means of managing currency risk; ease of use; a full range of hedge alternatives and comparisons; consideration of tax and accounting impacts; assessment of probabilities and degrees of certainty before trade decisions are made; evaluation of cross-rate exposure situations and base currency environments; updating to include new hedge instruments; and training capabilities for new staffs.

For more information: **Financial Research Company,** 30 Lincoln Plaza, New York, NY 10023, (212) 245-7200.

Futrak—Advanced Currency Trading System

The Futrak Advanced Currency Trading System (F.A.C.T.S.) provides technology for evaluating over-the-counter and exchange-traded currency options and performing sensitivity analysis on foreign exchange portfolios. Operating either as a stand-alone or as a part of the total Futrak integrated solution, the system provides traders with the facts. Highlights of F.A.C.T.S. include option pricing with all derivatives; user-defined matrices of prices and derivatives; sensitivity analysis on and across portfolios; trade capture, including the capture of simulated trades; unlimited portfolios and portfolio definitions; full cross-currency capability; sophisticated graphics; and rapid calculations; and long dates (25 data points, O/N to 30 years).

For more information: **Investment Support Systems, Inc.,** 1455 Broad Street, Bloomfield, NJ 07003, (201) 338-0321.

Futrak—Base System and Services

Futrak was created to provide solutions for companies managing their exposure in the demanding environment of financial risk management. It provides an array of quality features and services to answer the trading, hedging, and arbitrage needs of traders, as well as the accounting and transaction-processing needs of the operations staff. As Futrak is modular, companies can choose only the modules they need, creating a cost-effective and customized system. Futrak's base system and services are the foundation of the product line.

In reference to analytics, decision support, risk management, and operations, Futrak is an integrated system that provides traders, operations, and management with the on-line and hard copy information necessary to maximize profits and minimize risk in the areas of interest rate, foreign exchange, and commodity risk management.

Futrak's integrated approach maintains appropriate controls over operations and avoids duplicate trade entry, while allowing traders to maintain up-to-date positions and to analyze real and simulated trades under a variety of scenarios.

For more information: **Investment Support Systems, Inc.,** 1455 Broad Street, Bloomfield, NJ 07003, (201) 338-0321.

Futrak—Foreign Exchange Risk Management Back Office

The Futrak Foreign Exchange Risk Management Back Office system provides complete functionality for trading support, accounting, transaction processing, and report generation. Each module of the system can operate as a stand-alone or as a part of the total Futrak integrated solution. Each module is designed to present information in a clear, concise, and usable form. The system supports a wide range of foreign exchange instruments, including currency futures, over-the-counter currency options, exchange-traded currency options, and spot and forward contracts. It offers the back office an up-to-date method for comprehensive risk management.

The system includes these features: on-line inquiry capability by instrument type and/or portfolio; management reports, daily, month-to-date, and year-to-date, including P&L by portfolio, department, product group, trader, and hedge, realized and unrealized; operations reports, including broker reconciliation and position by broker and counterparty; margin management supporting the major exchanges and both SPAN- and strategy-based margining; confirmation for all over-the-counter instruments; multicurrency accounting; transaction-processing functions, including input, edit, amend, and back valuation; and table-driven functions.

For more information: **Investment Support Systems, Inc.,** 1455 Broad Street, Bloomfield, NJ 07003, (201) 338-0321.

Intex Solutions—Intex Option Price Calculations

Intex Option Price Calculations consists of ready-to-use functions for option buyers and sellers, including functions that compute theoretical value, implied volatility, historical volatility, the "Greek" sensitivity values (such as delta, gamma, vega, theta, phi, and rho), and the appropriate option expiration date. Both a modified Black-Scholes model and a binomial pricing model. The instruments covered include equities, futures, commodities, currencies, and short-term bond options. Intex Option Price Calculations is compatible with most PCs, minis, mainframes, and workstations.

For more information: **Intex Solutions, Inc.,** 161 Highland Avenue, Needham, MA 02194, (617) 449-6222.

Lester Associates—Futures Position Management System

The Futures Position Management System (FPMS) is a complete PC-based system that handles the complex job of managing a commodity position and satisfies the reporting requirements of hedgers, traders, trading support, management, and accounting. FPMS provides reports on all trading activity, including trades entered or changed and positions liquidated, as well as detailed and summary reports on the current trading position. It handles all U.S.-regulated futures markets, foreign commodity markets, futures options, currency options, and foreign exchange contracts. For non-U.S. market positions and foreign exchange positions, it provides cash flow projections, settlement reports, and payment instruction reports.

FPMS allows trading companies to identify and manage their trading performance and trading risk, including price risk, broker credit risk, settlement risk, and foreign exchange risk. The system runs on either a single PC or a local area network.

For more information: **Lester Associates, Inc.,** 11 South Passaic Avenue, Chatham, NJ 07928, (201) 635-2254.

MJK Associates—Data Services

MJK Commodity Data Services is a commodity and currency futures database. The database now includes complete historical and current daily price information for all foreign currency futures traded on the IMM as well as selected foreign currencies traded in London, cash prices for IMM futures, gold and silver futures and cash prices, and interest rate futures, both domestic and foreign. Options on the IMM currencies and interest rate futures have been scheduled for addition in 1992.

Time-shared access to the database, using a terminal or computer and a modem, is available with a local phone call in most U.S. cities and world capitals. Payment is made only for the data collected, which may range from individual dates to complete daily portfolios. Software can be built around MJK's standard transmission format, or MJK can customize a format to match the requirements of existing software packages. Historical data can be ordered on magnetic tape, $5\frac{1}{4}$-inch floppy disk, or $3\frac{1}{2}$-inch diskette (PC or Macintosh compatible). MJK can supply a partial or complete database and daily, weekly, quarterly, or yearly updates in these media.

For more information: **MJK Associates,** 1885 Lundy Avenue, Suite 207B, San Jose, CA 95131-1835, (408) 456-5000.

Montgomery Investment Group—Options XL, @Options, and OptionZ

Flexibility, speed, accuracy, and insight are characteristics that options traders and risk managers demand of today's profit-generating and risk control options analysis software. In order to meet these demands, Montgomery Investment Group has created Options XL, @Options, and OptionZ to serve the DOS, windows, OS/2, and MAC operating environments. These programs add option models and functionality to the dominant spreadsheets—Microsoft Excel, Lotus 1-2-3, and WingZ. Each of the programs is designed to be easy to use and requires minimal new training for current spreadsheet users.

Traders and risk managers evaluate different types of options and require varying degrees of precision. Therefore, the programs offer a choice of seven models for pricing options on equities, bonds, futures, foreign exchange, commodities, real estate, and more. Currently available are the Black-Scholes, Black, Garman-Kohlhagen, Modified Black-Scholes, Whaley (Quadratic), Pseudo-American, and Binomial (Cox-Ross-Rubenstein) models. Montgomery also offers custom models for exotic and over-the-counter options.

For more information: **Montgomery Investment Group,** 1455 Roman Drive, Rohnert Park, CA 94928, (707) 795-5673.

Naiditch Consulting—Micro Hedge

Targeted toward portfolio managers and options traders, Micro Hedge helps analyze currency options with mobility, as any variable may be changed, permitting instant analysis of the resulting position. Micro Hedge allocates user-defined volatility skews and cross-currency correlations and then calculates an all-encompassing global risk matrix. It is also able to integrate the core program with customized features, such as trading sheets and risk reports.

Micro Hedge runs either under windows or on a palm-top PC the size of a videocassette. A trader may therefore use it in an office or on the run.

For more information: **Naiditch Consulting,** 440 South LaSalle, Chicago, IL 60035, (312) 362-3577.

OMR Systems Corporation—The Trading Assistant

Created with a "Trade Anything . . . Anywhere" design philosophy, The Trading Assistant is a fully-integrated, multicurrency trade processing system that handles a wide range of financial instruments. It simplifies deal capture via motif-based trading blotters, and it supports back-office processing for virtually any type of traded instrument.

Upon entry of a transaction, The Trading Assistant will automatically update several on-line facilities to provide details on position exposure, limits, profit and loss, and gap analysis. After entry, The Trading Assistant will process the transaction through its entire life cycle until it is no longer part of the trading portfolio and has been purged from the system. By means of The Trading Assistant, options can be exercised and a transaction for the underlying commodity automatically generated, trades can be liquidated, rates can be fixed for upcoming periods, and more. Managers and operations groups may select from over 200 standard reports to assist them in managing their portfolios.

In addition, The Trading Assistant provides settlement instructions and confirmations for all trading activity in Swift, telex, and fax formats. It provides for daily or month-end accounting entries and for interfacing with the firm's general ledger.

For more information: **OMR Systems Corporation,** 101 Business Park Drive, Suite 220, Skillman, NJ 08558, (609) 497-2014.

Optionomics:—"Risk Has No Place to Hide"

Optionomics interfaces with three common data streams to show current price changes in a one-page format. As the market trades, it views the dynamics of chosen options and shows how implied volatility, alpha, delta, gamma, vega, and theta are affected by market changes. It also provides total portfolio analysis and equity graphs for over-the-counter options, forwards, futures, and futures options.

Optionomics answers "What if?" questions. It inputs positions from scratch or reads them from a file for speed and flexibility. It gives traders the freedom to change input parameters at any time and to display or print completed strategies in graphic form.

Optionomics plots graphs in a variety of formats. Its utility capability enables it to produce matrices for selected options, showing arrays of strike prices for changing levels of price and implied volatility.

For more information: **Optionomics,** 3191 South Valley Street, Suite 155, Salt Lake City, UT 84109, (800) 255-3374.

Orbit Software—Electric Scorecard II

Electric Scorecard II is a completely computerized record-keeping program for people who buy and sell foreign currency options. The program is a hedge success monitor that tells how much money one has made or lost as a result of buying or selling options. It can be used exclusively for foreign currency options or for any of 65 different commodity futures contracts. Its "What if?" feature calculates how much money one will make or lose when the price of an option goes up or down. Electric Scorecard II requires an IBM PC or compatible with a hard disk drive.

For more information: **Orbit Software, Inc.,** 1330 North 148 Plaza, Omaha, NE 68154, (402) 498-5712.

Pivotplus Trading Systems—PivotPlus

PivotPlus enables individuals and institutions to predict the most effective entry, exit, and stop points in all stock, index, and futures markets. Its ability to forecast turning points in the underlying futures instruments offers an advantage in executing futures options trades for the purpose of hedging or speculating with long positions, spreads, and premium writing strategies.

The PivotPlus system operates in its own windows environment, which serves data for over 47 separate algorithms that allow traders to capture profits in long- and short-term trading strategies. Validated in real-time trading by money managers and professionals, the system manages an entire database of price history and runs all of the calculations each day with just a few key or mouse strokes.

The system lets traders track as many symbols as desired, calculates the PivotPlus trading signals for each symbol, updates in real time to adjust for gaps or volatile price action, and calculates the theoretical value of the S&P futures contract as well as the actual versus theoretical spread against the spot cash index. PivotPlus was developed and is supported by a registered commodity trading adviser, and is used to trade futures and options on a daily basis.

For more information: **PivotPlus Trading Systems,** 5701 North Sheridan Road, Chicago, IL 60660, (312) 989-7151.

Revenge Software—An Option Valuator/An Option Writer

An Option Valuator and an Option Writer are two interactive software programs for evaluating options. An Option Valuator uses the Black-Scholes equations to predict the future fair market value of a call or put option and calculates option volatility and hedge ratios. An Option Writer evaluates covered option writing strategies, computing and displaying the total investment, maximum profit, maximum profit percentage, number of days to option expiration, investment percentage yield, annualized investment yield, yield if option is exercised, break-even price, and total profit. Special features include graphic displays, an options calendar giving the complete expiration date when only the month and year are entered, and an option editor permitting the user to change any option parameter so that the effect of the change on other parameters may be observed. The programs come with a comprehensive manual in a vinyl binder.

For more information: **Revenge Software, Inc.,** P.O. Box 1073, Huntington, NY 11743.

R.M.C.—Marketmaster

Marketmaster is a software program that creates leading indicators to forecast both the direction and the extent of future price movement. As such, it is different from systems that use lagging indicators. It can be used to forecast the prices of stocks, market indexes, futures, and virtually any other tradable instrument, but it has been applied to the trading of currency futures in particular. The manufacturer of Marketmaster has sought to make the program as powerful as possible and yet easy to use. The forecasts are always displayed graphically, and Marketmaster will run on any IBM PC or clone with at least 512K RAM. A hard disk is preferred but not mandatory.

For more information: **R.M.C.,** P.O. Box 60842, Sunnyvale, CA 94088-0842, (408) 773-8715.

Robert-Slade—Firstalert

The Black-Scholes, Black (futures), Cox-Ross-Rubenstein, Pseudo-American, and Adesi-Whaley option models are used. Theoretical and current profits and losses may be viewed in a tabular or graphic display on single positions or on a combined position for a complete portfolio. The number of positions that can be analyzed is nearly unlimited. Multiple "What if?" positions can be created by manipulating the volatility, interest rate, time, and projected price of the underlying. For each set of positions, such summary calculations as net delta, net vega, net theta, net rho, and net lambda are available.

Hedge exchange rate risk, delta risk (market exposure), gamma risk (change in delta), vega (volatility risk), and rho (interest rate risk) may be viewed in tabular and graphic formats.

Amost any type of spread combination can be created—ratio spreads (for cross rates) or combinations of cash versus future, cash versus cash, or cash versus cash future with an option hedge. Spreads can comprise up to five items. The spreads may be viewed in a tabular matrix display, as part of a portfolio, or as a high-resolution chart. In a graphic display, spreads are available for tick-by-tick data, data on any intraday interval, and daily, weekly, or monthy data.

Over 80 technical studies are available. Each of these studies can be customized to suit user preferences. Any of the studies can be run on a spread, a ratio, or another created position.

For more information: **Robert-Slade, Inc.,** 750 North Freedom Boulevard, Suite 301B, Provo, UT 84601, (800) 433-4276.

Software Options—C.O.T.S/BOSS

C.O.T.S/BOSS is a real-time back-office system encompassing accounting, audit, and control of off-balance sheet transactions. The system provides real-time position keeping and multicurrency revaluation, general ledger reports and interface, margin and brokerage accounting for house and clients, a flexible report generator, and other booking and settlement functions required for dealing in futures, options, bonds, equities and cash indexes, over-the-counter and traded currencies, forward rate agreements, and other cash instruments. Available for UNIX and DOS.

For more information: **Software Options, Inc.,** 473 Sylvan Avenue, Englewood Cliffs, NJ 07632, (201) 568-6664.

Software Options—C.O.T.S/DEALER

C.O.T.S/DEALER is a modular dealing support and risk management system designed for institutions that deal in options, fra's, and swaps. It provides comprehensive facilities to support market making in over-the-counter options and arbitrage and hedging involving exchange-traded options. DEALER is available for currency and physical commodity options (including exotics), interest rate instruments and options (including options on futures, cash bonds, and forward rate agreements), and equity and cash index options.

For more information: **Software Options, Inc.,** 473 Sylvan Avenue, Englewood Cliffs, NJ 07632, (201) 568-6664.

Systems Development Corporation—sdcRISK

sdcRISK provides trader/hedger support and risk management analytics designed specifically for trading in futures, securities, and listed options.

The features of sdcRISK include multiple-level password security; theoretical and actual positions saved by the user; automatic spread handling, option volatility valuation, and option expiration conversion to futures; full option support expressed as ticks or multicurrency monetary values; automatic handling of option volatility skew; dynamic volatility skew handling; user-selectable option valuation models, with provision for proprietary models; 3-D and 2-D graphic output of various factors; six standard theoretical value (delta) sheets; profit/loss calculation sheets providing position profit/loss, delta, gamma, theta, and vega; an option pricing calculator; transaction entry; and fully programmable ticker pages.

For more information: **Systems Development Corporation,** 141 West Jackson Boulevard, Chicago, IL 60604, (312) 408-1111.

Systems Development Corporation—sdcSENTRY

sdcSENTRY is SDC's real-time intraday risk management and SPAN-based margin support system. It is designed for use by FCMs and clearing members of futures, securities, and options exchanges worldwide.

Based on the sdcGARDS system designed for GLOBEX and the sdcLIFFE/GUARD system designed for the London International Financial Futures Exchange, sdcSENTRY receives transaction and position information intraday from a firm's back-office processing system. Utilizing real-time market prices, the system generates intraday profit/loss, available credit, and SPAN-based margin and risk management calculations. Current account risk is calculated as a percentage of available credit, with alarm thresholds for each account. All the values for all accounts are dynamically recalculated throughout the trading session. Account-by-account information is accessible through screen and printer output.

A true multicurrency system, sdcSENTRY supports margining and profit/loss calculations in multiple currencies, displaying the totals in the user's currency of choice. The user may change the base currency at any time during a session.

sdcSENTRY handles standard instrument update procedures through easy-to-use maintenance windows. It also offers a wide variety of other features.

For more information: **Systems Development Corporation,** 141 West Jackson Boulevard, Chicago, IL 60604, (312) 408-1111.

Technicom—Program Writer II

Program Writer II is a computerized program for either using or developing trading formulas. Each formula becomes an individual module that the program may call up quickly from the main menu. The program allows the use of up to four optimal parameters and automatically determines the optimum value for each of them. Full historical testing capabilities over any time period are included. High-resolution color graphics visually display the exact performance of a trading formula in any market over any period of time. Once optimum parameters have been determined, they are put into a file so that specific trading recommendations based on the trader's formulas may be automatically printed out each day. Program Writer II may be used on IBM or compatible computers.

For more information: **Technicom, Inc.,** 736 NE 20th Avenue, Fort Lauderdale, FL 33304, (305) 523-5394.

Terco Computer Systems—Option Master

Option Master is a powerful option analysis package that has been designed to help the individual option speculator and hedger. It allows the calculation of option premiums and deltas in a variety of report forms. By choosing the option contract to review, selecting a pricing model (Cox-Ross-Rubenstein or Black-Scholes), and calculating the implied volatility, Option Master can be used to generate a wide variety of reports that aid in spotting overvalued and undervalued option premiums.

Option Master can store an unlimited number of contracts, and it keeps all relevant market and option data on screen through its environmental window. Its "What if?" capabilities make scenario simulations easy. These simulate the effect that changing any one or more data items will have on the option contract.

For more information: **Terco Computer Systems,** P.O. Box 1803, Lombard, IL 60148, (708) 495-7123.

Track Data—TOGPLUS

TOGPLUS provides real-time mark-to-market sensitivity analysis of portfolios of any size, and it can maintain as many portfolios as desired.

Its "What if?" capabilities allow the user to set volatilities, time horizons, rates, and spread relationships for multiple scenarios that can be projected across any desired range of underlying price or rate movement. "What if?" projections can be displayed in either graphic or matrix form. P&L, net position, and other sensitivity measures can be projected across ranges of price, time, or volatility. The "Totals" row in the position display at the left side of the screen can be used to track the net price of any spread or combination.

TOGPLUS is fast, flexible, resourceful, and trusted.

For more information: **Track Data Corporation,** 95 Rockwell Place, Brooklyn, NY 11217, (718) 522-7373.

Track Data—TRACK/ONLINE

TRACK/ONLINE contains business and financial databases and quotes. Its users can retrieve real-time or delayed quotes on stocks, options, and futures from all of the major exchanges, including the Canadian and London exchanges. Other financial information includes mutual fund information and performance results; risk arbitrage; institutional holdings and 144 filings; earnings estimates; and equity analysis, technical indicators, economic and monetary projections, bond data, etc. from S&P MarketScope. TRACK/ONLINE also provides analysis on put/call option series, volatility analysis, market pulse, and scanning. TRACK/ONLINE's news databases provide current and historical news.

For more information: **Track Data Corporation,** 95 Rockwell Place, Brooklyn, NY 11217, (718) 522-7373.

APPENDIX C

A GRAPHIC PORTRAYAL OF
OPTION DELTAS

Graphs possess a logical form that enables a person to return to them from time to time and thus to see the gains in knowledge that he or she has made. This is why the graphs in Figures C–1 through C–6 have been provided. These graphs need not scare away even a person with no mathematical background.

The six graphs show the deltas for futures option calls and puts for three periods of time—zero to three weeks until maturity, two to three months until maturity, and five to six months until maturity. The slopes of the centerlines of the put and call graphs for a particular time frame are identical and intersect the horizontal axis at the value of 0.5. The horizontal axis varies from 0 to 1.0, the lower and upper limits of the delta—the degree to which an option tracks the underlying financial vehicle into which the option can be legally converted. The graph centerline is the steepest for the longest time period, which in our case is five to six months.

For each of the time periods, the width of the put graph is greater than that of the call graph. This is so because the number of people who are willing to trade puts is smaller than the number who are willing to trade calls. Many traders feel that a decline in price connotes a problem—failure rather than success. Rational traders do not hold this view, but the market is not confined to rational traders. It may be entered by anyone with the financial ability to trade. Rational traders do not hold this view because they know that in order to become consistently successful, they had to learn how to resist their gut impulses.

The shorter the time covered by the graph, the more closely the slope of the centerline approaches flatness. At zero time the slope would be zero. At infinite time, something we contemplate only at the end of our lives, the slope would be straight up. And it may not be too far from the truth to say that some will find options in Heaven.

The best way to monitor changes in the values of options seems to be to derive the means of these values from the computation of the standard deviation of the day-to-day differences in price closes for a 20-day period. This is perhaps the shortest time frame from which this statistic can be computed on a reasonable basis. The volatility of the means of the graphs

FIGURE C–1
Deltas for Futures Option Calls (zero to three weeks until maturity)

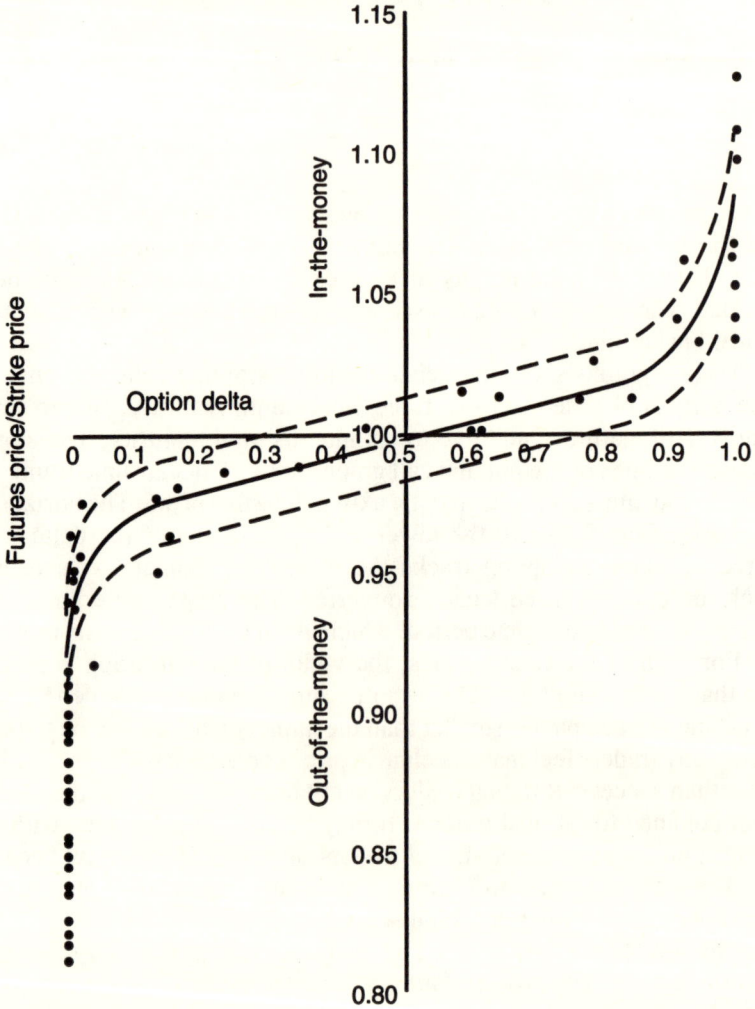

FIGURE C–2
Deltas for Futures Option Puts (zero to three weeks until maturity)

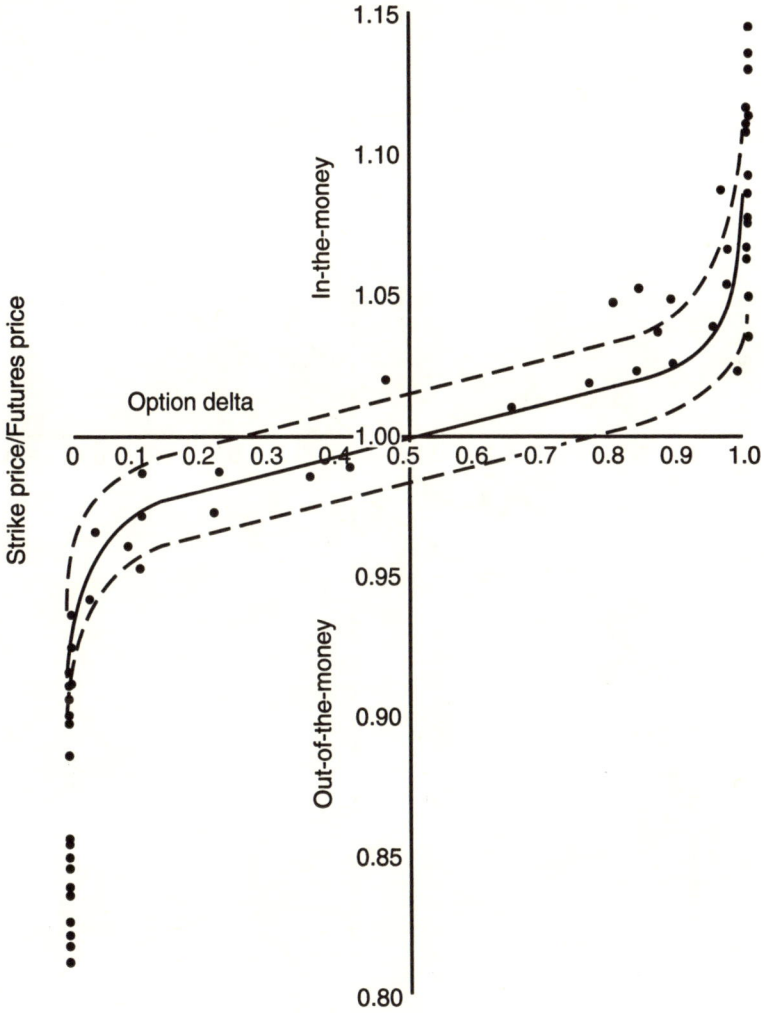

FIGURE C-3
Deltas for Futures Option Calls (two to three months until maturity)

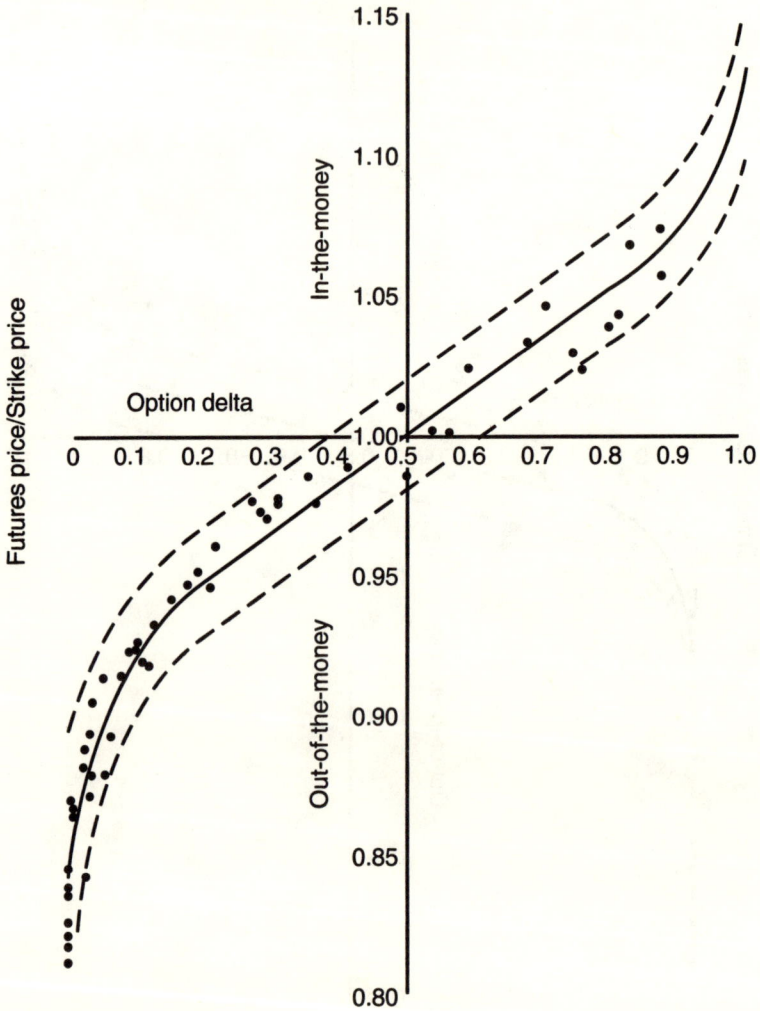

FIGURE C–4
Deltas for Futures Option Puts (two to three months until maturity)

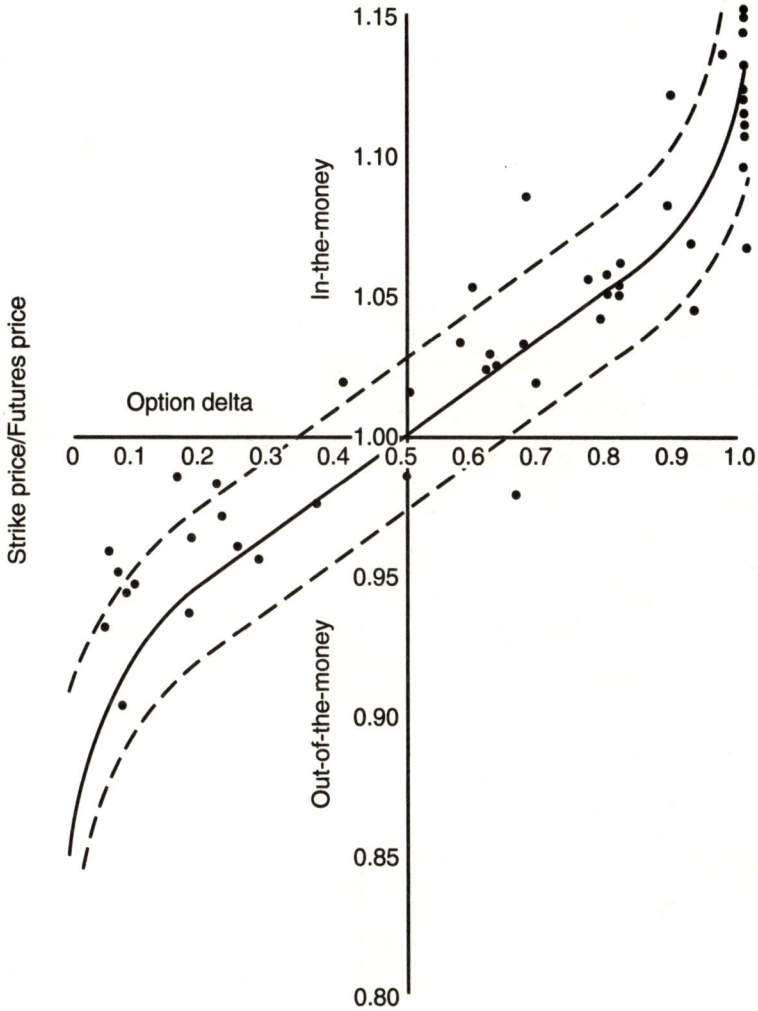

FIGURE C–5
Deltas for Futures Option Calls (five to six months until maturity)

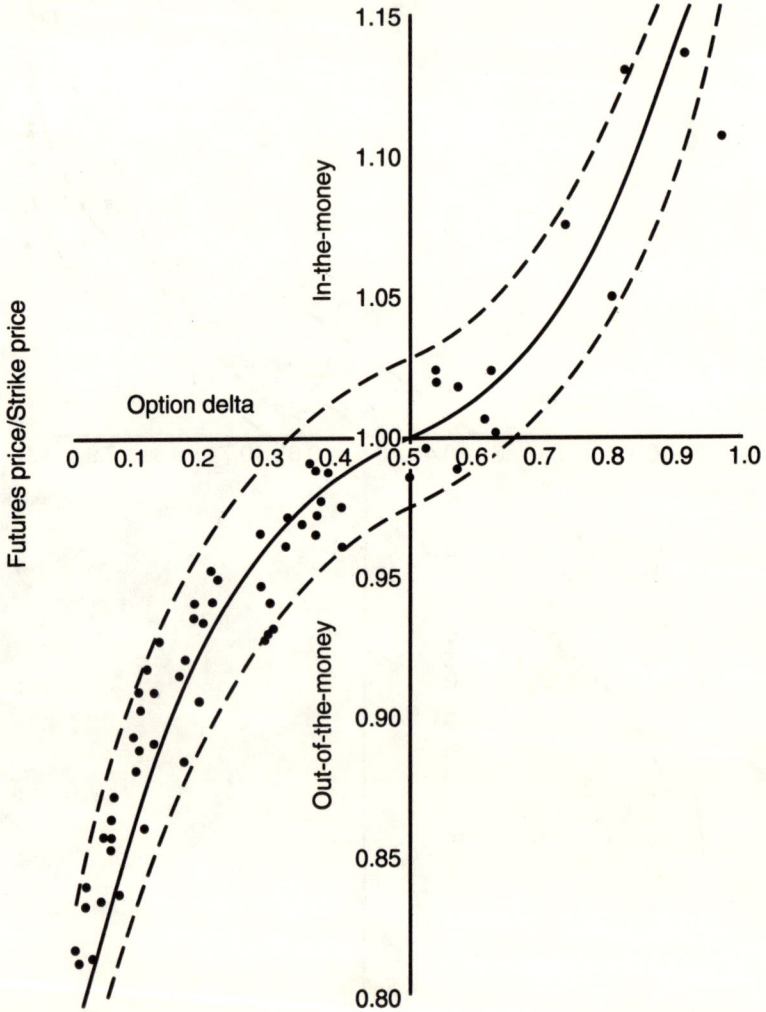

FIGURE C–6
Deltas for Futures Option Puts (five to six months until maturity)

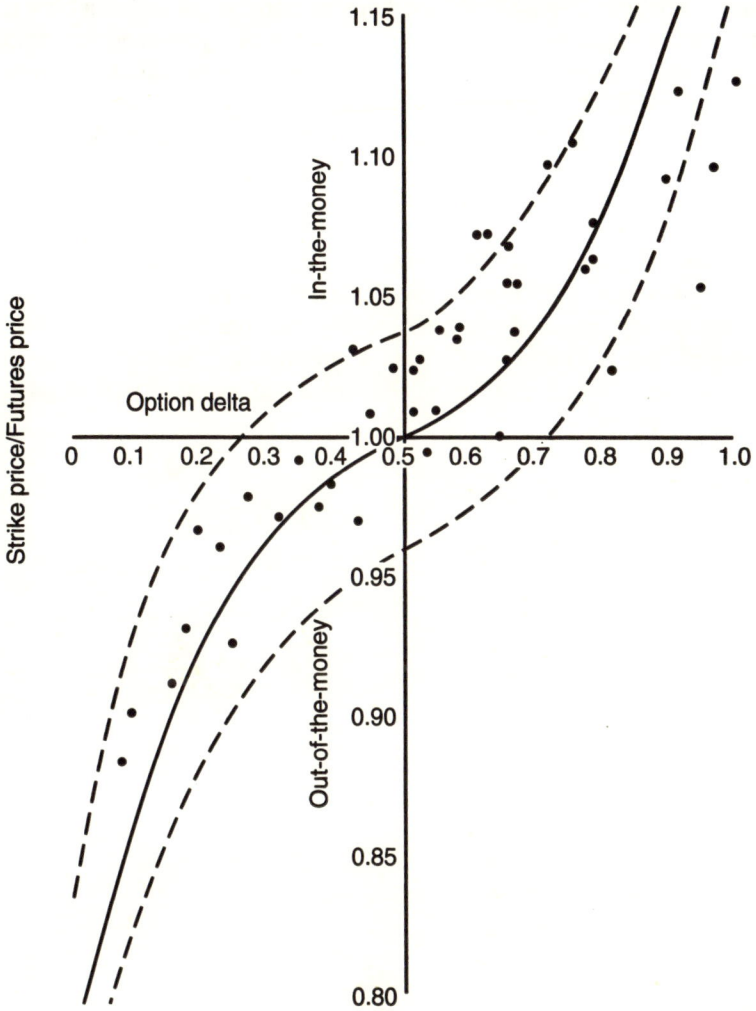

is close to a 20 percent value, with the lowest volatility being close to 10 percent, the highest close to 30 percent. An excellent way to trade options for a holding period of weeks and months is to monitor a graph of this volatility on a day-to-day basis, perhaps smoothing the graph a bit with a short-term moving average, such as a five-day moving average, and trading in a way that makes it possible to benefit from an unfolding increase or decrease in volatility. The most important caution that must be borne in mind, however, is that although price changes in trading markets can be monitored, the extent or duration of those changes cannot be accurately predicted with any consistency.

Note. Figures C–1 through C–6 originally appeared in "When to Strike," an article published in the October 1984 issue of *Intermarket,* a fine financial magazine. As happens to many of the fine things in life, the magazine died of the general lack of interest in wisdom that plagues America today, a lack of interest for which too many of us will pay the appropriate price.

GLOSSARY*

abandon   To elect not to exercise an option contract. The holder of a long options position has the right to exercise or abandon an option contract.

account executive   An individual who is engaged by a member of an exchange and approved by the exchange to act as a sales representative for futures and options contracts, and who is subject to all exchange rules. A commission fee is charged for each transaction. Also referred to as a *registered commodity representative* (RCR).

accumulate   To acquire more futures or options positions.

actuals   The physical cash market commodity/instrument upon which a futures contract is based.

aggregation   In commodities, the accumulation of futures and options positions owned or controlled by the same or related parties, to ascertain compliance with regulated position limits.

all or none   An order that includes a stipulation by the customer instructing the broker to execute no more or no less than the exact number of contracts specified in the order; the broker is instructed to cancel the order if it cannot be filled in its entirety.

alternative order   An order that is designated for execution only if another order cannot be filled; if the original order can be executed, the alternative order is canceled.

American-style option   A classification of options that allows the bearer to exercise at any time prior to expiration. In contrast, a European-style option can be exercised only on the day of expiration.

anticipatory hedge   A hedge of a probable future financial transaction that an enterprise expects but may not be legally obligated to enter into.

arbitrage   The simultaneous purchase of cash, futures, or options in one market against the sale of cash, futures, or options in a different market in order to profit from a price discrepancy.

---

* The terms in this glossary have been drawn from *The CME English/Japanese Dictionary of Futures and Options Terms* (Chicago: Chicago Mercantile Exchange, 1991). Terms used by permission.

arbitrage account   An account of a Class B clearing member containing transactions in foreign exchange, as a result of a specific arrangement between the member and its approved bank whereby the member has simultaneously taken a position with the bank opposite to that of the IMM transactions contained in said account.

arbitration   The process by which a panel or committee settles a dispute between two parties; both parties submit evidence for their case and agree to be bound by the decision of the panel or committee.

ask   The price at which a market participant is willing to sell.

asked/offer   A declared willingness to sell, usually at a stated price; the price at which a seller is willing to make a trade.

assign   To require an option seller to fulfill his obligation to assume a short futures position (in the case of a call option) or a long futures position (in the case of a put option).

assignment—delivery   The process by which the Clearing House selects the long position to accept delivery of a contract for which a seller has submitted a delivery notice.

assignment notice   A written notification that assignment of options has occurred and that assumption of a position in the underlying futures contract will occur.

assignment—options   The process by which the Clearing House, in response to a long exercising its option, randomly selects a seller to fulfill its obligation to buy or sell the underlying futures contract at its strike price. The assigned seller of a put must buy the underlying futures contract; the assigned seller of a call must sell the underlying futures contract.

at-the-money   A term used to describe an option whose strike price is arithmetically closest to the price of the underlying contract.

audit trail   A physical record of trading information, typically identifying the brokers participating in a trade, the firms clearing the trade, the terms and time of the trade, and the customers involved in the trade.

automatic exercise   A process by which all in-the-money long option positions are exercised at expiration.

backspread   An option spread strategy in which calls are sold at a lower strike price than those bought. The backspread is looking for volatility in the underlying currency to increase. Its results are opposite to those of the ratio spread. Also known as a *reverse ratio spread*.

bar chart   A graphic depiction of the range of prices that were traded in a particular time period. The top of a vertical line represents the highest price for the time period; the bottom of the vertical line represents the lowest price for the time period; a short horizontal line fitting at a right angle to the vertical line shows the last price traded for the time period. Usually, one bar or vertical line represents one day's trading data.

base currency The currency unit used to measure the price of a second currency (e.g., for 2.9525 DM/BP, DM is the base currency).

basis The difference between the futures price and the underlying cash price for a specific instrument, usually expressed as cash price minus futures price. For example, if the cash S&P 500 is at 300 and the December S&P futures is at 298, the basis would be 2. Basis reflects the carrying cost.

basis contract A contract between a long hedger and a short hedger, in which payment is made on the agreed-upon basis.

basis risk In a hedge, the risk that the change in the value of the futures position will not be equal to the change in the value of the hedge position.

bear market A market in which prices are falling, investor confidence for the short term is poor, and further declines are anticipated. A market in which the recent price behavior and/or future expected price behavior is characterized by decline.

bear spread A spread that is initiated in the expectation that the futures price will decline.

bear strategy Any investment approach designed to capitalize on the decline in price of a given investment product or a given group of investment products. Examples of bear strategies include short selling of securities, short call options positions, short futures positions, long put options positions, bear spreads, bear squeezes, and bear raids.

beta—beta coefficient With regard to hedging an equity portfolio, to establish the exact hedge coverage, one first determines the portfolio beta—a statistic that describes the portfolio's tendency to rise or fall in value along with the market. The beta coefficient is a product of statistically comparing the portfolio's changes in value over time with changes in the relevant stock index value. A portfolio beta of 1.0 indicates that the portfolio value has moved in the same proportion as the index; a beta of 0.7 indicates that the portfolio value has moved with the index, but only 70 percent as far on average.

bid An offer to buy a specific quantity of a commodity at a stated price.

bid and asked The price offered by a potential buyer of a contract, countered by the price offered by the owner of the contract.

bid-ask spread   The range or difference between the highest current buying price (bid) and the lowest current selling price (ask).

Black-Scholes or **Black-Scholes Option Pricing Model**   Named after Fischer Black and Myron Scholes, the Black-Scholes Option Pricing Model evaluates the theoretical value of put and call options using such variables as time to expiration, dividends, the strike price, the underlying price, interest rates, and price volatility.

box spread   A complex options arbitrage position in which the spreader is long a bear spread with puts and simultaneously long a bull spread with calls, using the same strikes. Can also be viewed as simultaneously short a synthetic underlying at one strike price and long a synthetic underlying at another strike price. A box spread at expiration is always equal to the difference between the strikes involved.

break-even point   The price at which an options position simply pays for itself. If a call option buyer has paid $1 for the right to buy the underlying futures at a price of $10, then the option's break-even point is $11. When the futures price moves up to $11, the option holder can (1) exercise the option and thereby buy the futures contract at a price of $10 or (2) simultaneously offset the futures position by selling it at a price of $11; or (3) the $1 profit from the sale of the futures contract will serve to exactly offset the $1 cost of the options position.

broker   A person or firm that is paid a fee or commission for executing buy or sell orders for a customer. In futures trading, the term may refer to one of several entities: (1) a floor broker—a person who actually executes the trade in the trading pit; (2) an account executive (AE), an associated person (AP), or a registered commodity representative (RCR)—a person who deals with customers in the offices of a futures commission merchant (FCM); or (3) a futures commission merchant (FCM).

brokerage fee   The commission charged by a brokerage firm when it places an order for a customer. (In the futures industry, because positions are customarily offset prior to a contract's expiration, this commission covers a round-turn trade, i.e., both an initial long position and an offsetting short position or both an initial short position and an offsetting long position.) The funds paid by a customer to a brokerage agent in consideration of either investment advice or the execution of a futures market transaction.

brokerage house   A firm whose primary purpose is to execute trades for customers.

bull market   A market in which the recent price behavior and/or the expected price behavior is characterized by increases; a rising market.

bull spread   With calls, a spread in which one is long a lower strike option and simultaneously short a higher strike option in the same expiration month. With puts, a spread in which one is short a higher strike option and simultaneously long a lower strike option in the same expiration month.

butterfly spread   An option spread strategy in which an investor assumes a long or short position at a given strike price and the opposite position at strike prices of equal distances above and below this price. Three strike prices are involved, the lower two being utilized in the bull spread and the higher two in the bear spread (e.g., long one 50 call, short two 55 calls, long one 60 call). In a butterfly spread, two positions at the "inner" strike price must be linked with one position at each of the "outer" strike prices. In addition, all of the options in the spread must have the same expiration.

buyer   A market participant who enters into an agreement with another market participant (the seller) to accept a specified quantity of an investment product in consideration of an agreed-upon price. In the futures and options industry, buyers typically fall into one of the following categories:

options buyer   An investment agent who has entered into a unilateral agreement under which he or she has paid in full for the right, but *not* the obligation, to purchase a specified quantity of a specified investment product at a predetermined price in the future.

spread buyer   An individual who has engaged in the simultaneous purchase and sale of related investment products; for instance, futures contracts based on the same underlying commodity but with different delivery months.

cabinet trade   A transaction that allows options traders to liquidate deep out-of-the-money positions at a value less than what is normally the minimum price fluctuation.

calendar   The selling of a nearby futures or options (put or call) contract and the buying of a more deferred futures or options contract with the same strike price.

calendar spread   The simultaneous purchase and sale of identical futures or options (put or call) contracts with different delivery or expiration dates. One could be short the near-term future or option and simultaneously long the deferred future or option.

calendar straddle   With options, a straddle in which one is short a near-term straddle while at the same time long a straddle with a more distant expiration.

call option A contract between a buyer and a seller in which the buyer pays a premium and acquires the right, but not the obligation, to purchase a specified futures contract at the strike price on or prior to expiration. The seller receives a premium and is obligated to deliver, or sell, the futures contract at the specified strike price should the buyer elect to exercise the option.

call price The cost associated with buying a call option. The most the buyer of a call option stands to lose is the premium, while the potential gains from the position are unlimited. The call price is often referred to as the option's *premium*.

capital requirements Minimum levels, or minimum percentages of total sources of funds, that owners of an enterprise are required to contribute by regulators or insurers. The value of assets belonging to an economic entity, unencumbered by obligations of any kind, necessary for that entity to participate in specific financial activities. In the futures and options industry, regulatory bodies (specifically the Commodity Futures Trading Commission and the Securities and Exchange Commission) have set minimum levels of capital necessary for brokerage firms to conduct futures and options business. However, futures and options exchanges typically require amounts far in excess of regulatory minimums for their fully active member firms.

cash forward sale A sale of a cash commodity for delivery at a later date.

charting Plotting or graphing commodity prices to depict trends in price movement.

class of accounts For the purpose of assessing margin, futures and options exchanges have established three distinct account classifications: member, hedge, or speculative. A member or hedge account typically receives minimum margin rates, while the minimum margin rates of a speculative account are somewhat higher than these minimums.

class of options A term used to describe options of the same type (either put or call) and with the same expiration date.

clean float An exchange rate mechanism in which currencies move freely against each other—without central bank intervention.

cleared trade A transaction for which both the purchase information and the sale information have been entered correctly into a clearing system. Once the system has successfully matched such transactions, the clearinghouse or association becomes the buyer to each seller and the seller to each buyer, and assumes responsibility for the financial performance of the transactions and for the timely and accurate transfer of funds associated with them.

clearing   The procedure through which a clearinghouse or association matches corresponding buy and sell records and, having done so, becomes the buyer to each seller of a contract and the seller to each buyer. In addition, the clearing process evokes the clearing organization's responsibility to protect buyers and sellers from loss by assuring the financial integrity of each contract open on its books.

clearinghouse   1. An adjunct to a commodity exchange through which all transactions on the exchange are settled. In addition, the Clearing House of the CME is charged with the responsibility for assuring the timely and efficient transfer of funds associated with CME transactions and with guaranteeing the financial performance of each open contract on its books. 2. The department of the CME through which all trades on the CME are adjusted and cleared.

clearing margins   Minimum margin rates as determined by an exchange's governing bodies and applied to clearing member brokerage firms.

closing out/offsetting   The liquidation of an existing position. An offset is achieved by establishing a position of equal quantity in the identical commodity on the opposite side of the market (e.g., the liquidation of a purchase of futures or options contracts through the sale of an equal number of contracts of the same delivery or cash settlement month or the liquidation of a sale of futures or options contracts through the purchase of an equal number of contracts).

closing price   The final settlement price or "last trade" price of the trading session.

Commodity Futures Trading Commission (CFTC)   The federal agency empowered by Congress to regulate the American commodity futures industry. Established in 1974 under the Commodity Futures Trading Commission Act, the CFTC has five commissioners, each of whom is appointed by the president and subject to Senate confirmation. The CFTC, though independent of any branch of the federal government, is overseen by the Senate Agricultural Committee.

commodity price discovery   One of the economic functions of the futures market is price discovery. Price information from market participants around the world is collected and distilled in the trading pit. In this fashion, the prices of various commodities/instruments are discovered. Once price has been discovered in the trading pit, it is disseminated around the word virtually instantaneously via quote vendors.

competitive devaluation   The process by which a currency is officially caused or allowed to depreciate vis-à-vis the currencies of trading partners in order to (theoretically) stimulate exports.

condor spread   An option spread strategy under which an investor assumes a long or short position at two adjacent strike prices and the opposite position at strike prices of equal distances above and below these strike prices. In a condor spread, two positions at the "inner" strikes must be linked with individual positions at each of the "outer" strike prices. In addition, all of the options in a condor spread must have the same expiration.

confirmation statement—customer   A report that a commodity brokerage firm issues each day to each of its customers in which the various elements of each transaction (contract, price, quantity, etc.) and the market value of each open position are confirmed.

contract month/year   The month and year in which a given contract becomes deliverable if it has not been liquidated or offset before the date specified for termination of the trading of that contract month.

contract specifications   Key trading details for each commodity listed in the rules of an exchange, including such things as (1) trading hours, (2) contract size, (3) months traded, (4) price quoted, (5) minimum fluctuation, (6) last trading day, (7) standards or grades that must be met when delivering cash commodities against futures contracts.

contract unit   The specific amount of the commodity represented by the futures contract. For example, one Swiss franc futures contract consists of 125,000 Swiss francs.

correction   A small market movement against the prevailing trend.

covered call write   A situation in which one is long the underlying futures and simultaneously short a call option. The short or written call provides the covered writer with premium income.

covered option   An option in which the holder of a long or short option position has an equivalent position on the opposite side of the market in the underlying product.

covered put   Essentially a situation in which one is short the underlying and short a put option.

covered put write   A situation in which one is long the underlying futures and simultaneously short a put option. The short put provides the covered writer with premium income.

covered straddle   Similar to a covered write. However, instead of being long the underlying and short a call, the covered straddle trader is long the underlying and short both a put and a call, thereby significantly increasing his income.

covered straddle write   A situation in which options straddles are sold and the underlying futures are simultaneously bought.

covered write   The sale of a call or put option in conjunction with the purchase of the underlying futures.

cross currency   A set of futures contracts recently developed by the CME that track the changing relationship between currencies other than the U.S. dollar.

cross hedging   Hedging one instrument with another instrument that serves as a close substitute. For example, given that no futures contract based on commercial paper exists, market users could attempt to neutralize a portion of the interest rate risk associated with commercial paper rates by hedging with Eurodollar or Treasury bill futures contracts.

cross margining   A newly developed system under which multiple clearing organizations share position data for the purpose of calculating a single, portfolio-based margin requirement for brokerage firms and their customers. The CME has participated in a cross margin program with the Options Clearing Corporation since October 1989. From that time until the present, the cross margin system has proved to be an exceedingly efficient way to identify the true risks of a portfolio and hence to assign the appropriate margin requirement.

cross rate   The value of one currency expressed in terms of another.

customer margin   1. The margin that a brokerage firm requires from a customer. This margin may be larger than the one that an exchange requires from its clearing member firms, so that the brokerage firm, which is dealing directly with the customer, is provided with a margin cushion. 2. The minimum value of the assets that a brokerage firm requires from a customer to cover the risks associated with the initiation or maintenance of a given set of futures and options market positions (customer margin requirement) or the value of the assets that a customer places in the hands of futures commission merchants or clearing organizations to meet this liability (customer margin deposits).

customer spread margin   The margin rate assessed to speculative customer accounts holding simultaneous long and short positions in markets deemed by margin-setting authorities to exhibit similar price movement tendencies. Margin authorities set the requirements for spreads in such a way as to reflect the reduced risk associated with these positions.

cylinders   A method used to hedge exposure in the foreign exchange market. One could be long puts and short calls or long calls and short puts. (The short options help offset some of the premium expended on the long options.) Also called *fences* or *synthetics*.

dealer option   A generic name for an over-the-counter option. Because OTC options are largely traded by dealers, they are also called *dealer options*.

deep out-of-the-money   With call options, a situation in which the futures price is substantially below the strike price of an option; with put options, a situation in which the futures price is substantially above the strike price of an option. Out-of-the-money options have no intrinsic value.

delivery   The tender and receipt of the actual commodity, or of a delivery instrument covering the commodity, in settlement of a futures contract.

delivery month   The contract month during which delivery takes place.

delivery notice   The written notice in which a seller informs the Clearing House that he intends to make delivery against an open short futures position on a particular date. This notice is separate and distinct from the warehouse receipt or other instruments that are used to transfer title during the actual delivery.

delta   1. A derivative that describes the change in an option's premium compared with the change in the price of the underlying. Deltas range from 1 percent to 100 percent. The underlying always has a delta of 100 percent. At-the-money options generally have deltas of 50 percent. 2. A statistic that measures the pricing behavior of a given option relative to the pricing behavior of its underlying contract. The value of delta can vary from −1 to +1, depending on the time remaining until an option's expiration, the relationship of the option's strike price to the current price of the underlying, and whether the option is a put (negative delta value) or a call (positive delta value).

delta neutral   1. A statistical characterization indicating that the risks of a portfolio are evenly balanced between the rising and declining prices of an underlying contract. 2. A trading strategy in which the deltas of short and long futures and options positions offset each other.

delta spread   1. A risk-limiting ratio spread. The ratio of the spread is determined by dividing the delta of the option to be bought by the delta of the option to be sold. 2. A spread created to obtain a delta-neutral state—for example, long one futures, short two at-the-money calls. Delta of long futures = +100%; delta of two short at-the-moneys = −100%; 100 − 100 = 0, or delta neutral.

diagonal time spread   An options calendar or time spread containing long and short positions of different strike prices and expiration dates (e.g., long June 300 call, short March 290 call).

differential   In commodities, the algebraic difference between the market prices of two related products. Also, a characteristic or average difference between two related market prices.

downside protection   A pricing position strategy that anticipates falling prices.

dynamic early exercise   The act of converting an in-the-money American-style option to its corresponding position in the underlying contract on any business day prior to its expiration day.

efficiency   1. Producing the most product for a given cost or producing a given amount of product for the least cost. Producing the highest return for a given level of risk. 2. Incorporating information into market prices as quickly, currently, and completely as the available technology economically allows.

even lot   A futures transaction in which the quantity is rounded in even multiples of 10, 50, or 100.

exchange rate   The price of one currency expressed in units of another currency.

exchange rate futures   Standardized contracts for future delivery of a currency in exchange for payment in a second currency.

exercise   The process by which a long option holder involves the right granted by the option contract. Call holders exercise to buy the underlying futures contract, while put holders exercise to sell the underlying futures contract. The CME assigns exercise of a short option position by a process of random selection. The Clearing House cancels the option and creates the futures positions on the firm's books on the day following exercise.

exercise limit   A limit that is placed on the number of options contracts that can be exercised.

exercise notice   A specific form that the holder of a long option position submits to the Clearing House to indicate his intention to convert the position into the corresponding position in the underlying contract.

exercising an option   See *exercise*.

exotic currencies   The currencies of countries outside the group of major industrial nations.

expiration   The time at which an option contract is no longer valid.

expiration date   1. The last day of trading for an option contract, after which that contract is no longer valid. 2. The last day upon which a given option contract can either be traded or converted into a position in its underlying financial instrument.

extrinsic value 1. The element of an option's price over and above what the option would be worth were it to expire immediately. Extrinsic value is calculated by subtracting an option's in-the-money value from its price (the extrinsic value of out-of-the-money options is exactly equal to their price). Extrinsic value is a reflection of what the market perceives to be the likelihood of favorable price trends in the underlying financial instrument over the option contract's life. 2. The part of an option premium that is determined by the current futures price, the amount of time until expiration of the option, short-term interest rates, the volatility of the underlying futures contract, and the expectations of buyers and sellers. Total option premium = Intrinsic value + Extrinsic value. Extrinsic value is also referred to as *time value*.

flat position A situation in which one has no position (i.e., one is neither long nor short).

foreign currency All currencies not accepted as the official legal tender of a given country.

foreign currency exchange rates The values of nondomestic currencies versus a country's official currency at any given moment in time. Unless not freely convertible, these values are determined by market forces.

forward contract See *cash forward sale*.

forward market The market quoted today for products that will be delivered or offset on a future date. The delivery time and quantity are determined between a seller and a buyer.

forward-forward swap A deal involving an exchange of two currencies between two forward dates.

futures The standardized contracts covering the purchase and sale of commodities for future delivery on an organized exchange.

futures contract 1. A bilateral agreement between two parties to transfer from the seller to the buyer a specific quantity of a given commodity or financial instrument at a particular price as determined under the rules of the Commodity Exchange Act. The futures contract seller is obligated to deliver the commodity or instrument and the futures contract buyer is obligated to accept such delivery under the terms of the original agreement unless either party elects to transfer this obligation through the execution of a subsequent, offsetting futures transaction. In contrast, under an option contract the purchaser has the right, but *not* the obligation, to make or take delivery. 2. An obligation to deliver or take delivery on a specified quality and grade of a commodity during a designated month at a designated price.

futures-type option An option contract whose "deep in-the-money" status (strike price significantly below underlying trading price for calls, significantly above underlying trading price for puts) gives it a high probability of being exercised and whose pricing behavior is therefore extremely similar to that of a futures contract.

FX Foreign exchange.

gamma A statistic measuring the impact of time on the pricing behavior of a given option contract. Specifically, gamma measures the extent to which an option's delta (the tendency of the option's prices to move in tandem with the prices of its underlying contract) changes over time.

hedge Generally refers to a "bona fide hedging transaction," which CFTC Rule 1.3(z) defines to include futures transactions that (1) represent a temporary substitute for cash market transactions that are to take place at a later time and (2) are economically appropriate to the reduction of risks. Hedging to transfer risk is the primary economic function of the futures and options markets.

hedge adjustment Modification of one or more hedge positions that serves to reduce risk.

hedge exemption An exemption from the normal futures and/or options position limits that is granted to bona fide hedgers on a case-by-case basis.

hedge ratio A measure that equalizes the dollar value of a change in the cash market instrument with the dollar value of a change in the derivative instrument that is being used to reduce the risk associated with the cash market instrument.

hedgers Individuals or institutions that hedge as a means of reducing or eliminating price risk.

hedging 1. Taking a futures market position that is opposite to a position held in the cash market in order to minimize the risk of financial loss from an adverse price change. 2. A purchase or sale of futures as a temporary substitute for a cash transaction that will occur later.

hedging effectiveness A measure reached by comparing the rate targeted when a hedge was placed with the rate that actually resulted once the hedge was lifted. This measure can take into account the margin cash flows that occurred over the course of the hedge and the slippage between the movement of cash market prices and the movement of futures market prices.

IMM The International Monetary Market Division of the Chicago Mercantile Exchange.

implied volatility The annual level of price fluctuation that can be expected in the financial instrument that underlies an option contract, given the strike price and market value of the option, the market value of the underlying financial instrument, the option's time to expiration, and the prevailing interest rates. Implied volatility statistics, which are employed by options traders as an indication of current options market trends, are a key feature of all options pricing models. In contrast to implied volatility, historic volatility measures one standard deviation price change using historic price data on the underlying, not the option.

import hedging The means employed to reduce or eliminate the risk that the cost of an import will increase because of a decline in the value of the importer's currency as compared to the value of the exporter's currency.

in-the-money A call option with a strike price lower (or a put option with a strike price higher) than the current market value of the underlying commodity.

initial margin 1. The amount of "good faith" collateral that a futures and options exchange or regulatory body sets as a minimum deposit requirement for any customer that wishes to engage in futures or short options trading, to ensure performance of the customer's obligations. 2. The minimum deposit that a clearing firm must require from customers for each contract. The contract specifications indicate the amount of this deposit.

interbank market A market in which trading is conducted between banks via telephone and telex. In contrast, a futures market conducts all trading at a centralized location.

intercommodity spread A spread that consists of a long position in one commodity and a short position in a related commodity.

interdelivery (or intramarket) spread The purchase of one delivery month of a particular futures contract and the sale of another delivery month of the same contract at the same time and on the same exchange.

interest rate parity theorem A theorem stating that the differential between the risk-free, short-term interest rates of two countries is exactly equal to the differential between the cash and forward currency rates of the two countries.

interexchange (or intermarket) spread A spread that consists of a position at one exchange and an opposite position for the same commodity at another exchange.

intermarket spread The purchase and sale of related commodities in the same or different markets or in the same or different delivery months.

intracommodity spread   A spread that consists of opposite positions of the same commodity in different contract months. The spread may involve contracts of the same year or of different years.

intrinsic value   An option whose underlying price is above the strike price (for calls) or below the strike price (for puts).

leverage   1. The control of a large amount of securities with a small amount of funds. 2. In the futures industry, the control of large dollar amounts of an underlying commodity with a relatively small amount of capital.

liquidate   1. To convert an existing trading position into cash by executing an offsetting transaction (a sale for a long position, a purchase for a short position) in a financial instrument of identical specifications. 2. To offset an existing position.

listed option   An option listed for trading on a regulated futures, option, or stock exchange.

long   One who has bought a futures or options contract to establish a market position.

long hedge   A risk management technique that involves buying a futures contract to offset a short cash position (e.g., a cattle feeder who needs to buy feeder cattle in the future would buy feeder cattle futures now to protect his intended purchase against a possible increase in prices).

long position   1. A market position that obligates its holder (in the case of a futures contract) or gives its holder the right but *not* the obligation (in the case of an options contract) to accept the underlying contract or financial instrument. 2. An obligation to receive delivery of a futures contract.

maintenance margin   The minimum equity that must be maintained for each contract in a customer's futures account subsequent to the customer's deposit of the initial margin. If the equity drops below this level, the customer must make a deposit to bring the account back up to the initial margin level.

margin   The amount of money or collateral deposited by a client with his broker, or by a clearing firm with the Clearing House, to insure the broker or the Clearing House against loss on open futures or options contracts. The margin is a performance bond, not a part payment on a purchase.

initial margin.   The total amount of margin per contract required by the broker when a futures position is opened.

maintenance (variance) margin.   An amount that must be maintained on deposit at all times. If a customer's equity in any futures position drops to or under the maintenance level because of adverse price action, the broker must issue a margin call to restore the customer's equity. For specific margin requirements, consult the specifications of particular contracts.

mark-to-market   The daily adjustment of all open positions to reflect the settlement price of the contract. Each position is credited with profit or charged with loss, and the next trading day is begun at the settlement price.

married put   A situation in which an investor or futures trader is long a futures contract or stock and long a put for protection against downward movement of the contract or stock. Similar to a covered write.

minimum price fluctuation   The cash value of the minimum amount by which the price of a commodity may fluctuate, as described in the contract specifications. Also known as a *tick*.

model   A set of relationships that explains and predicts market behavior. A model captures the essence of a problem but need not describe all of the detail. For example, option pricing models use a few simple relationships to capture the essence of how markets price options.

monthly statement   A document that details a customer's opening balance and position, purchases and sales during the month, money or securities deposited or withdrawn, and closing balance and position. This document is typically issued by a brokerage house.

naked   A position in one market that is not offset by a position in another market.

naked call   A position in which one sells or writes call options without owning the underlying securities.

naked option   An open option contract that is not covered by an offsetting position in the underlying commodity or by another option contract against which it can be spread.

naked position or naked writing   A position in which one is short options without being long or short the underlying instrument. This is a position of unlimited risk.

naked put   A position in which one sells or writes put options without owning the underlying securities.

net change   The difference between the current price of a commodity and the previous day's settlement price.

net long   The total number of long contracts held.

net long/short   The market position expressed as the difference between the total number of long contracts held and the total number of short contracts held.

net margining   Allowing one trader's long position in a given contract to offset another trader's short position in the same contract before calculating the margin for the combined positions.

net position   The difference between the long open contracts held and the short open contracts held in any futures or options contracts.

net short   The total number of short contracts held.

offer   An offer to sell a specific quantity of a commodity at a stated price. The opposite of a bid.

offset   1. To remove a position from an account by establishing an equal but opposite position, making or taking delivery, or exercising an option; 2. To report reductions of a firm's inventory of open long purchase dates to the Clearing House.

open position   A long or short position that has not been liquidated.

optimal hedge   The hedge vehicle that performs the hedging function best. For example, in using S&P futures as a hedge against a decline in a portfolio, the optimal hedge would incorporate an adjustment that takes into account the beta and/or correlation of the portfolio.

option   A derivative instrument that gives one the right, but *not* the obligation, to go long or short (calls and puts) an underlying instrument. An option buyer pays a price (the premium) in exchange for this right.

option buyer, option holder, or option taker   A purchaser of calls, puts, or any combination of calls and puts.

option contract   A contract that gives the buyer (or holder) the right, but *not* the obligation, to be long or short a futures contract at a specified price within a specified time period. The specified price is called the *strike price*. The futures contract that the long may establish by exercising the option is referred to as the *underlying futures contract*.

option premium   The price that a buyer pays, and a seller receives, for an option.

option seller, option grantor, or option writer   The person who, in return for receipt of premium, incurs the obligation to fulfill the terms of an option contract upon assignment by the Clearing House.

option spread   A position in which one is simultaneously long or short various options or combinations of options. Futures contracts may also be used in constructing spreads.

OTC option   An option contract that is not bought or sold on a regulated commodity exchange but is usually marketed by banks or large financial institutions.

out-of-the-money   A term used to describe an option that has no intrinsic value—for example, a call option with a strike price higher (or a put option with a strike price lower) than the current market value of the underlying commodity. Because an option's value depends on current prices, it can vary from in-the-money to out-of-the-money with market price movements during the life of the option contract.

position   1. An obligation to perform in the futures or options market. A long position is an obligation to buy; a short position is an obligation to sell. 2. The result of an initiating financial transaction that carries with it the rights and obligations associated with the given contract market, as outlined in the contract specifications. See also *call option* and *put option*.

premium   1. The price paid by the purchaser of an option to the grantor (seller). 2. The amount by which a cash commodity price exceeds a futures price or another cash commodity price.

processor hedging   Hedging conducted by processors to guard against price increases of inputs and/or price declines of outputs. See *hedging*.

producer hedging   Hedging conducted by producers to guard against price increases of inputs and/or price declines of outputs. See *hedging*.

purchase date   The date on which a long position is established on a clearing firm's books.

purchase price   The amount of money asked or paid for establishing a long futures or options position.

purchasing hedge   See *long hedge*.

purchasing power parity (PPP)   The situation that exists when a second currency into which a currency has been converted purchases the same quantity of goods or services in the country in which the second currency is used as is purchased by the original currency in the country in which it is used.

purchasing power parity theorem (PPPT)   The theorem that purchasing power parity should be the long-run equilibrium level for currencies, all other things being equal.

put option   An option that provides the purchaser with the right, but *not* the obligation, to sell a futures contract at an agreed price (the strike price) at any time during the life of the option. A put option is bought in the expectation of a decline in price.

quantity   The number of futures or options contract increments that are associated with a bid, offer, or actual transaction.

range   The difference between the highest and lowest price recorded during a given trading session, a week, a month, the life of a contract, or any other given period.

ratio hedging   The protection of a portfolio or an option position by means of hedge ratios or deltas.

ratio spread   A spread in which the trader is short more options than he is long (e.g., long one 300 calls, short two 305 calls. The opposite of a backspread.

ratio write   A situation in which one is long the underlying and short two or more call options in an appropriate ratio. Similar to a covered call write.

risk   1. The possibility of loss. 2. The dollar difference between the current price of open positions and the price at which their liquidation would occur.

risk management   The continuous monitoring and subsequent adjustment of a position of risk. In following up a hedge position, the risk manager must manage the position by offsetting it, adding to it, or modifying it in order to better control risk.

risk preference   Preferences with regard to risk. The risk preferring would pay to accept more risk and would require payment to avoid more risk. The risk neutral are indifferent between accepting and avoiding more risk. The risk avoiding would pay to avoid more risk and would require payment to accept more risk. Financial economists use risk preference to study choices between risk and return.

risk/reward ratio   The ratio between the potential for profit and the potential for loss.

selective hedge   A futures position that may be placed or lifted against a long-term cash position, depending on the short-term price outlook.

seller   A market participant who enters into an agreement with another market participant (the buyer) to provide that participant with a specified quantity of an investment product for a mutually acceptable price. In the futures and options industry, sellers typically fall into one of the following categories:

  options seller   An investment agent who has entered into a unilateral agreement under which he has received cash in consideration of a binding obligation to provide a specified quantity of a specified investment product at a predetermined price in the future. An options seller is subject to margin/performance bond requirements.

  seller   A person who takes a short futures position or who grants (sells) a commodity option. An option seller is also called a *marker* or *grantor*.

  spread buyer   An individual who has engaged in the simultaneous purchase and sale of related investment products (e.g., futures contracts based on the same underlying commodity but with different delivery months).

selling hedge   The act of selling futures contracts for protection against possible price declines of commodities that will be sold in the future.

settlement date   The date on which the buyer becomes the owner and the seller relinquishes ownership.

short hedge   See *selling hedge.*

SPAN margin system   The Standard Portfolio Analysis of Risk™ (SPAN™) margin system. This computer system determines options and futures portfolio margin requirements. It is a portfolio-based approach to risk margin calculations that may be applied easily to any exchange's margining methods, either gross or net, and incorporated into any firm's bookkeeping system. The CME Clearing House uses SPAN™ to margin clearing firms, and clearing firms use it to margin their customers.

speculate   To take a position in futures or options for the purpose of financial gain rather than risk management.

speculation   The assumption of a futures or options position with significant risk by a market participant that has fully examined both the risks and the potential rewards of doing so. Speculation differs from gambling in that the speculator does not create artificial risk; he merely accepts the transfer of another economic agent's market exposure. Speculation differs from investment in that a greater magnitude of risk is associated with it.

speculator   An individual who does not hedge but who trades in commodity futures or options with the objective of achieving profits through the successful anticipation of price movements. The speculator is a risk-taker who enhances the liquidity of futures markets.

spread   An investment position containing multiple, related financial instruments with some degree of offsetting risk. In futures markets, there are four basic types of spreads: (*a*) interdelivery spread—the simultaneous purchase and sale of a single commodity in different delivery months; (*b*) interexchange spread—the simultaneous purchase and sale of identical commodities on different exchanges; (*c*) intercommodity spread—the simultaneous purchase and sale of related commodities (such as Treasury bills and Eurodollars); and (*d*) product spread—the simultaneous purchase and sale of a raw commodity and its by-products. There are also many types of spreads that involve options positions and futures and options positions in combination.

stack hedge   A hedge in which contracts with the same expiration month are bought or sold. Contrast with *strip hedge*.

straddle—options   One short call option and one short put option with the same strike price and the same expiration.

strangle—options   One short out-of-the-money call option and one short out-of-the-money put option with different strike prices and the same (or different) expiration.

strike price   The price agreed upon between the seller and buyer of an option to become the price at which the option may be exercised. Strike prices on options are at exchange-designated intervals.

strip hedge   A situation in which a hedger uses successively deferred futures contracts to implement a hedge; thus, instead of using one contract month, the hedger may buy or sell successive delivery months (e.g., short June and short September and short December, instead of being short three June). The successive contracts create a strip of expirations, one succeeding another. The strip hedge is used to create a synthetic longer term hedging vehicle.

strong currencies   The currencies perceived to be likely to maintain value over time—generally those of industrialized countries whose central banks tend to maintain a noninflationary monetary policy.

swap   A transaction in which two or more parties agree simultaneously to the terms of both the initial purchase and sale of a commodity, financial instrument, or currency as well as the subsequent repurchase and resale of the same commodity, financial instrument, or currency.

synthetic futures   An options position involving a long call and short put position (long the synthetic) or a short call and long put position (short the synthetic) that duplicates the profit/loss characteristics of a futures contract. Conversions and reversals are synthetic futures positions offset by actual futures positions. These arbitrage positions are created only when the market is mispricing one of the component instruments.

synthetic long (short) put   The short selling (purchase) of a futures contract and the simultaneous purchase (short sell) of a call.

theta   The measure of an option's time decay—the amount of premium that is lost as another day passes, all other things remaining the same.

tick   The minimum price fluctuation specified by the contract terms in an exchange's rule book.

time and sales   A database on all futures and options fluctuations that contains the time and price associated with each transaction executed on an exchange floor. This database is available to customers who wish to verify whether an order executed on their behalf was filled at a price that accurately reflected the prevailing prices at the time the order was placed.

time value The amount that an option's premium is above the option's intrinsic value. Time value plus intrinsic value equals the total value of an option's premium. Time value is subject to decay that accelerates as expiration nears.

trade (transaction) The purchase or sale of a specified number of contracts on an exchange trading floor made in accordance with the rules of the exchange.

uncovered option See *naked option.*

uncovered sale The sale of an option without a position in the underlying futures contract.

underlying commodity The commodity represented by a futures contract (e.g., a live hog futures contract represents a certain quantity and quality of live hogs).

underlying futures contract The futures contract that may be purchased or sold upon the exercise of an option.

utility Happiness. Economic theory assumes that people try to maximize their happiness, and economists use this assumption to model how people make choices.

variable ratio write A situation in which one is long the underlying and short options of several strike prices.

variance A standard statistical measure of variability around a mean (average) value. The formula for variance is Variance $(X) = E[X - E(X)]^2$. E is the statistical expectation, which is a probability-weighted average of all values. The square root of variance is the standard deviation.

vega A measure of the amount of an option's premium change for a 1 percent move in the implied volatility.

vertical spread A spread of one short option against one long option of the same expiration and of different strikes in which both options are of the same type (either both puts or both calls).

volatility An expression of the underlying movement of a commodity, security, or financial instrument. When price movements are large, volatility is said to be large. Mathematically, volatility is the annualized standard deviation of the price movement of an instrument.

warrant A financial instrument that gives the bearer the right, but *not* the obligation, to purchase (call warrant) or sell (put warrant) a specific quantity of a security at a specific price. The duration of warrants differs from that of options. Many warrants are perpetual. Those that are not typically have a significantly longer contract life than is normally associated with an option.

weak currencies   The currencies of countries whose economic conditions are generally perceived to be poor—high inflation, trade balances in deficit, high unemployment, etc.

write   To sell an option.

writer   Another name for an option seller.

zero-sum game   A characterization that is often applied to futures and options markets because there are always an equal number of long and short positions for any given contract. Thus, a price fluctuation will by definition have a net cash benefit of zero. However, this simplistic view does not take into account the fact that the risk transfer and price discovery aspects of futures and options markets, among other things, do create a net benefit to the economy.

zeta   See *vega*.

REFERENCES

Figlewski, S.; W. Silber; and M. Subrahmanyam. *Financial Options from Theory to Practice.* Homewood, Ill.: Business One-Irwin, 1990. Pp. 281–313.

Joseph, M. *Hedge Accounting Puzzle Clarified.* Cedar Falls, Iowa: Corporate Risk Management, 1991. Pp. 8–9.

Kato, H. *The CME Dictionary of Futures and Options Terms.* Chicago: Chicago Mercantile Exchange, 1991.

Labuszewski, J., and J. Nyhoff. *Trading Options on Futures.* New York: John Wiley & Sons, 1988.

Mayer, T. *Commodity Options.* New York: New York Institute of Finance, 1983.

Natenberg, S. *Option Volatility and Pricing Strategies.* Chicago: Probus, 1988. Pp. 116, 220.

Rachleff, M., and R. Herz. *Hedging with NYMEX Energy Futures, Operational and Accounting Controls, Financial Reporting, and Federal Income Taxes—A Practical Guide.* New York: Coopers & Lybrand, New York Mercantile Exchange, 1989.

Rachleff, M., and K. Piccoli. *NYMEX Natural Gas Futures: A Practical Guide to Development and Management of a Hedge Program.* New York: Coopers & Lybrand, New York Mercantile Exchange, 1989.

Tharp, Van K. *The Investment Psychology Guides.* Cary, N.C.: Investment Psychology Consulting, 1991.

Trading and Hedging with Currency Futures and Options. Chicago: Chicago Mercantile Exchange, 1989.

INDEX